DI014885

DISCARD

THE
POLITICS
OF
DECEPTION

THE
POLITICS
OF
DECEPTION

JFK's Secret Decisions on
Vietnam, Civil Rights, and Cuba

PATRICK J. SLOYAN

Farmington Public Library
2101 Farmington Avenue
Farmington, NM 87401

THOMAS DUNNE BOOKS
St. Martin's Press
New York

002000482372

THOMAS DUNNE BOOKS.
An imprint of St. Martin's Press.

THE POLITICS OF DECEPTION. Copyright © 2015 by Patrick J. Sloyan. All rights reserved. Printed in the United States of America. For information, address St. Martin's Press, 175 Fifth Avenue, New York, N.Y. 10010.

www.thomasdunnebooks.com
www.stmartins.com

Designed by Phil Mazzone

The Library of Congress Cataloging-in-Publication Data is available upon request.

ISBN 978-1-250-03059-7 (hardcover)
ISBN 978-1-250-03060-3 (e-book)

St. Martin's Press books may be purchased for educational, business, or promotional use. For information on bulk purchases, please contact the Macmillan Corporate and Premium Sales Department at 1-800-221-7945, extension 5442, or write to special markets@macmillan.com.

First Edition: February 2015

10 9 8 7 6 5 4 3 2 1

For Phyllis, the blue-eyed girl with the friendly smile

CONTENTS

THE
POLITICS
OF
DECEPTION

Prologue

JFK

JOHN FITZGERALD KENNEDY WAS ELATED. He walked toward me, grinning. He wore a brown pinstripe too big for his shoulders, a rep tie, and a white handkerchief in his lapel pocket. He fingered the center coat button. His face had a springtime tan, and the sun had created reddish highlights in his thick, light brown hair. I was one of a handful of reporters who had just listened to his inspirational use of history and wit to awaken University of Maryland students to a life of public service. Senator Kennedy, replete with cheers and applause, was ready for our questions.

I was spellbound by his speaking style and sparkling humor. To illustrate the joy of politics, Kennedy had recounted the journey of Thomas Jefferson and James Madison prior to the 1800 presidential election. The two founding fathers claimed not politics but the study of flowers and ferns, birds and bees, were the reason for their trip through Hudson River Valley and most of New England. Village by village, town by town, Jefferson and Madison proved the success of personal contact with voters by winning the White House. Kennedy responded to the student roar with a toothy smile. He was the most sought after speaker of the day, with looks and style that stirred both men and women. It was April 27, 1959, and Kennedy was on the verge of his bid for the presidency of the United States.

"I do not come here today in search of butterflies," Kennedy said. More cheering.

I understood his ambitions only vaguely that day. While a professional journalist since leaving the U.S. Army in 1957, I was enrolled at Maryland on the GI Bill. But I worked part-time for the *Washington Evening Star* and the *Baltimore News-Post* and would file stories to both newspapers on Kennedy's speech. I knew enough to ask a serious question of a politician. And, because of his command of history in the day's speech, I recalled the 1928 campaign of Al Smith, the Democratic presidential candidate defeated by Republican Herbert Hoover. Many say Smith's Catholicism played a role in his defeat, I noted. Do you think it will hurt your candidacy? He had heard the question before, but I wanted my own answer. I was unprepared for his reaction. The humor washed from his face. His eyes and mouth hardened. His elation from the crowd's applause vanished. He looked at me and then said firmly, "No, my religion will be an asset. America is a religious nation and Americans will respect my religion." His gaze shifted to the next questioner, who was interested in pending Senate legislation. Then he shot me another dirty look before handling the new question. Who the hell is this kid? the glare seemed to say.

At that moment, I was unaware Catholicism was his political millstone. Three years earlier at the Democratic Convention in Chicago, Adlai Stevenson, the nominee, rejected Kennedy's bid for the vice-presidential nomination. "America is not ready for a Catholic yet," Stevenson told Jim Farley, himself a Catholic and political adviser to President Franklin D. Roosevelt. While backing Kennedy's bid in Chicago, Tennessee senator Albert Gore told Stevenson that Catholicism was an "insurmountable" problem for the Democratic ticket. Also objecting was House Speaker Sam Rayburn. "Well, if we have to have a Catholic, I hope we don't have to take that little pissant Kennedy." Most of those very same political players would leap to their feet and cheer four years later when Kennedy seized the presidential nomination in the 1960 Democratic Convention in Los Angeles.

Kennedy's outward energy, sunny good looks, and quick tongue made him an easy choice over the dark and dour Richard M. Nixon. Kennedy won handily with the electoral vote that decides presidential elections—303 to Nixon's 219. But the popular vote, which provides a deeper measure of American sentiment, left him with a fingernail of 118, 574 votes out of 68 million cast, the smallest plurality since the 1884 election seventy-six years earlier. Of course, Virginia senator Harry F. Byrd won 500,000 votes that year as a third party candidate. But at dawn that day of victory, Kennedy was in the minority, with only 49.7 percent of the popular vote. Former president Harry Truman was mystified. "Why, even our friend, Adlai, would have had a landslide running against Nixon," Truman told a friend. While Kennedy's election was a breakthrough for religious tolerance, a close look at the vote showed him the first president to be elected with a minority of Protestant voters. Voter perception of his Catholicism had undercut Kennedy once again.

The closeness of that election was never far from his thoughts while he was president and planning for his second term. Every move, every speech, every White House visitor, every presidential trip, every decision was connected to his 1964 presidential reelection campaign. For modern American presidents, the struggle to prevail for a second term begins when the left hand is on the Bible and the other in the air for the inauguration of their first term. As he prepared for reelection in 1963, events in Cuba, the civil rights movement, and Vietnam were eroding his chances for a second term. How he responded to these challenges was hidden from the world by a docile, at times worshipful Washington media. The president could count on an array of powerful journalists as personal friends in those years. There were exceptions. Frontline reporters such as Lloyd Norman, *Newsweek*'s Pentagon reporter, so upset Kennedy that he ordered that the Central Intelligence Agency trail Norman and embarrass leakers.

David Halberstam, the *New York Times* reporter in Saigon, caused Kennedy almost daily fits. He pressured the newspaper's publisher to yank Halberstam. Almost any criticism pierced the president's thin skin. "It is almost impossible to write a story they like," said Ben Bradlee of *Newsweek* and a personal friend of the president. "Even if a story is quite favorable to their side, they'll find one piece to quibble with." But Kennedy had no reason to complain about me. I was in the press section only a few feet from Kennedy on that snowy January 20 inauguration. Once again, Kennedy's address and the electricity of the day enthralled me. For the next two years and eleven months, I would have a front row seat as Kennedy delivered one dynamite speech after another. There were some clunkers. But for the grand moments there were grand performances. My Irish-American Catholic background did a mind meld with Jack Kennedy.

I had joined the Washington bureau of United Press International in September of 1960 and soon gained unimaginable power and influence. Journalism was the intersection between politicians and their voters. The UPI A Wire stories sent by teletype over telephone wires at sixty words per minute were delivered to the editor of newspapers around the globe. The first time I heard CBS anchorman Walter Cronkite, a UPI veteran, read the exact words I had written—well, it was a trip. Clippings from newspapers including the *New York Times* and the *Washington Post* swelled my ego. My perceptions of a news event were in direct competition with those from the Associated Press. My dispatch was delivered well ahead of other Washington bureau reporters. Often their editors would demand facts matching or better than Sloyan's UPI account. At UPI, we doted on Kennedy, who seemed to dominate our daily report. My colleague, Helen Thomas, elevated his wife and children to a news category reserved for Britain's royal family.

Three months after his inauguration, Kennedy made a decision that haunted his presidency. His approval of the April 17 Central Intelligence Agency invasion of Cuba turned into the Bay of Pigs fiasco that left American-trained invaders unprotected as they were killed and captured by Fidel Castro. Kennedy took responsibility for the failure in a town where buck-passing is an art form. At a news conference—an almost weekly event in the new administration—he held off questions placing blame. "There's an old saying that victory has a hundred fathers and defeat is an orphan," Kennedy said. "I am the responsible officer of the government." Once in the White House, Kennedy ordered the CIA to form standby assassination teams. They were after Castro until Kennedy's final day in office.

Pretty quickly, reporters found Kennedy to be both naïve and reckless in approving the CIA plan, which, on casual inspection, was ridiculous. "How could we have been so stupid," Kennedy confessed to *Time*'s Hugh Sidey. Still, his voter approval rating rose in polls at home. Abroad, his refusal to employ a U.S. Navy armada within striking distance of Castro indicated weakness to Soviet premier Nikita Khrushchev. Perhaps it emboldened the Soviet leader, the hardened commissar of Stalingrad, to test the forty-five-year-old American. In 1961 in Vienna and in 1962 in Cuba, Khrushchev threatened Kennedy with nuclear warfare. The world-shaking confrontation in October 1962 ended when Kennedy's brandishing of U.S. superior strategic weapons forced Khrushchev into a humiliating retreat. At least that was my perception along with other journalists who told the world how the Soviet leader blinked when he was "eyeball to eyeball" with the cool but daring Kennedy. But this was all cunning manipulation by Kennedy. Instead, he secretly followed Khrushchev's path away from nuclear confrontation. In fact the Russian leader achieved his objective of eliminating fifteen U.S. nuclear warheads in Turkey only minutes from Moscow. Kennedy and his handlers would hide the truth from the world for more than thirty years. In doing so, they covered up Kennedy's finest moment as president when he ignored his top advisers to avoid the first step on the way to nuclear warfare. In-house historians perpetuated the fabrication that it was Khrushchev, not Kennedy, who was rolled. As late as October

10, 2013, the *Washington Post* recounted how "Kennedy coolly stared down Soviet leader Nikita Khrushchev and barely averted the war."

In many African-American homes, particularly among the poor, there is often a picture of Martin Luther King Jr. flanked by a photo of Kennedy and even of his brother Bobby. The place of honor stems from news accounts by me and others that the Kennedy brothers took up King's cause against racist hate and segregation. This perception is not quite accurate. In hopes of retaining Southern voters, Kennedy opposed civil rights legislation and had a hostile relationship with King. Both brothers hoped to halt what became the historic March on Washington. Kennedy and brother Bobby, the attorney general, ordered telephone wiretaps and the bugging of hotel rooms in an effort to intimidate the civil rights leader. But King refused to bend even after the FBI, in the most extensive federal smear campaign in history, circulated recordings of him and other women.

Another news report I helped fabricate was Kennedy's opposition, surprise, and dismay over the assassination of President Ngo Dinh Diem of South Vietnam. As an editor on the night desk at UPI, I had developed an interest in Saigon chaos. When connections blocked Neil Sheehan of the UPI Saigon bureau from reaching New York or Tokyo, he would call me in Washington to file his dispatch. As a result, I followed Vietnam events in both Saigon and Washington. The day Diem was killed, the following went out on the UPI wire to clients: "I can categorically state that the United States government was not involved in any way," said State Department press officer Richard Phillips. "It's their country, their war and this is their uprising." Few believed him. As the *Washington Star* editorial said, the people who did believe him, "would fit in a very small phone booth." However, it would be more than forty years before facts showed the depth of Kennedy's involvement that left Diem's blood on his legacy and opened the door for the involvement of 8 million Americans in ten years of the Vietnam War. Diem's influence and a reluctant military in Saigon forced Kennedy to personally organize and execute the overthrow of government in the midst of the hottest battle in the cold war. Kennedy bribed the key officer who enabled reluctant generals to overthrow Diem. And Kennedy set the stage for Diem's assassination, which Kennedy knew was likely weeks before it happened. The dirty work was handled by Henry Cabot Lodge Jr., a Republican given a free hand in Saigon as U.S. ambassador. Lodge refused to rescue Diem two hours before he was murdered. Lodge's closest aide likened it to a gangland slaying. Kennedy's brother Bobby sought to blame Lodge with the whole bloody business. Diem's death may seem a blip in the scheme of things. I now see it as the destruction of the stability of the Saigon government, which led American combat troops into a jungle slaughterhouse. The U.S. Army was corrupted and defeated by a war that divided American citizens to an extent not seen since the Civil War. From Washington, I watched the American government lie and squirm for eleven years while the war tore away the American soul.

As a reporter, I covered the White House closely from the end of Lyndon Johnson's tenure to the end of William Clinton's term. One thing I learned is that when a president's words are in quotation marks as having said something pithy, nasty, insulting, or even angry, rarely did the words come directly from the president. Some third party—a senator or a press secretary—has provided the reporter with the quotation. Hearsay, of course, does wonders for history. In this book, I have strived to quote only words that actually passed the lips of Kennedy and his advisers. There are some secondhand quotes, but these are minimal. A sharper focus on these events in 1963 come from White House tape recordings Kennedy made secretly in the Cabinet Room (a microphone in a light fixture and beneath the table) and the Oval Office (a microphone in his desk well). Kennedy, a student of history, was organizing a record of his presidency. None of those recorded knew of Kennedy's taping system, which he turned on and off at will. There were hidden switches in the Oval Office and a third beneath the Cabinet Room conference table.

Contrast that with Richard M. Nixon's voice-activated tape recorder, which captured the vindictive, angry, boozy, paranoid president trying to lie his way out of the Watergate scandal. Nixon could easily forget history was listening, but not Kennedy. Hours of Kennedy recordings are still classified even though most of the participants are dead and the secrecy labels have lapsed under federal law. The Kennedy family and his presidential library continue to hide the darker side of Camelot. Kennedy's actual words during the Cuban missile crisis, the civil rights struggle, and dealing with Diem offer insight into an inspired, devious, ruthless man, more pragmatic than principled—in other words, a politician.

Kennedy's illnesses, drug use, and serial seductions I have left to others. Instead, my focus is on presidential machinations as Kennedy duped me and other journalists into misleading readers, librarians, schoolteachers, historians, and filmmakers. Many are still unaware of how Kennedy handled these major issues in the final year of his life. That reality was buried with him at Arlington National Cemetery. I was there for that, too. With his burial, myth overtook reality. This is not a mea culpa, although it may sound like it. Actually I am just cleaning up my early accounts from fifty years ago. Another lesson I learned at UPI was how to handle news or facts as they changed over time. On an important story used by newspapers and broadcasters around the world, there was an early version. As new facts came along, there was a "first lead," perhaps "first lead (correct)" (which identified and eliminated a gross error). By the end of day, after many new leads, there was a write-through—including a note to editors—with facts freshened, a little better writing, and logic that would satisfy critics on the other end of the teletype clicking out the truth. At UPI, we never made mistakes—at least ones that we couldn't eventually clean up.

So this book is a write-through of President Kennedy's last year in office as he prepared for the 1964 reelection bid—in effect, his last campaign. Cuba, the civil rights movement, and Vietnam were akin to a Wack-a-Mole game at the White House. Just as Kennedy focused on the political erosion of Vietnam, civil rights would explode on television to undercut him with conflicting ideologues. Killing Fidel Castro was high on his agenda. Kennedy's last campaign is a story of a desperate politician determined to overcome events conspiring to erode his chances for a second term as president of the United States. Assassination and smear became the tools of the responsible officer of government.

Patrick Sloyan
Paeonian Springs, Virginia
July 2013

1

General LeMay's Threat

FOR PRESIDENT KENNEDY, JANUARY 1963 was not too early to prepare for his 1964 reelection campaign. Ever since his stunning upset of Republican Henry Cabot Lodge Jr. in the 1952 Senate race in Massachusetts, Kennedy always got an early start.

"My chief opponents followed the old practice of not starting until about two months ahead of the elections. By then, I was ahead of them. In 1952, I worked a year and a half ahead of the November election before Senator Lodge did," Kennedy said. "I am following the same practice now."

Kennedy's head start philosophy ignored the latest polls. They showed you where you were today but were no predictor of future standing. More important was a checklist of advantages and disadvantages, strengths and weaknesses, positives and negatives. Even so, the poll released January 20 showed Kennedy with a scintillating approval rating by 76 percent of voters interviewed by George Gallup's American Institute of Public Opinion. Much of it stemmed from his triumphal resolution of the Cuban missile crisis four months earlier. But in 1963, Kennedy's biggest advantage had the potential of turning into a devastating weakness. That chilling prospect hit home during a meeting with Defense Secretary Robert S. McNamara. After disposing of some issues related to Pentagon hardware, McNamara shifted to the 1964 reelection campaign.

"LeMay and Power could cause real trouble during the campaign next year," McNamara told Kennedy. He was speaking of General Curtis LeMay, the Air Force chief of staff, and General Thomas Power, commander of the Strategic Air Command. Both generals knew the truth about the 1962 Cuban missile crisis that Kennedy had hidden under layers of deception, manipulation, and mendacity. Kennedy had secretly agreed to Khrushchev's demand of a missile swap—U.S. Jupiter rockets in Turkey for Soviet missiles in Cuba. Since Kennedy had deployed the Jupiters in 1961, the Russian leader had raged at the U.S. warheads only a quick flight from Moscow. The cunning Russian's gambit in Cuba was designed to remove the American threat in Turkey.

To the world, Kennedy presented a very different story. He made it seem that Soviet premier Nikita Khrushchev had overplayed his hand by secretly deploying Russian nuclear-tipped missiles in Cuba that could strike targets in the southern United States. The showboating communist leader, famous for pounding his shoe on the podium at the United Nations, blundered and then stepped back from nuclear warfare in the face of a steely determination demonstrated by the young American president. "We're eyeball to eyeball, and I think the other fellow just blinked," said Secretary of State Dean Rusk. That quote, underlining a Kennedy victory and Khrushchev's retreat, first appeared in an inside account of White House deliberations published in the *Saturday Evening Post* two months after the 1962 crisis. It portrayed a president ready to launch devastating air strikes and send 140,000 troops into Cuba if Khrushchev did not remove the offending missiles. The article set the factual standard for historians, librarians, moviemakers, and teachers, and the global perception of crisis outcome.

In those days before television news became predominant, the *Post* and *Life* magazines were in millions of American homes, barbershops, hair salons, and doctor's offices. They were national publications with an impact equal to today's penetrating *60 Minutes* reports based on exclusive facts from the lips of the insiders, including the president. The publications were crucial to voter perceptions. The magazine article, entitled "In Time of Crisis," was just one more example of Kennedy's burying the reality of what was the pinnacle of the cold war between the United States and the Soviet Union. Kennedy and his staff had duped one of the authors of the article, Charles Bartlett, into writing a total fabrication of White House decisions. Bartlett, Kennedy's chum since their prep school days and a reporter for the *Chattanooga Times,* would not learn the truth himself until decades later. The cover-up was so complete and lasting because Kennedy demanded—and got—Khrushchev's silence as a condition of the missile swap. What really happened would not emerge on the public record for more than thirty-five years with the declassification of White House tape recordings and Soviet documents. Both show Kennedy quickly conceding to Khrushchev's offer of a nuclear weapons exchange—Russian missiles in Cuba for American missiles in Turkey that the Soviet leader so bitterly resented.

Kennedy not only embraced Khrushchev's missile swap the day it was offered, he ordered the Air Force to defuse the fifteen Jupiter rockets in Turkey that had so angered the Soviet leader. American Air Force troops stationed near Izmir where the missiles were deployed were ordered to remove all of the W49 warheads, each with an estimated blast of 1.44 megatons. "We could not take them out unilaterally, " Rusk said twenty-three years later, explaining how the Jupiters were technically under the control of the North Atlantic Treaty Organization. "So Kennedy had them remove the warheads from the missiles in Turkey during the Cuban missile crisis." The crisis ended on Sunday, October 28, the day after Kennedy's secret agreement with Khrushchev. Kennedy, Rusk, McNamara, and McGeorge Bundy, in top secret discussions on October 27, seem to think the order to remove the warheads was done that day. It was a different story at Cigil

Air Force Base in Turkey, where Airman Fred Travis, then twenty-one, had a more accurate version. "The order came down October 27, but you couldn't remove fifteen warheads in one day," Travis said. "We could lock them down, make them safe. But it took days to remove the warheads. This was a sixty-five-foot rocket that you had to lay down on its side on a special truck. Then another crew removed the nose cone that contained the warhead." Work was under way well after Khrushchev announced removal of Russian rockets from Cuba.

Those Jupiters were never the focus of the showdown between Kennedy and Khrushchev, according to the White House rewrite of history for the *Saturday Evening Post.* Kennedy would lead Bartlett to believe that it was Adlai Stevenson, his ambassador to the United Nations, who pushed for the missile swap while the president was standing firm against it. "Adlai wanted a Munich," said an unidentified source quoted by Bartlett, referring to Britain's craven diplomatic surrender to Adolf Hitler in 1938. In fact Stevenson first raised the idea of the missile exchange that Kennedy swiftly accepted from Khrushchev. And it was Kennedy himself who manipulated Bartlett into smearing Stevenson, according to McGeorge Bundy, the president's national security affairs adviser.

Kennedy and McNamara's concern about these truths leaking into the 1964 presidential campaign was a legitimate fear. General LeMay, a table-pounding critic of Kennedy's handling of the Cuban missile crisis, knew of the secret Jupiter disarmament and the missile swap. Also, LeMay was close to Senator Barry Goldwater, the conservative Arizona Republican. Goldwater, already seen in 1963 as the GOP standard-bearer in 1964, was a leading critic of Kennedy's policy toward Cuban leader Fidel Castro. While diplomatic spin could—and eventually would—mute suspicions of the Jupiter removal from Turkey, a leak about defusing the warheads would underscore a Kennedy concession and a political cover-up.

Before their removal, the thermonuclear Jupiter warheads—a

hundred times more powerful than the weapon that incinerated Hiroshima—were less than a fifteen-minute flight from Moscow. The brevity of the flight time posed a first-strike threat to Kremlin military planners—destroying Soviet weapons with a sneak attack before bombers and missiles could be used or dispersed. In those days, according to the CIA, Russia had only ten rockets that could threaten the United States. Kennedy's Jupiter deployment in 1961 was done over the objections of his defense chief, Congress, and other experts. While a dubious addition to the American strategic arsenal, the deployment outraged the Russian leader. Khrushchev ignored thirty Jupiters deployed in Italy during the Eisenhower administration. Nor did he mention sixty American-made Thor missiles based in the United Kingdom. His personal ire was reserved for the fifteen Jupiters in Turkey that he objected to in person when first meeting with Kennedy in Vienna. Surrounding Russia with nuclear weapons was unwise, the Soviet leader told Kennedy at their 1961 summit meeting. "We must be reasonable and keep our forces within our national boundaries," Khrushchev told Kennedy. "This situation may cause miscalculation."

However, Khrushchev's threats to seize Berlin within six months stunned Kennedy at Vienna, who resolved to deploy the Jupiters as a show of strength. The deployment was completed by March of 1962. The Soviet leader saw the Jupiters in Turkey as a personal insult. To illustrate his anger, Khrushchev put on a little show for visitors, including American newspaper columnist Drew Pearson, at his vacation home at Sochi. The site of the 2014 Winter Olympics, the town is a Russian resort on the Black Sea that borders Turkey. Khrushchev would hand binoculars to guests and ask them to look at the sea's horizon. Saying they saw nothing, the guests would return the binoculars. With a flourish, Khrushchev would hold them to his eyes. What did he see? they asked. "U.S. missiles in Turkey aimed at my dacha!" Khrushchev would bellow. The CIA picked up the Russian's outbursts and Kennedy knew of Khrushchev's anger over the Jupiter deployment. When it became apparent that the Soviet missile deployment was under way in Cuba, Kennedy understood it was linked to the U.S. missile deployment in Turkey. When the White House sent out the first alarm to the Pentagon, the CIA, and the State Department about the Cuban deployment, Kennedy asked for advice on how the Jupiters could be removed. "What actions can be taken to get the Jupiter missiles out of Turkey?" demanded McGeorge Bundy, Kennedy's national security affairs adviser, in an all-points memo on August 21, 1963.

"We were not inventing anything new," Khrushchev would say years later about his secret missile deployment in Cuba. "We were just copying methods used against us by our adversaries." The Americans, he said, "would learn just what it feels like to have enemy missiles pointing at you; we'd be doing nothing more than giving them a little of their own medicine." Starting in January of 1962, the Soviet leader personally directed the covert deployment in Cuba of forty-two Sandal missiles that could explode nuclear warheads over dozens of American cities 1,200 miles away in the South and Southwest. The Sandal could reach Washington, Atlanta, Miami, Houston, Dallas, San Antonio, and smaller cities in that region. Soon, according to Kennedy, longer-range Russian rockets in Cuba could reach every city in the western hemisphere. But American intelligence never spotted in Cuba the Skean rocket that could fly 2,800 miles to strike New York or other major U.S. cities.

In the end, Khrushchev's stealthy deployment of rockets and ninety nuclear warheads in Cuba was the fulcrum to leverage the threatening missiles out of Turkey and off the Russian doorstep, out "of the left armpits of the Russians," as one American missile expert put it. Kennedy and his advisers discussed the possibilities of such a deal, but it seemed beyond their reach until the Soviet leader laid it on the table Saturday, October 27. In Moscow the day before, Khrushchev told his executive board, the Presidium, for the first time that the Cuban deployment was aimed at elevating the Soviet status in the world and removing the Turkish missiles. "If we could achieve additionally the liquidation of the bases in Turkey, we would win," said the party chairman as he outlined the missile exchange proposal sent to Kennedy. Khrushchev made the stark swap public, placing it before the eyes of global public opinion. Even Kennedy admired the politically shrewd end game by the Russian leader when it unfolded in the Oval Office on Saturday morning, October 27, 1962. "This trade has appeal," Kennedy told his advisers. "He's got us in a pretty good spot here. Because most people will regard this as not an unreasonable proposal. I just tell you that." Disagreeing were Secretary of State Rusk, Defense Secretary McNamara, Attorney General Robert F. Kennedy, Army General Maxwell Taylor, chairman of the Joint Chiefs of Staff, and National Security Adviser McGeorge Bundy. They and five others in the deliberations made for a lopsided majority against the missile swap. To them, the Kremlin solution was so laden with potentially disastrous political and diplomatic consequences. To American voters, it would seem Kennedy had sacrificed a NATO ally after being outfoxed by the communist leader. Instead of humiliating Khrushchev for taking the world to the edge of a nuclear abyss, Kennedy would be capitulating to the Soviet leader. By pulling the Jupiters out of Turkey, the rest of NATO would forever doubt American solidarity. "Kennedy's concession" was how Bundy would later characterize the agreement. Bundy had demanded that Kennedy reject the Soviet proposal outright the day it arrived. "This should be knocked down publicly," Bundy said.

Dominating the discussions was the president's brother, known to most as Bobby. He worried about the image of the United States attacking the tiny nation of Cuba because of Soviet actions. "You're going to kill an awful lot of people and we're going to take an awful lot of heat on it," Bobby told his brother. Even then, Khrushchev could send replacements for missiles damaged by air attacks. Bobby argued only an invasion of Cuba would end the Soviet threat. To whip up American support for such an invasion, Bobby recalled the sinking of the USS *Maine* in Havana harbor under mysterious circumstances in 1898. "Remember the *Maine*" became the battle cry that led the United States into war with Spain. At one point on October 16, Bobby suggested staging an American attack on U.S. warships that could then be blamed on Cubans—an American-generated provocation at the U.S. naval base at Guantánamo, Cuba. Bobby said he wondered "Whether there's some ship, you know, that . . . sink the *Maine* again or something." Bobby led the hawk contingent against the missile exchange.

The exceptions—siding with Kennedy in the crucial hours—were Vice President Lyndon B. Johnson, Undersecretary of State George Ball, and Director John McCone of the CIA. All three had taken hawkish positions when the crisis started. But they were transformed to doves after the shocking word that an American U-2 spy plane had been shot down over Cuba and the surge among other advisers for quick retaliation. Their attitudes changed after a convoluted scenario by McNamara that included an attack on Cuban sites followed by the public announcement that the Jupiters had been disabled. The defense chiefs hoped the defusing of the Jupiters would keep the Soviet Union from attacking the Turkish rockets in retaliation for U.S. air strikes in Cuba, a tortured idea designed to prevent a tit-for-tat escalation that could lead to nuclear warfare.

The vice president quickly offered the logic that if the Jupiters were to be disabled anyway, why not forgo the air strikes and just swap the missiles in Turkey for those in Cuba. "Why not trade?" interjected Johnson upon hearing McNamara's scenario. Ball applauded the vice president's common sense. "And save a few hundred thousand lives," Ball added. "Make the trade," Ball shouted at another point. "Make the trade then!" McCone also supported the vice president's logic. "I don't see why you don't make the trade then," McCone said. Later he added: "And, I'd trade these Turkish things out right now. I wouldn't even talk to anybody about it." A few hours later, Kennedy would do exactly as McCone recommended.

Johnson, Ball, and McCone wanted to avoid the launch within hours of five days of massive air attacks on Cuba. Five hundred warplane sorties a day would be followed by a landing of 140,000 troops to destroy the Soviet threat, oust Fidel Castro, and establish an anticommunist government. Most of the others in the pressure-packed Cabinet Room were supporting the military strike. Brother Bobby dismissed the president's blockade of Russian ships from entry into Cuban ports. "Slow death" was Bobby's view of the naval tactic, which delayed a conflict but did not remove the missiles from Cuba. The attorney general, Rusk, and Bundy kept clinging to a secret Khrushchev offer Friday that suggested a simple U.S. pledge to never invade Cuba would result in the removal of the Russian weapons. The president, his voice impatient, reminded them that Khrushchev's emotional Friday-night solution was no longer on the table. "Now he's got something completely new," Kennedy said of the Soviet leader's public announcement. "I think you're going to have it very difficult to explain why we are going to take hostile military action in Cuba against all these sites . . . when he's saying, 'If you get yours out of Turkey, we'll get ours out of Cuba.'

"I think we've got a very tough one here," Kennedy said.

The president was in and out of the Cabinet Room when Johnson, Ball, and McCone became the three advisers to openly favor the missile swap. The other twelve advisers favored the attack on Cuba even though Kennedy was pushing acceptance of Khrushchev's final offer. "Save all the invasion . . . lives . . . everything else," Johnson said after again urging the missile swap. He also argued that Turkish leaders would go along after they realized that removal of the Jupiters would take them off the Soviet target list. And Turkey would get the protection of the U.S. nuclear umbrella with the Polaris submarine fleet—without needing a base in Turkey. "We're going to give you more protection than ever with Polaris with less advertising," Johnson said. "And it's going to make it less likely you'll get hit. Why wouldn't [the Turkish prime minister] buy that?" Ball again pushed for the swap. "I'd say, 'Sure, we will accept your offer,'" Ball said. "We can work it out."

Johnson's support of the president's preference to accept the missile trade has been largely ignored by historians. Most accounts are influenced by Bobby Kennedy's claim that Johnson contributed nothing to the crisis except hawkish statements. And even after instigating Ball and McCone's support for the missile swap, Johnson continued to warn Kennedy of the potential drawbacks. It could lead to demands for total withdrawal—U.S. planes and troops as well as missiles—from Turkey. In effect, Moscow would be dictating limits to American support for a NATO ally. "Why then, your whole foreign policy is gone," Johnson said sharply to Kennedy. "You take everything out of Turkey—20,000 men, all your technicians and all your planes and all your missiles . . . and crumble." "How else are we going to get those missiles out of there, then?" Kennedy replied calmly. "That's the problem." Despite his ambivalence, Johnson agreed to lobby the military in behalf of Kennedy's acceptance of Khrushchev's missile swap. At the Pentagon, the Joint Chiefs were pushing for an attack on Cuba, as were the majority of Kennedy's civilian advisers. Shortly after the Russian leader's missile exchange proposal arrived at the White House Saturday morning, October 27, Johnson urged a four-star general who influenced the top military commanders to endorse the missile swap.

Army General Lyman Lemnitzer, who had just stepped down as the chairman of the Joint Chiefs on October 1, said the vice-president called him to the White House. Even though he was no longer chairman, Lemnitzer huddled with the Joint Chiefs throughout the crisis. He had been succeeded by Taylor, a Kennedy favorite, three weeks earlier. "Johnson stated that he thought the Khrushchev proposal was a reasonable one and should be accepted," Lemnitzer said. Lemnitzer recalled the White House meeting with the vice-president in a letter and conversations with Dino A. Brugioni, a CIA official who prepared briefings for the chiefs that accompanied photographic intelligence of Soviet missile bases in Cuba. "I had great difficulty in convincing Vice President Johnson that our Jupiter missiles were an important part of NATO's deterrent posture," Lemnitzer said in a letter to Brugioni. Johnson became belligerent, saying, "since we damn well gave them to the Turks, we can damn well take them back," Lemnitzer continued. "Then Johnson, in his inimitable manner, said: 'We can make it up to the Turks.'" The substitute for the Turks would be Mediterranean patrols by new American submarines with nuclear-tipped Polaris missiles. After being softened up by Johnson, Lemnitzer met with Kennedy about five P.M. After that meeting, Lemnitzer shared the White House position with the other service chiefs at the Pentagon. With nuclear war still possible, the chiefs viewed eliminating any U.S. warheads as a mistake. "Lemnitzer would say it was a most stupid move," Brugioni said.

There is no White House record that Kennedy and Johnson planned an approach to the Joint Chiefs. But Johnson stressed that he reserved his best advice for private meetings with Kennedy. Both Johnson and Rusk favored the one-on-one channel, which often eluded the White House tape recording system and attacks by other advisers in bigger group settings. Johnson's forceful lobbying of the former chairman of the Joint Chiefs was likely not done on his own. The vice president was probably acceding to Kennedy's request. Lemnitzer's letter and the White House tape recordings challenge Bobby's contention that Johnson played no role in ending the crisis.

Defusing the warheads made moot another part of the secret proposal to Khrushchev—pledging to remove the Jupiters within five months. Bobby delivered the deal to Khrushchev via the Soviet ambassador in Washington along with a demand for total secrecy: If Russians made public the missile swap agreement, the whole deal was off. But Bobby made no mention of the Jupiter warhead removal, according to American and Soviet documents. Perhaps that would have been a form of instant gratification for Khrushchev that Kennedy was not ready to grant. Rusk's disclosure of Kennedy's order on

October 27 to disable the Jupiters was made during interviews in 1984. But the president's order also may have been based on fear of an accidental launch during the crisis. Control of the Jupiters depended on commercial telephone from Paris, a long-distance network of landlines that was easily compromised and notorious for disruptions and poor sound quality.

The missile swap pact was kept secret until 1971, shortly before Khrushchev's death. The Soviet government said secrecy was the key aspect of the Kennedy agreement for a missile swap negotiated by Kennedy's brother Robert and the Russian ambassador to Washington, Anatoly Dobrynin. But there was no proof to back up the Soviet claim. One reason was the refusal by the Americans to sign any documents outlining the missile swap. Khrushchev asked for a written agreement to replace what had been only an oral pledge to remove the missiles from Turkey. According to Dobrynin, two days after the secret agreement, Khrushchev wanted the deal spelled out in a formal document. The Soviet leader's appeal was directed in a letter to Bobby Kennedy. After consulting with his brother, Bobby returned the letter. According to Dobrynin, Kennedy said he could not sign a document that might become public at some future date. "The appearance of such a document could cause irreparable harm to my political career in the future," Robert Kennedy said, according to Dobrynin. Or to the 1964 reelection campaign of his brother, John—a campaign Bobby planned to manage. The matter was dropped, Rusk confirmed later. Bobby Kennedy was later elected as U.S. senator in New York and was killed in 1968 while campaigning for the Democratic presidential nomination.

The American version of events did not start to emerge until the release of White House tape recordings in 1997. Rusk's revelation about removing the Jupiter warheads was made in a 1984 interview with his son, Richard, who was preparing to write a book. Richard did not reveal the removal of the warheads in Rusk's recollection of the missile crisis. In hiding these concessions to the Soviet leader, Kennedy also covered up his finest moment as president. He led the minority in favor of concessions to protect the world from Armageddon. At times he seemed almost alone in the clear-eyed perception that events were eroding his best efforts to avoid a nuclear conflict with a death toll in the millions and staggering destruction to both nations. Kennedy was immersed in a chess match of escalation:

What would be the Soviet reply to an attack on their missiles in Cuba? A Soviet strike on the American missiles in Turkey?

What would be the American reply? A U.S. attack on Russian forces that attacked Turkey?

Or would Khrushchev grab the western sectors of Berlin as he had vowed to do a year earlier? The German capital had been divided among allies at the end of World War II. What then?

One miscalculation could quickly evolve into a holocaust. Most of the men in the Cabinet Room offered muddled advice that always came back to a military attack and the first step toward Armageddon. Kennedy, however, rejected every suggestion that risked escalation. Kennedy let everyone in on the stakes involved in a televised speech—the first nationwide broadcast of a crisis—with words that sent chills up the spine of all. After hearing from the military and briefing congressional leaders, Kennedy faced the cameras on October 22, his baritone unwavering, his eyes unflinching. Most who heard it would never forget that there really was a chance for a sudden, fiery death.

"It shall be the policy of this nation to regard any nuclear missile launched from Cuba against any nation in the western hemisphere as an attack on the United States, requiring the full retaliatory response upon the Soviet Union," Kennedy said. "The 1930s taught us a clear lesson: aggressive conduct, if allowed to go unchecked, ultimately leads to war. I call upon Chairman Khrushchev to halt and eliminate this clandestine, reckless and provocative threat to world peace. We will not prematurely or unnecessarily risk the costs of worldwide nuclear war in which even the fruits of victory would be ashes in our mouth—but neither will we shrink from that risk at any time it must be faced." He portrayed Khrushchev as a cowardly sneak who brought the world to the edge of a nuclear abyss with a deployment of nuclear weapons hidden behind a string of clumsy lies. When Kennedy finished, it was easy to pick out the world's savior from the archvillain—the kind Ian Fleming produced in his James Bond novels that Kennedy so admired.

In the confines of the Cabinet Room, however, Kennedy made clear he would do just about anything to avoid nuclear war—including politically unpalatable concessions and blatant mendacity that could cripple his reelection if the body of lies began to crumble. If ever there was a time when the ends justified the means, it was later that Saturday night in the Oval Office. "Now the question is really what action we take which lessens the chances of nuclear exchange, which obviously is the final failure," Kennedy told the newly created executive committee made up of his senior advisers.

The Saturday (October 27) Khrushchev's solution arrived, Kennedy had American strategic nuclear forces on war footing. DEFCON 2, the Pentagon acronym for defense readiness condition, had been issued for B-52 bomber pilots circling within striking distance of the Soviet Union. The red alert of DEFCON 2 was only one step below the white alert of DEFCON 1—nuclear war is imminent. Most B-52s carried four hydrogen bombs with a destructive force equal to 4 million tons of TNT explosives. At Malmstrom Air Force Base in Great Falls, Montana, the men of the 341st Missile Wing began spinning the gyroscopes that would guide 150 Minuteman intercontinental ballistic missiles to their Soviet targets. Each missile had a warhead with an explosive yield equivalent to 170,000 tons of TNT. Six Polaris submarines—each with sixteen nuclear-tipped missiles—were moving silently and unseen toward Soviet targets. One warhead from these *Ethan Allen* class subs was the equivalent of 600,000 tons of TNT. Never again were American strategic forces to be on such a hair-trigger alert.

As part of a series of nuclear tests approved by Kennedy earlier in the year, Air Force B-52s detonated three hydrogen bombs at the Johnston Atoll test site in the South Pacific during the missile crisis. Nearby Soviet "trawlers" relayed details of the tests to Moscow. The third B-52 test, code-named *Calamity,* was conducted at dawn on Saturday, October 27. The ten-engine jet dropped the same sort of hydrogen bomb carried by SAC bombers flying racetrack formations near the Soviet Union. *Calamity* produced an orange fireball that eerily reflected on the ocean. It was the scariest form of saber rattling. A mushroom cloud rose 63,000 feet. Kennedy was told of the successful test as he began a Saturday of fateful decisions that risked a real-world calamity. The United States had a lopsided advantage in strategic weapons, and Kennedy was confronted with a recommendation to launch a preemptive first strike—launched without warning—that would destroy most of the Soviet missiles and bombers. This "counterforce" strategy envisions the destruction of most Soviet weapons, minimizing Moscow's ability to retaliate against the United States.

A leading advocate was General LeMay. "If there is to be war, there's no better time than the present," LeMay said at the Pentagon. "We are prepared and the [Russian] 'bear' is not." LeMay was the likely role model for actor George C. Scott, who played the scary Air Force General "Buck" Turgidson in Stanley Kubrick's *Dr. Strangelove or: How I Learned to Stop Worrying and Love the Bomb.* It was filmed two years later, and the general favors an all-out surprise strike on the communists to degrade their retaliation. The general tells the president that there would still be a Soviet response on American cities. "Mr. President, I'm not saying we wouldn't get our hair mussed," Turgidson says. "But I do say no more than ten to twenty million killed, tops. Uh, depending on the breaks." The same cold-blooded proposal came from Senator Richard B. Russell, the Georgia Democrat who was chairman of the Senate armed services committee. Russell said he talked to LeMay and supported the Air Force chief's aggressive solutions to the crisis.

"It's a very difficult choice that we're facing together," Kennedy told Russell and the congressional leadership during an October 22 meeting.

"Oh my God!" Russell said, interrupting the president. "I know that. Our authority and the world's destiny will hinge on this decision. But it's coming someday, Mr. President. Will it ever be under more auspicious circumstances? I don't see how we are going to be better off next year."

By invoking LeMay's name, Russell clearly irked Kennedy. The Air Force chief had undoubtedly influenced the president's advisers, including the defense secretary. During World War II, Captain McNamara did statistical studies showing the effectiveness of LeMay's fire-bombing campaign against Japan. More than 40 percent of sixty-six Japanese cities were destroyed; 500,000 people were killed and 5 million left homeless. It was this warrior's ferocity that LeMay brought into the White House deliberations. At times LeMay bordered on open contempt for the president. He dismissed Kennedy's suggestion for a naval blockade of Cuba.

"I think that a blockade and political talk would be considered by a lot of our friends and neutrals as being a pretty weak response to this. And I'm sure a lot of our own citizens would feel that way, too." LeMay then implied Kennedy had blundered into crisis. "In other words, you're in a pretty bad fix at the present time," LeMay said.

"What'd you say," Kennedy asked evenly.

"I say, you're in a pretty bad fix," LeMay said.

"You're in it with me," Kennedy said, adding with a laugh, "personally."

LeMay kept boring in. "I just don't see any other solution except direct military intervention," LeMay said. Instead of a reply such as seizing Berlin, LeMay predicted the Russians would do nothing rather than risk devastation. In fact, avoiding an attack on Cuba would be an invitation for Khrushchev to grab Berlin. Moscow would feel "they've got us on the run," LeMay said. As for the naval blockade, it was another incentive for bolder Soviet action. "It will lead right into war," LeMay said. "This is almost as bad as the appeasement at Munich."

That was a deep dig at Kennedy. His father, Joseph P. Kennedy, as U.S. ambassador to Britain in 1938, had supported Prime Minister Neville Chamberlain's effort to satisfy Adolf Hitler's Nazi ambitions by flying to Munich. Chamberlain had agreed to Hitler's occupation of the Sudetenland in Czechoslovakia in exchange for what turned out to be a worthless peace agreement. Munich was forever seen as worst form of statesmanship. It encouraged Hitler to seize Poland, an invasion that launched World War II. Every man in the room realized LeMay had just implied that the president would rather placate Khrushchev than challenge the Soviet provocation. LeMay was challenging Kennedy's guts. After the October 19 meeting was over, other members of the Joint Chiefs lingered in the Cabinet Room, unaware that their comments were being recorded. "You pulled the rug right out from under him," General David Shoup, the Marine commandant, said to LeMay in a voice filled with congratulation.

The president had held his tongue until he got outside the Cabinet Room. In private, he produced an angry explosion for Deputy Defense Secretary Roswell Gilpatric. "He was just choleric," Gilpatric recalled later. "He was just beside himself." This situation was nothing new between LeMay and Kennedy. Whenever LeMay briefed the president in earlier meetings, it left Kennedy boiling. "He ended up in sort of a fit," Gilpatric said. "I mean, he just would be frantic at the end of a session with LeMay because, you know, LeMay couldn't listen." This was partly because LeMay was becoming increasingly deaf and refused to wear a hearing aid, Gilpatric said. "He would make what Kennedy considered—we all considered—perfectly outrageous proposals that bore no relation to the state of affairs in the 1960s."

Still, LeMay was on the same track as former president Eisenhower. McCone, who personally briefed Eisenhower on the Cuban crisis, reported to Kennedy that the old general saw an offensive Soviet

base in Cuba as "intolerable from the standpoint of this country."
He favored all-out military action going "right for the jugular first"
by destroying Havana and Castro, McCone reported. To Kennedy,
Eisenhower's support was crucial in domestic political terms. If the
World War II commander supported Kennedy, there was little room
for Republicans in Congress to second-guess his handling of the crisis.
Kennedy personally telephoned his predecessor during the crisis to
seek his advice—and support.

LeMay, Taylor, and McNamara told Kennedy he must give
the order Saturday or Sunday if OPLAN 312 were to be launched
on Monday or Tuesday—500 warplane sorties against Cuban sites.
That level of assault would be maintained for five days. Then OPLAN
316 would begin with an invasion by air and sea of 90,000 Army
and Marine troops. Another 50,000 would join the invasion force
within two weeks. Kennedy's advisers were all struggling to avoid
public actions that would signal uncertainty. "I don't think at this
particular point we should show a weakness to Khrushchev," Mc-
Namara said. He was urging combat planes to support surveillance
flights over Cuba by unarmed U-2 spy planes and other photorecon-
naissance aircraft. It was these flights that first spotted the Soviet
missile deployment October 16.

About four P.M. Saturday, word arrived that a Soviet surface-to-
air missile had shot down an American U-2. "The wreckage is on
the ground and the pilot's dead," General Taylor said. "They've fired
the first shot," said Paul Nitze, an assistant secretary of defense.

"Well now, this is much of an escalation by them, isn't it," Kennedy said evenly. It was not a question. The news rattled the Cabinet
Room. The death of one man—identified later as Air Force Major
Rudolf Anderson Jr.—underscored the reality that it was not just diplomacy and strategy being discussed but human life and death. Vice
President Johnson, Undersecretary Ball, and McCone of the CIA
began openly endorsing Khrushchev's missile exchange. "That's when
everybody's color changed a little bit," Johnson observed. Khrush-

chev, too, he predicted, would understand the gravity that flowed from downing the American spy plane. "It was sure as hell that's going to make the impression on him," Johnson said. "Not all these signals that each one of us write. He's expert at that palaver."

General Taylor reminded Kennedy that he had authorized an automatic Air Force strike on the offending antiaircraft site in Cuba in the event of a U-2's being shot down. Kennedy quickly countered the standing order and said his personal approval would be needed before any Air Force retaliation. When he got Kennedy's new order at the Pentagon, LeMay hung up the phone in disgust. "He's chickened out again," LeMay told an aide.

With deadlines looming, Kennedy took it all in, tapping his prominent front teeth with first his finger, then a pencil. "We are running out of time," Kennedy said twice during the final meetings Saturday night. After hearing everyone out, the president signaled he had made up his mind.

"This is a pretty good play of his," Kennedy said of the Khrushchev proposal. "Most people will think this is a rather even trade, and we ought to take advantage of it. We can't very well invade Cuba with all its toil and blood . . . when we could have gotten them out by making a deal on the same missiles on Turkey. If that's part of the record, then you don't have a very good war." Then Kennedy turned the Oval Office into a woodshed. He ended the opposition to the missile swap by his most trusted advisers. Bobby got his marching orders. The attorney general was instructed on what to tell Soviet ambassador Dobrynin to relay to Khrushchev.

In a diary, Bobby would admit the president's offer hinged on removal of the Jupiters in Turkey. The diary was used as the basis for his posthumous book *Thirteen Days: A Memoir of the Cuban Missile Crisis*. Bobby was quite specific about the swap, according to Theodore Sorensen. He was the president's speechwriter, confidant, and a participant in the super-secret Oval Office session when Bobby was told what to tell the Russians. And it was Sorensen who put together Bobby's best-selling book after he was assassinated on the 1968 campaign trail. Sorensen said he penciled out the truth of the deal. "His diary was very explicit that this was part of the deal; but at that time it was still a secret even on the American side, except for the six of us who had been present at that meeting," Sorensen confessed at a 1989 Moscow conference on the crisis. "So I took it upon myself to edit that out of his diaries." Nor did Sorensen disclose the backroom deal in his biography of Kennedy. Sorensen was part of a cottage industry of authors who knew the truth about Kennedy's missile exchange but hid it. Another was Arthur Schlesinger Jr., Kennedy's in-house Pulitzer Prize–winning historian. In his best-selling *A Thousand Days*, which was published in 1965, he said Kennedy rejected the missile exchange as soon as it was proposed. Khrushchev, Schlesinger said, backed down. "It was clear that he had thrown in his hand," the historian wrote.

In a 1988 book, Bundy rationalized the secrecy but not the truth of the swap. "Concerned as we all were by the cost of a public bargain struck under pressure at the apparent expense of the Turks, and aware as we were from the day's discussion that for some, even in our own closest councils, even this unilateral private assurance might appear to betray an ally, we agreed without hesitation that no one not in the room was to be informed of this additional message," Bundy wrote. "Robert Kennedy was instructed to make it plain to Dobrynin that the same secrecy must be observed on the other side. Any Soviet reference to our assurance would simply make it null and void."

The defusing of the Jupiter warheads, however, was not part of a specific quid pro quo between Kennedy and Khrushchev. While McNamara proposed removing the warheads during the Saturday deliberations, there is no evidence of the action in either American or Soviet documents released decades later. According to the Russian diplomat, Bobby was red-eyed and exhausted when they met at the Justice Department. The president wanted an answer from Khrushchev by Sunday—not an ultimatum but a request. Bobby made no mention of defusing the Jupiters in Turkey but said the president agreed to their removal by April of 1963. "The greatest difficulty for the president is the public discussion of the issue of Turkey," Kennedy said, according to Dobrynin. "However, President Kennedy is ready to come to agree on that question with N. S. Khrushchev. However, the president can't say anything in public," Kennedy reiterated, the Soviet diplomat said.

Kennedy and the world breathed a sigh of relief when Khrushchev, as requested, made a Sunday announcement that Russians missiles were coming out of Cuba after the American president pledged never to invade the communist island. But in a later secret letter to the president, Khrushchev stressed his public assurances on the removal of the Cuban missiles "were given on account of you having agreed to the Turkish issue." Now Kennedy was still concerned about Republicans on his domestic political flank. One of his first calls that Sunday was to Eisenhower. Kennedy stressed his rejection of Khrushchev's public offer to swap missiles. "We then issued a statement that we couldn't get into that deal," Kennedy told Eisenhower. Only an agreement not to invade Cuba, he said.

"Any other conditions?" Eisenhower asked.

"No," Kennedy said, adding later, "This is quite a step down for Khrushchev."

Eisenhower, who had dealt with ruthless Russians in the past, was clearly mystified by the Soviet leader's retreat. "This is a very, I think, conciliatory move he's made," he told Kennedy. Ten days after Kennedy's bald-faced lie to his predecessor, Democrats avoided the traditional off-year losses in the congressional elections. They even gained four seats in the House and wound up with two-thirds of the Senate. Kennedy's aura of victory had extended to the polls.

After dealing with Eisenhower, Kennedy plotted one of the most durable cover-ups in American history. He would manipulate the media's perception of the crisis with one of its own. He invited newsman Charles Bartlett to bask in the glow of victory with a dinner at the White House. Bartlett, a Pulitzer Prize–winning reporter, had a long personal relationship with the president. Bartlett had introduced Kennedy to Jacqueline Bouvier and attended their wedding. Bartlett was also a frequent guest during the Cuban crisis in the White House family quarters for dinner with the president and his wife.

"I think the pressure of this period made him desire more to have friends around," Bartlett recalled later. "I think I was over there for dinner three times in the week, or something like that." Bartlett was also one of five working journalists who agreed to provide Soviet embassy officials with ostensibly inside information during the crisis at the behest of the White House. At one point, Bartlett showed one Russian contact actual U-2 photographs from the White House to show that the Americans had solid evidence of the Soviet missiles in Cuba.

October 29, the day after the crisis ended, Bartlett said he had the idea to write about the crisis after talking with a White House press office aide, Ralph Dungan, who encouraged him. "It would be a good magazine article because the president certainly looks good from everything I know," Bartlett told Dungan. That Monday night he went to dinner with Kennedy at the White House and described his plan to write a magazine article. Kennedy said others were also writing inside accounts. "My role, I've decided, in all these articles will be not to talk to the writers," Kennedy said, according to Bartlett. "There's no point sitting around and patting myself on the back." Instead, Bartlett was turned over to McGeorge Bundy, Kennedy's adviser on national security affairs and other participants in the crisis, including Bobby Kennedy. Along with coauthor Stewart Alsop, the *Saturday Evening Post* article led off with the historic "eyeball to eyeball" quote.

It was supposed to be something Rusk reportedly whispered to Bundy when they learned Soviet ships had gone dead in the water off Cuba rather than defy Kennedy's blockade. Vice President Johnson—who urged the missile swap—was not even included by Bartlett as one of the "nine men who made the live-or-die decisions when the chips are down." Singled out for searing criticism was Stevenson, the ambassador to the United Nations. He was likened to Chamberlain, the appeaser of Hitler, for favoring a missile swap instead of an all-out military strike on Cuba. On October 17—the day after the missiles were discovered in Cuba—Stevenson sent Kennedy a note saying the world would see the Soviet missiles in Cuba as quid pro quo for U.S. missiles in Turkey. While refusing to talk with a gun at his head, Stevenson said Kennedy should remain open to negotiations on "the existence of nuclear missile bases anywhere."

According to Bartlett, Kennedy was ready to destroy the Russian rockets and invade Cuba if Khrushchev decided to run the naval blockade. There was no hint that Kennedy agreed to Khrushchev's missile swap—just the opposite. "Only Adlai Stevenson dissented from the [White House] consensus," Bartlett reported. He quoted an unidentified official as saying, "Adlai wanted a Munich. He wanted to trade the Turkish, Italian, and British missile bases for the Cuban bases." Two decades later, Bartlett recalled for one author that the attack on Stevenson stemmed from a White House lunch with Bundy and his deputy Michael Forrestal. Every newspaper and broadcast network carried a version of Bartlett's report, forcing Stevenson into a series of embarrassing denials. Two years later, Bundy would blame the president for Bartlett's attack on Stevenson. "I will say for myself that I never saw that damned thing [the Bartlett article] before it appeared, but Jack Kennedy did," Bundy said. "That article wouldn't have happened if the president hadn't at one point, and for a period, been very irritated with Adlai," Bundy said. "But it was a case where he let himself go, or let others go." According to Bundy, it was in the aftermath of the crisis when Stevenson balked at Kennedy's orders on negotiations to remove Soviet bombers from Cuba. That irked the president.

But there were other reasons Kennedy would malign Stevenson. Kennedy resented Stevenson for rejecting him as a running mate in the 1956 presidential race. It was too soon to put a Roman Catholic on the ticket, Stevenson had concluded. And when Kennedy offered him the assignment as UN ambassador, Stevenson did not readily accept but asked for time to think it over. "The president never liked him," Bobby said of Stevenson. "He put up with him." Stevenson, a liberal and articulate former Illinois governor, was the Democratic presidential candidate twice defeated by Eisenhower. Schlesinger, who was close to Stevenson, was directed by Kennedy to deny that the president leaked the details. "Will you tell Adlai that I never talked to Charlie [Bartlett] and that this piece did not represent my views," Kennedy said, according to Schlesinger.

Khrushchev, too, reacted to the *Post* account. He noted that it was no accidental leak but an aggressive media campaign. "This evidently is done for the purpose of informing the public in a one-sided way," Khrushchev wrote Kennedy. To his senior advisers and the White House staff, Kennedy cautioned against public boasting about Khrushchev's retreat. But in private Kennedy bragged to friends, including newsmen that he left Khrushchev battered. "I cut his balls off," Kennedy said. Kennedy's success in spinning the world's media to his advantage could prove temporary and fragile if the truth leaked. When the Jupiters were finally removed in April 1963, there was plenty of speculation that it was part of a deal to get missiles out of Cuba. "Most Turks believed we had made a secret deal with Russia to scrap offensive weapons," C. L. Sulzberger reported from Ankara in the *New York Times*. But that was just speculation. Most accepted Kennedy's cover story that the Jupiters had become irrelevant as American Polaris submarines began patrolling the Mediterranean off the Turkish coast. The USS *Sam Houston*, with its sixteen nuclear-tipped rockets, surfaced at the port of Izmir on April 15, 1963.

For Kennedy, however, the Air Force generals remained a ticking time bomb. No one was more unhappy with Kennedy's secret missile swap with Khrushchev than the Air Force chief of staff. "The greatest defeat in our history," LeMay said, slapping a Pentagon table for emphasis, according to General Taylor. When Kennedy invited the chiefs to the White House to thank them for their support during the crisis, LeMay rudely rejected the president's gratitude. "We lost," LeMay said sharply to Kennedy. "We ought to go in there today and just knock them off." Through General Lemnitzer, LeMay knew of Kennedy's acceptance of the Soviet missile swap. The order to remove the Jupiter warheads also passed through LeMay's chain of command, including the Strategic Air Command, which was headed by General Thomas Power. Both senior officers took secrecy labels seriously and were unlikely to expose Kennedy's backroom deal. They also faced punishment if they violated security regulations.

But LeMay was duty bound to tell Congress as much as possible in closed-door hearings where members were cleared to hear top secret details. In heavily censored testimony made public in February 1963, LeMay cryptically hinted that "other factors" were involved in the Jupiter withdrawal. LeMay suggested Congress ask McNamara about these "other factors." Mr. Conservative, Senator Goldwater, was on the armed services committee. He had first met LeMay during World War II when Goldwater was flying supply planes in Asia. As senator, Goldwater remained in the Air Force reserve, rising to the rank of brigadier general. LeMay made sure Goldwater could take spins in the latest Air Force jets, including the Mach 3 SR-71 Blackbird spy plane. They were personal friends.

After LeMay had testified in secret, Goldwater took to the Senate floor for another speech lambasting Kennedy's Cuban policies. "Mr. President, what goes on?" Goldwater said. Were the Jupiter removals "part of some kind of deal involving Cuba and disarmament plans"? The order to remove the Jupiter warheads on October 27 was the sort of evidence that could reveal Kennedy's cover-up. Reporters with the right tip could hunt down the American airmen who just might tell how they raced to disable the Jupiters in Turkey. Even more unnerving for Kennedy was the fact that LeMay and Power were about to leave the restraints of active duty. They could prove a disaster in the 1964 reelection campaign, McNamara warned Kennedy.

"They will retire July first," McNamara said, explaining why Le-May and Power could cause real trouble in 1964.

"Power fortunately can be held until 30 November without difficulty. So we can keep him, all right. I would like—if you agree . . ."

Kennedy anticipated his next words.

"Keep LeMay on?" Kennedy said.

"I could think of a job between July first and January," McNamara said. "Something like that." That would be two months after the 1964 presidential election.

"Do it well in advance," Kennedy said. "Will you speak to him some time soon?

"I would rather have them in than out," the president said.

LeMay's service was extended for a year. For the rest of his life, including a stint as a vice-presidential candidate in 1968, the removal of the Jupiter warheads and the missile swap remained top secret. But in a 1968 campaign book, he alluded to a secret deal between Kennedy and Khrushchev.

"If so, we definitely came out on the short end of the bargain in a confrontation which has been hailed as a great diplomatic victory," LeMay wrote. "Only the revelations of history will clear this up."

2

ZR/RIFLE

SEE THE POLL?" BOBBY KENNEDY asked his brother over the telephone. "You're down to 70 percent."

"What?" said the president.

"Down to 70 percent," said Bobby. Attorney general was his day job. But he was also his brother's campaign manager, and that was his continual preoccupation.

"When was that?" Kennedy asked.

"Gallup poll. About two days ago," said Bobby. "From 76 to 70. You break 50–50 with the Republicans, 18 percent against you." That meant half of the Republicans approved of Kennedy's performance, good news along with only 18 percent of all voters surveyed disapproving. But Kennedy focused on the bad news.

"We have dropped 6 percent in a month, have we?" Kennedy said.

"Since January," Bobby said.

The March 2, 1963, poll was the beginning of a steady and frightening decline for the candidate and his campaign manager for the next ten months. The direction of a poll—up or down—was most important. And a direction downward triggered all kinds of reappraisals. What was causing the drop? Both men had their eyes on 1964, when New Hampshire's primary was set for the second Tuesday in March, the start of voter involvement in the presidential sweepstakes.

One reason for the decline was constant attacks by Republicans in Congress over Kennedy's failure to oust Fidel Castro. And Kennedy remained dedicated to either killing or compromising with Castro to the end of his presidency. Ironically, Castro caused the president's highest approval rating ever. It soared to 83 percent of voters interviewed as they rallied behind the inexperienced young president who had been humiliated in 1961 at the Bay of Pigs by Castro. His predecessor, Eisenhower, and his opponent in 1960, Richard M. Nixon, were among the Republicans who took part in a solidarity meeting with Kennedy. When the poll was published after the Cuban debacle, he could only marvel. "The worse you do, the better they like you," Kennedy said.

Eisenhower's support came with a slice of humiliation. The general took the Navy lieutenant to task during a walk in the woods of Camp David. Ike's orders during World War II had sent countless Americans to certain death. He challenged Kennedy's refusal to order a nearby U.S. Navy armada to destroy Castro and his army as they repelled the CIA-organized invasion of Cuba. Kennedy said the use of carrier-based warplanes would have exposed American involvement. "My advice was that we must try to keep our hands from showing in this affair," Kennedy said. Ike was incredulous. "How could we expect the world to believe that we had nothing to do with it?" Ike said. Where did the invasion ships come from? Where did the invaders get weapons? Communication gear? Kennedy lacked the guts to spill the blood. "I believe there is only one thing to do when you go into this kind of thing: It must be a success," Ike told Kennedy. Also, Kennedy said, the U.S. air strike by the USS *Essex* was canceled out of fear that the Soviet Union would make trouble in Berlin. "That is exactly the opposite of what would really happen," Ike said. "The Soviets follow their own plans, and if they see us show any weakness, that is when they press us the hardest. The second they see us show strength and do something on our own, that is when they are very cagey."

Using U.S. Navy warplanes to bomb Castro was probably Kennedy's last best chance to remove the Cuban revolutionary from power through collateral damage. A more direct attack on Castro had been launched by Eisenhower with orders to the Central Intelligence Agency. But it seemed to go nowhere. Senior CIA officials banned "bad words" and tiptoed around the orders to assassinate the Cuban leader. Director Allen Dulles of Central Intelligence was briefed on a plan to hire American mobsters to kill Castro. In looking at the record of the briefing, the CIA inspector general, John Earman, found Dulles only nodded but didn't actually speak. "It is appropriate to conjecture as to just what the director did approve," said Earman. "It is safe to conclude given the men participating and the general subject of the meeting that there was little likelihood of misunderstanding—even though details were deliberately blurred and the specific intended result was never stated in unmistakable language." Murder, liquidation, killing, and assassination were banned from the director's office. "It is reasonable to conclude that the pointed avoidance of 'bad words' emphasized to the participants the extreme sensitivity of the operation," Earman said. And a lack of bureaucratic enthusiasm. The tap dance continued for the next four years as plots were hatched only to fizzle. One official had the temerity to demand Deputy Director Richard Helms explain what he meant by "getting rid of Castro." Helms eyed the man and snapped: "Use your imagination."

Army Colonel Sheffield Edwards, director of security, had been the first one tasked with Ike's order to eliminate Castro. Shortly before his death in 1963, Edwards testified secretly to Senate investigators that Dulles personally ordered him to assassinate Castro. Edwards served in both world wars before joining the Central Intelligence Group, an Army forerunner of the CIA. At Langley, most called him Shef, and his pronounced stutter was a cover for his ruthlessness. Edwards wound up retaining Johnny Roselli of Las Vegas and Sam Giancana of Chicago, both certified gangsters. As patriots, both refused the $150,000 the CIA offered to kill Castro. Edwards

expected them to give Castro the old rat-tat-tat in the Plaza de la Revo-
lución. "Apparently the Agency had first thought in terms of a typical gangland-style killing in which Castro would be gunned down,"
the IG Earman said. Giancana, a mob boss, quickly refused this ploy
as too risky. He insisted on poison, a quick-dissolving pill that a con-
federate in Havana could slip into Castro's tea. Edwards turned to
Dr. Edward Gunn, chief of the Office of Medical Services for the
CIA dirty tricks division. Gunn had turned upside down the Hip-
pocratic oath of first do no harm; Gunn was Dr. Do Harm at the
CIA. He would fashion weapons to exterminate Castro for four years.
His favorite poison was the deadly botulinum toxin. Gunn fashioned
it into pills that would be passed to Giancana. But first Colonel Edwards tested one pill in a glass of water. Instead of instantly dissolv-
ing, it would not even disintegrate. Edwards demanded Gunn test
the pill. Guinea pigs were fed the pills and were still whistling hap-
pily the next day. It turned out that the pigs had a special immunity.
When the pills were fed to monkeys, they died horribly as expected.
The pills never made it to Castro's teacup. According to Giancana,
his hit man in Havana got cold feet.

Dr. Gunn was ordered to come up with an alternative. He dusted
a box of fifty Cohibas—Castro's favorite cigar—with the botulinum
toxin. "Merely putting one in the mouth would do the job," the inspector general reported. Gunn spent hours rewrapping each long and
fat Esplendido and repairing cigar box seals to hide signs of tam-
pering. The cigars, like the pills, never got to Castro. Still, they were
an excellent product. Gunn kept one cigar in his safe and tested its
toxicity for Inspector General Earman. "It was still 94 percent effective" in 1967 when Earman was conducting his probe of assassination
attempts on Castro.

Under Kennedy, pressure to get rid of Castro became severe, Earman said. Richard Bissell, the number two man at the CIA, was contacted shortly after Kennedy's inauguration. There was a demand for
a standby assassination team. "The White House has twice urged me

to create such a capability," said Bissell. He set up an Executive Action Capability, given the cryptonym ZR/RIFLE. Kennedy speechwriter Richard Goodwin recalled McNamara at a two-hour postmortem on the Bay of Pigs. McNamara put his hand on Goodwin's shoulder. "The only thing to do is eliminate Castro," McNamara said.

"You mean?" Goodwin replied.

"I mean it, Dick," McNamara said. According to the inspector general, ZR/RIFLE soon became synonymous with assassinating Castro. He traced the order to the defense secretary during an August 15, 1962, meeting in the conference room of Secretary of State Dean Rusk. "Liquidated" was McNamara's word for getting rid of Castro and his government. All of Kennedy's senior men attended the session—Rusk, General Taylor, McGeorge Bundy, John McCone, and others. This special group morphed into Operation Mongoose, headquartered in the White House and overseen by brother Bobby, the attorney general. The executive director was Edward Lansdale, an Air Force general celebrated for his direction of CIA support for the president of South Vietnam and other Asian leaders. President Kennedy envisioned a $50 million per year program in a November 30, 1961, eyes only order to his national security team. "We will use our available assets to go ahead with the discussed project in order to help Cuba overthrow the communist regime," the president wrote.

With Bobby in charge of ZR/RIFLE, the CIA provided a detailed briefing on past plans to get rid of Castro, including the hiring of mobsters Roselli and Giancana. At the end of the May 7, 1962, meeting, Bobby Kennedy needled the CIA men. "I trust that if you ever try to do business with organized crime again, you will let the attorney general know." Then Bobby quickly approved of another attempt by Roselli and Giancana to kill Castro with Dr. Gunn's poison pills. This time Giancana used an anti-Castro leader in Miami to relay the pills—hidden in a pencil carved out by Dr. Gunn—to Havana. Once again no attempt was made in Havana. "The plot was aborted and the pills returned," said the inspector general.

In 1963, Desmond Fitzgerald took over the CIA Cuban task force. Fitzgerald came up with an array of schemes: A midget submarine would plant an explosive-filled sea mollusk near Castro's favorite skin-diving area. Or dust the interior of a skin-diving suit with Madura foot, a fungus that would cause Castro to erupt in tumors. Maybe infect the oxygen regulator used for diving with tubercle bacilli. As each far-out idea was dropped, Fitzgerald came under more intense pressure from the White House. "We cannot overemphasize the extent to which responsible Agency officers felt themselves subject to the Kennedy administration's severe pressures," Earman said. "The fruitless and, in retrospect, often unrealistic plotting should be viewed in that light." The IG Earman's 1967 report was an effort to spin four years of failure by the CIA to kill Castro into ruthless mismanagement by the Kennedy White House.

While these CIA misfires were going on out of sight, Castro was given the Republican spotlight in Congress. Goldwater, Senator Kenneth Keating of New York, and other Republican leaders were hammering away at Kennedy's inability to topple Castro, even after the Cuban missile crisis. Led by Goldwater, the Republicans charged that Castro was still hiding nuclear weapons in Cuban jungles. The GOP attacked the continuing buildup of Russian troops in Cuba even though the Soviets had removed intermediate range nuclear-tipped rockets. The Republican attacks were followed by more White House pressure on the CIA. Complicating the issue was Republican McCone of the CIA. The president and his brother suspected McCone was the source of intelligence on Russian activities in Cuba being used by Goldwater on the Senate floor. "Some thought he [McCone] is disloyal," Bundy said in a February 18, 1963, national security memo. Mongoose director Lansdale repeatedly pushed for a ZR/RIFLE end to Castro, according to IG Earman. The cold-blooded plotting of Castro's assassination made the CIA director queasy. McCone was a devout Catholic who objected to McNamara's proposal to "liquidate" Castro. He called the Defense chief to complain after the first meeting in 1962. McCone feared joining in murder could jeopardize his immortal soul. "If he were involved in such a plot, McCone said he would be excommunicated," Earman said. McCone characterized talk of removing Castro, knocking off Castro, and disposing of Castro to mean overthrowing the communist government of Cuba. "McCone's recollection is probably faulty," IG Earman concluded.

By the fall of 1963, the CIA revived contact with a Castro insider who might become the ideal assassin. He was Major Rolando Cubela Secades, who had become involved while a medical student in efforts to overthrow the dictator Fulgencio Batista. Once Castro took over, Cubela was already the number two man in Directorio Revolucionario Estudantil, an elite group of leftists dedicated to cleaning up Havana government. He also had the rank of major, the highest in the Cuban army after the revolution. In 1959, a CIA source reported that Cubela had frankly expressed his dissatisfaction to Castro with the revolutionary government. "Cubela privately told intimates that he was so disgusted with Castro that if he did not get out of the country soon, he would kill Castro himself," Inspector General Earman said. In later contacts, Cubela talked of defecting to the United States. By October 17, 1963, Cubela told his CIA contact that he wanted to meet with Bobby Kennedy or a senior U.S. government official.

The CIA Cuban desk chief, Desmond Fitzgerald, agreed to meet Cubela in Paris. Cubela emphasized two points: If Castro was overthrown, he wanted American support for himself in any new Havana government. And two, he wanted a high-powered rifle with a telescopic sight. To kill Castro at a distance, he explained. He did not wish to sacrifice his life while killing Castro. Desmond said later that he told Cubela the United States would have no part in the attempt on Castro's life. "Be that as it may," said IG Earman, "the written record tells a somewhat different story." He quoted a report by Néstor Sánchez, who attended the session with Fitzgerald and acted as interpreter. According to Sánchez, Fitzgerald approved a shipment of weapons to Cubela in Cuba. To Sánchez, Cubela asked what CIA "technical assistance" he would get to kill Castro. As a doctor, Cubela said, he could devise means to kill Castro other than a rifle. That alerted Dr. Gunn at CIA headquarters on November 19, 1963. Perhaps a disguised syringe full of poison? "Gunn says that he went immediately to his workshop and spent the rest of the day and most of the night fabricating the device," the IG report said. After several failures, Gunn finally managed to gut the inside of a Paper Mate ballpoint pen. Inside, Gunn had devised a syringe with a point so fine that the person injected would barely feel it. "He compared it with the scratch from a shirt with too much starch," Inspector General Earman said. Gunn recommended the syringe be filled with Black Leaf 40, a common insecticide that would kill Castro. It was mostly nicotine sulfate, a powerful toxin. Néstor Sánchez took the Paper Mate and flew back to Paris on the night of November 21. Cubela had agreed to meet him at a hotel on November 22.

That same month—on November 5—Kennedy learned of another solution to the Castro problem. William Attwood, who had served as ambassador to the West African country of Guinea, had gotten hints from UN diplomats that Castro might be willing to break with Moscow and reestablish ties with Washington. Attwood, a journalist by trade, had interviewed Castro in 1959 for *Look* and now proposed a secret meeting with the Cuban leader. "It was an outside chance," Attwood would say later. "But it just might work. Castro would have to expel the Russian soldiers in Cuba. There were about 17,000 at the time. But we heard Castro was still angry over the way [Premier Nikita] Khrushchev treated him—treated Cuba—during the missile crisis." When Kennedy learned of Attwood's proposed secret mission, he immediately became concerned that such a meeting would leak to the press.

"Any word that gets out," Kennedy said, "we'd have to have an explanation. Can we get him off the payroll?" Attwood had the status of ambassador on the staff of the U.S. delegation at the United Nations. McGeorge Bundy explained if there was a meeting, it would not be in Havana. "Send a plane over to Mexico," Bundy told Kennedy. Through Averell Harriman, Attwood had urged Kennedy to meet with a French journalist who would be interviewing Castro in Havana. Kennedy told the journalist, Jean Daniel, that Castro was acting as the Soviet agent in Latin America. Kennedy asked Daniel to return after his meeting with Castro.

If Castro was truly interested in a new deal, Kennedy said he must end Moscow's domination. Two weeks after the Attwood mission was proposed, Kennedy spelled out the U.S. position in a November 18 speech in Miami before the Inter American Press Association. Castro, he said, has "made Cuba a victim of foreign imperialism, an instrument of the policy of others, a weapon in an effort dictated by external power to subvert the other American republics," Kennedy said. "This and this alone divide us. As long as this is true, nothing is possible. Without it, everything is possible."

After Kennedy's Miami speech, Castro called in journalist Daniel to hear what messages he carried from Kennedy. Their six-hour Havana conversation covered a number of subjects and Castro said he saw "positive elements" in some of the American president's words. While still critical of Kennedy, Castro told Daniel that he could live with the American leader. "Anyone else would be worse," Castro said with a jab at Khrushchev. In Washington, Bundy made a telephone call to Attwood. "He said the president wanted to see me and discuss what he might say to Castro," Attwood said. The call was on November 18. Attwood said the meeting would take place after Kennedy returned from his November 22 Dallas trip. The Kennedy-Johnson ticket carried Texas in 1960, and the president hoped his Dallas visit would unite feuding Democrats in time for the 1964 presidential race.

Agent Néstor Sánchez arrived in Paris on the morning of November 22 with Dr. Gunn's diabolical Paper Mate. Major Cubela was waiting for him in a hotel room. Cubela was the CIA's best hope for an assassin who could get close enough to Castro to inject death with the click of a ballpoint pen.

3

The Crocodile

THE WALLS IN WILLIAM AVERELL Harriman's uptown Manhattan apartment would make any museum curator salivate. Fifty years of collecting meant a rotating selection of gems from around the world. One he bought on a Paris honeymoon with his second wife—Vincent van Gogh's *Roses*—was bequeathed to the National Gallery of Art, where it was valued at $50 million. The day president-elect John F. Kennedy came for lunch, Pablo Picasso and André Derain caught the eye.

Ostensibly, the lunch was for a secret meeting with Hugh Gaitskell, leader of the British Labour Party. It was a diplomatic no-no for a new president to be meeting with the opposition of the British government. The proper form was for Kennedy to first see Prime Minister Harold Macmillan, head of the Conservative Party. But Gaitskell asked Harriman to arrange the confidential session with the new American leader. The real topic, however, was the future of Averell Harriman in the New Frontier. The young president-elect was eyeing the old party war-horse for a powerless and almost honorary post in the New Frontier. Instead, Harriman's ambitions would drag Kennedy into the most sordid government business of his administration and open the door to the ten-year American war in Vietnam.

No one—most of all Kennedy—could foresee what would grow

out of lunch that day in Manhattan. Gaitskell first met Harriman while he was in Paris disbursing another $13 billion in U.S. dollars under the Marshall Plan to rebuild Europe after World War II. It was the second American gift to those wrecked societies since the war ended. Before the plan, named for Secretary of State George Marshall, had been put in place, Washington had already supplied $13 billion to clear the rubble. While acting as the Marshall Plan ramrod in Paris, Harriman suffered a major setback. He seemed on the verge of becoming the secretary of state after eight years of being America's most distinguished diplomat. Then an aide at the Talleyrand Hotel brought him a dispatch from the United Press teletype: Truman had selected Dean Acheson for the post. Harriman's face sagged with disappointment. The consolation prize was to become the first White House adviser on national security affairs.

But that was 1948. This was 1960. Kennedy had yet to name anyone to the most important foreign policy portfolio. Harriman's qualifications quickly surfaced when the table discussion turned to dealing with the Soviet Union and its new premier, Nikita Sergeyevich Khrushchev. A year earlier, as a mere tourist, Harriman was the first American to conduct a lengthy meeting with the new Soviet leader— ten hours that began in the Kremlin and wound up in the Russian's Moscow dacha for dinner. Harriman gave a 6,000-word report to the grateful U.S. ambassador, who had yet to meet the new Russian leader. For Kennedy, who relished reading about the past, Harriman was a historic figure. In almost every photo, every newsreel of Cairo, Tehran, Yalta, and Potsdam, Harriman can be picked out in the background. There he is on the deck of a warship off Newfoundland, standing behind President Franklin Delano Roosevelt as the Atlantic Charter is hammered out in 1941 with Prime Minister Winston Churchill. Or at Churchill's side as they witness Adolf Hitler's bombers set London afire during the blitz. And with Churchill again as they are greeted by Joseph Stalin in Moscow.

As FDR's personal representative in London and later as ambassador to the Soviet Union, Harriman was in every meeting aimed at destroying Nazi Germany and Japan as well as rebuilding the world's shattered economies. He had become the communists' favorite capitalist, the font of $11 billion in wartime Lend-Lease—everything from coffee to war planes, trucks, guns, and bullets. Stalin, the mass murderer, stood up and smiled for Comrade Averell. For Harriman, the Kremlin door was always open. That could be an important asset for a new president confronted with the uncertainty of the cold war with the Soviet Union.

Against Harriman's selection was Bobby Kennedy. Harriman favored Senator Stuart Symington of Missouri for the 1960 presidential nomination. Also, Harriman thought the time was not right for a Roman Catholic president. When Kennedy fund-raisers approached the heir to a fortune second only to the Rockefellers, Harriman offered only a pittance of $10,000. Worse, he had a public dislike for Joseph P. Kennedy Sr., whom Harriman viewed as a nouveau riche brigand. Harriman's biggest impediment was his age. At seventy, his hearing had gone from bad to worse, but he refused a hearing aid, that symbol of elderly weakness. As governor of New York, Harriman had selected a budget director who also had a hearing problem. Their public meetings were shouting matches that reminded Albany reporter Jack Germond of the children's game "Sounds Like."

To fill out the luncheon table, Harriman had included one of his protégés, Michael Forrestal. He was the son of Defense Secretary James Forrestal, who had overworked himself into a depression and other mental problems that ended in suicide. The fifth at the table was Harriman's executive secretary, Jonathan Bingham. When dessert was served, Harriman offered an analysis of Khrushchev's mindset and the Soviet intervention in the Congo. Gaitskell offered a few words of dissent. Harriman's hearing again betrayed him. He thought the dissent came from Bingham. With a flash of anger, he reprimanded Bingham as ignorant and inexperienced. Kennedy stared into space and Gaitskell looked at his coffee cup. The brief display of temper had underlined Harriman's failing. On the way out, Kennedy called Forrestal aside. "Jesus," thought Forrestal. "He's going to make Averell Secretary of State!"

Instead, Kennedy began with a little laugh. "Now, this is very serious," Kennedy told Forrestal. "Averell's hearing is atrocious. If we're going to give him a job, he has to have a hearing aid, and I want you to see that he does." The job of secretary of state went to Dean Rusk. Some last-minute lobbying by old friends helped Harriman get a post that seemed almost honorary, a selection for past deeds. John Kenneth Galbraith, Kennedy's professor from Harvard, told the new president it would be a mistake to bypass an insider from two shooting wars, the reconstruction of Europe and the cold war. So Harriman's appointment was characterized as that of a roving ambassador and troubleshooter without portfolio. "An act of sentiment," said Bobby Kennedy.

What Kennedy had done out of sympathy was akin to melting a block of ice enclosing a saber-toothed tiger who suddenly sprang to life. With razor-sharp claws, Harriman shredded friend and foe alike as he moved from rover to the number three post at the Department of State. As undersecretary of state, Harriman would issue what became the death warrant for Ngo Dinh Diem, the president of South Vietnam and the leader of the American crusade against communism. Kennedy would bitterly resent Harriman for manipulating the president into approving Diem's overthrow.

Harriman's use of a hearing aid quickly transformed his perceptions of the world around him. Or more accurately, he was transformed by his wife Marie. She bought him the latest in hearing aids, a small flesh-colored plastic device with an on-and-off switch that fit within and behind the contours of his ear. Sometimes it would whine noisily when the volume was too high. Soon Harriman turned this symbol of infirmity into a sword. He would use the hearing aid to shock, insult, intimidate, or even cut down anyone who challenged him. He slashed his way through the Washington jungle with the skill of a master bureaucrat. In close combat, Harriman would become rude, savage, relentless, and overbearing. Confrontations with him would leave civil servants or foreign government leaders flustered, struggling to figure out just the right response. Just as the unwitting victim was about to respond, Harriman would shut off his hearing aid, sit back, and glare—or even worse, shut his eyes.

William Colby, who had become Harriman's counterpart at the Central Intelligence Agency, got the full treatment. As were many, Colby was deferential because of Harriman's age, his long career in government, and his personal connection with the president. "[Harriman] put me directly to the test," Colby recalled. "He would sharply—sometimes almost insultingly—jab questions at me, scarcely leaving me time to reply. He insisted on direct answers, some impossible to give, and [would] then turn away and ignore the answers. If a subject I was reporting on struck him as not that important, he would ostentatiously turn off his hearing aid and leave the matter to his aides to follow. On more than one occasion, he baited me sufficiently to cause me to shout my answers in apparent anger at him."

In his first year, Harriman ascended from a rover without portfolio to a post in control of American policy in the Far East as one of five assistant secretaries of state. His harsh treatment of subordinates on the Far East desk earned Harriman a new and lasting nickname—the Crocodile. They gave him a silver replica of the beast that was inscribed "From His Devoted Victims." Harriman won the post by enabling Kennedy to avoid a hopeless war that was dropped in his lap the very day before his inauguration as the 35th president of the United States.

The 34th president, Dwight D. Eisenhower, left his young successor in a bind. Perhaps the old soldier delighted in taking the wind out of Kennedy's sail. After all, Kennedy had maligned Ike's leadership throughout the 1960 campaign. It was Eisenhower, Kennedy said, who let the Soviet Union gain superiority in the number of nuclear-tipped missiles that could strike the United States. "I don't want that goddamned son of a bitch sitting in this seat," Eisenhower told one aide in the Oval Office during the campaign. The genial general was not beyond political revenge. Richard M. Nixon, who suffered for eight years as his vice president, saw Eisenhower as a subtle manipulator. "He was a far more complex and devious man than most people realized," Nixon said. "In the best sense of those words."

Eisenhower bequeathed Kennedy two bombshells. One, with a delayed fuse, exploded on April 17, 1961, when the CIA's invasion of Cuba floundered in failure before the world. The Bay of Pigs would show Kennedy to be reckless, naïve, and unwilling to use the naval armada that Ike had planned to crush Fidel Castro, Moscow's man in Havana. Following Ike's plan, the U.S. Navy had situated an aircraft carrier, Marines, and other warships within striking distance of Cuba. But Kennedy vetoed their use even as CIA-backed Cuban invaders were killed and captured by Castro. Underpinning the invasion was the idea that Cubans would rise up in revolt against Castro, a notion that seemed ridiculous in hindsight. The plot was handcrafted by Ike's director of Central Intelligence, Allen Dulles, and his deputy, Richard Bissell Jr.; Kennedy would fire them both. But it was Kennedy, on nationwide television, who took the fall for the fiasco at the Bahía de Cochinos.

The second bombshell produced more dread than noise in the Oval Office on January 19, 1961. Laos, a tiny isolated country of mountains and jungles, was about to fall into the communist orbit. With airlifted Soviet arms, the communist faction, the Pathet Lao, with support of Hanoi's Viet Minh army, was on the verge of seizing all the strategic locations. It could become a staging base for a communist takeover in the neighboring countries of Burma, Thailand, and Cambodia to the east and South Vietnam to the west. Communist China sat on the northern border of Laos. Eisenhower had pumped millions of dollars into competing factions, including enough to build a 29,000-man army equipped with America's weapons. But it was not enough.

"This is the cork in the bottle of the Far East," Eisenhower told Kennedy. "If Laos is lost to the free world, in the long run we will lose all of Southeast Asia." Ike was restating his domino theory—if one country turned red, the rest would topple in a row. Initially, the thought was that the Philippines, Indonesia, and India would fall to the red menace as well. This idea fell into disfavor decades later. But Kennedy had become a true believer of this theory.

"You are going to have to put troops in Laos. With other nations if possible—but alone if necessary," Ike said.

Kennedy paused before replying. "If the situation was so critical," he asked Ike, "why didn't you decide to do something?"

"I would have, but I did not feel I could commit troops with a new administration coming to power," Ike replied.

At first Kennedy rattled the American saber at a White House news conference. Maps of all Southeast Asia were displayed, and Kennedy vowed to confront communist-backed gains. The Laotian communist offensive was slowed after Kennedy ordered the U.S. Seventh Fleet deployed to the Gulf of Siam. This same March order sent three hundred U.S. Marines to Thailand, where they serviced twenty new helicopter supply ships flown by the CIA to Laos in support of anti-communist forces. Marine combat troops were landed later on the Thai–Lao border. But Kennedy quickly retreated after a closer look at Laotian geography. He must have wondered about Eisenhower's advice after a series of briefings by his top military advisers on the Joint Chiefs of Staff. How could a five-star general favor fielding U.S. soldiers in the face of a logistical nightmare? There was no effective way to support American ground troops in landlocked Laos. Two small airports could not handle an aerial invasion—one likely to come under fire by communist troops. There was no way to ship arms, food, and other equipment except from Vietnamese ports and then over mountain ranges on dirt roads that turned to mud in monsoon rain. Army General Lyman Lemnitzer, chairman of the Joint Chiefs, told Kennedy that the only certain way to remove the communist threat was the use of tactical nuclear weapons, particularly if Communist China intervened, as they had done in Korea. Kennedy, still stung by military advice on the ill-fated Bay of Pigs invasion a month earlier, was reluctant to accept the Pentagon's invasion plans for Laos.

Rather to stand and fight in Laos, Kennedy decided the better solution was to leave. The best way out of Laos was a diplomatic deal announced May 13 with the Soviet Union, Communist China, and the five neighboring countries. But this had to be done without its being viewed as another retreat by Kennedy from a communist challenge. Things were going from bad to worse in Laos just after Kennedy avoided the use of military power during the disaster at the Bay of Pigs. Outwardly, Kennedy's goal was for establishment of a neutralist government after all foreign forces withdrew from Laos. In reality, neutrality meant concessions to the communists—primarily to Hanoi and its relentless goal to seize South Vietnam.

With American diplomacy and the president's political stature on the line, Kennedy turned to his roving ambassador without portfolio. By late April, Harriman was off like a shot to Vientiane, Luang Prabang, and even smaller villages, where he met with princes and generals. Eleven days in Laos and then on to Rangoon, Phnom Penh, Bangkok, and Saigon. Harriman explained the political dimension of his mission in a letter to Winthrop Brown, the American ambassador to Laos. "Our job is not to confront the president with a situation requiring a decision on whether to permit Laos to be overrun by the Commies, or introduce American combat forces," Harriman said. In Geneva, Harriman reestablished his friendly working relationship with the Soviet delegate to the talks. In past administrations, he had been free to make decisions on his own. But Rusk bound Harriman to strict instructions that chafed. At one point, Harriman wanted to meet privately with the Communist Chinese delegate.

Rusk vetoed the move. There has been no diplomatic relations with Beijing since Mao Zedong came to power in 1949. Harriman did an end run around Rusk. He complained about the State Department's strictures in a letter to John Kenneth Galbraith, then ambassador to India. Harriman knew Galbraith would pass along the complaint to Kennedy. Soon Kennedy told Rusk that Harriman could do anything he wished at Geneva. But by the time the carte blanche arrived in Geneva, the Chinese delegate had left the talks. Reopening ties with China would have to wait until Richard M. Nixon was president.

As the diplomatic smoke screen began to evaporate in Geneva, the governments in Bangkok and Saigon began to balk at Harriman's handiwork. He had accepted a series of concessions that eliminated international enforcement of troop withdrawals by Hanoi. And Hanoi was known for reneging on solemn promises. For Ho Chi Minh, Laos provided the ideal route for arms and food supplies to his guerrilla army in South Vietnam. The supply line also was protected by an international border: The treaty prohibited cross-border attacks by Saigon to interdict Ho's supply line. Hanoi was already paving parts of a jungle highway that became known as the Ho Chi Minh Trail. Pressed by the British and French in Geneva, Harriman also agreed to withdraw CIA operatives from Laos who were fostering attacks by primitive mountain tribes on Hanoi's supply line. Included was a ban on South Vietnamese forces crossing the Laotian border to attack North Vietnamese infiltrators.

To the president of South Vietnam, Harriman's quest for neutrality in Laos was exposing his country's flank to an unchallenged assault by the communists in Hanoi. Ngo Dinh Diem's agitation was clear to the new American ambassador in Saigon, Frederick Nolting. He spoke flawless French with a soft Virginia accent and was polite and mannerly, while his predecessor had been rude and confrontational with Diem. Just as Geneva got under way, Diem had been reelected as president by a landslide. Nolting, a star in the U.S. Foreign Service, was under orders from Kennedy to drop the hard line and coax and cajole Diem into accepting American policy. Nolting shared Diem's dismay over Harriman's concessions in Geneva. "The effectiveness of this agreement depended entirely on the good faith of the parties involved," Nolting said. "If Laos did not really become neutral, South Vietnam's flank would be exposed, its defenses greatly endangered." Nolting approached Harriman with Diem's misgivings about the Geneva concessions during a conference in Bangkok. Harriman reminded Nolting that he was working for Kennedy, not Diem. And the president had "directed" Harriman to get a diplomatic settlement and "that he was determined to do so." According to Nolting, his meeting with Harriman grew heated. In an effort to reassure Nolting, Harriman said his talks with the Soviets gave him a "fingertips feeling" that the Russians would enforce a withdrawal of Hanoi's troops from Laos. "Even so, I said that my fingertips gave me precisely the opposite impression," Nolting said.

It soon became clear that protests by Saigon and Bangkok would do little to change the outcome in Geneva. Through his delegate to the conference, President Diem announced he would not sign the treaty. Now Harriman could become as obsequious as any fawning diplomat in the service of his country. When Cambodia's leader, Prince Norodom Sihanouk, bolted from Geneva in protest, Harriman chased after him. Learning Sihanouk was driving to Italy, Harriman flew ahead to Rome and greeted the prince as he checked into his hotel. Harriman's cajoling led to Cambodia's ambassador returning to Geneva.

But there would be no soft soap and kid gloves in Saigon for Diem, who was struggling against a growing communist onslaught. Diem's refusal to sign could jeopardize Harriman's pledge to Kennedy. So Harriman arrived in Saigon with an ultimatum for Diem. Nolting recalled the confrontation that took place in a steamy palace room on September 20, 1961: Diem launched into one of his monologues about Vietnamese history, stretching back to the 1930s, detailing the communism penetration into Southeast Asia and a trail of broken agreements and bad faith. "The historical record was impressively long and accurate," Nolting said. "Its relevance to signing the treaty on Laos without safeguards was clear."

But when Diem was in mid-monologue, Harriman drew his sword. "Harriman had turned off his hearing aid and closed his eyes," Nolting said. "Diem noticed this with some annoyance but continued." Nolting wondered if the long flight had tired the old man, who was now asleep. He nudged Harriman. The Crocodile opened his jaws. "I have a fingertips feeling, Mr. President," Harriman snapped. "The Russians will police this agreement and make the others live up to it. We cannot give you any guarantees, but one thing is clear: If you do not sign this treaty, you will lose American support." Then, looking at the small, plump man in the white sharkskin suit, Harriman said with a tone of finality: "You have to choose."

After much hand-holding by Nolting, Diem—or at least his representative—did sign the 1962 Geneva Treaty on the Neutralization of Laos. But he never recovered from being slapped down by Harriman. "They took a violent dislike to each other from their first meeting in 1961," said Diem's presidential secretary, Nguyen Dinh Thuan. "It was very unfortunate. Diem did not understand Harriman's role in the Democratic Party and Harriman did not understand Diem."

Harriman, too, would never forget Diem's threat to block the Geneva agreement. The effrontery of the challenge by this Asian pip-squeak was lodged forever in Harriman's memory, particularly when some issue arose about South Vietnam. Nolting would also be savaged later by the Crocodile for his opposition. Two months after their meeting, Harriman was in Geneva putting the finishing touches on the treaty that permitted Kennedy to avoid Eisenhower's edict for a ground war in Laos. The secretary of state called Harriman with news of his promotion. Kennedy had made him one of the five assistant secretaries of state. But his hearing aid didn't quite pick up which post Rusk had mentioned. Harriman called Rusk back and learned he would take over U.S. policy for the Far East—that meant South Vietnam and Diem.

Little more than a year later, Harriman's name was being sardonically celebrated in Saigon. As predicted by Diem, Ho Chi Minh quickly violated the Laos treaty. Moscow had washed its hands of Laos. Hanoi reinforced its troops in Laos and the pipeline to South Vietnam was soon overflowing with men and equipment for the guerrilla war against Saigon. At the American embassy in Saigon, the trail through Laos no longer bore the name of Ho Chi Minh. Instead, it was called the Averell Harriman Memorial Highway. By 1963, Kennedy was secretly financing an army of 20,000 Meo tribesmen to attack the highway and Hanoi's troops headed for South Vietnam.

Kennedy's escape from Laos soon turned into another international defeat one month after the Bay of Pigs. Journalists and academic experts in Southeast Asian politics sided with Diem in viewing the treaty as surrender to the communists. *Time* magazine recalled Kennedy's inaugural pledge to "pay any price" on behalf of liberty.

"The price in Laos seemed too high," *Time* said in its June 5, 1961, edition.

4

Miracles

AVERELL HARRIMAN WAS JUST ONE of a long list of opponents who confronted the president of South Vietnam. Ho Chi Minh, the leader of communist North Vietnam, was determined to eliminate Ngo Dinh Diem, his archrival for leadership of the former French colony. Ho, who issued a death warrant for Diem in 1945, finally arranged for an assassination in 1957. This was a messy third world affair lacking a sophisticated assassin with a high-powered rifle, a telescopic sight, and a guarantee of success. Instead, an unpaid teenager with a dirty pistol was assigned the job. The death warrant was issued after Diem had fled Vietnam. It was ordered in absentia after Diem refused Ho's offer to serve in his communist government in Hanoi. Ho recognized Diem as a nationalist with an impeccable reputation. But Diem rejected Ho just as he had rejected the French in Saigon. He despised both communism and colonial government. Twelve years later, in 1957, the world had turned. Diem, the fugitive exile, had returned to Saigon, tamed South Vietnam's warring factions, and was building a powerful army with American money that just might mean the guillotine for Ho. Diem favored beheading, French style, for his opponents. He owed his position at least in part to determined backing by Senator John F. Kennedy.

At every turn in Diem's fight for power, Kennedy joined in blocking U.S. diplomats who wanted to get rid of the defiant Saigon leader. Kennedy teamed up with Senator Mike Mansfield to foil U.S. abandonment of Diem. As leading Democrats on the Senate Foreign Relations Committee, Kennedy and Mansfield repeatedly threatened to cut off all U.S. aid if French and American opponents in Saigon succeeded in ousting the leader of the shaky new South Vietnamese government. At the time, French colonial leaders depended on American millions to retain their tenuous grip on Saigon. Efforts by Kennedy and Mansfield proved crucial as President Eisenhower and Secretary of State John Foster Dulles backed Diem in the face of a political turmoil in Saigon.

State Department representatives were angered by Diem's blunt defiance of their demands for a more democratic government. The heads of the U.S. mission in Saigon urged Eisenhower to dump the embattled Diem. But in almost every instance, Eisenhower and Secretary Dulles would reject their pleas. From Dulles, the cables to Saigon were always the same: Senators Kennedy and Mansfield would block aid authorizations, even organize a Foreign Relations Committee vote to withdraw from Vietnam if Diem was deposed. "The U.S. should stick to its guns in continuing to support Diem," Mansfield said in one memo relayed by the State Department during a crucial moment in 1955. "Ngo Dinh Diem and Ho Chi Minh are the only two national leaders in Vietnam. To eliminate Diem would leave the field to Ho. If Diem quit or was overthrown, there would very likely be civil war and as a result Ho could walk in and take the country without any difficulty."

By 1956, Senator Kennedy became the leading member of Congress to promote the Catholic president of South Vietnam. His father, Joseph Kennedy, and Francis Cardinal Spellman, the New York Catholic leader, provided the financial foundation of the American Friends of Vietnam. Senator Kennedy became a founding member along with men who later became part of his New Frontier administration—historian Arthur Schlesinger Jr., speechwriter Ted Sorensen, and Angier Biddle Duke, chief of protocol. Kennedy gave the Friends inaugural address at Washington's Willard Hotel in 1956. Kennedy's theme was the amazing success of President Diem. "Vietnam represents the cornerstone of the Free World in Southeast Asia, the keystone to the arch, the finger in the dike," Kennedy said. "Burma, Thailand, India, Japan, the Philippines, and obviously Laos and Cambodia are among those whose security would be threatened if the Red Tide of communism overflowed into Vietnam." Kennedy's father, Joseph, along with Francis Cardinal Spellman enlisted Catholic leaders and parishioners in Diem's anticommunist crusade. Spellman's repeated attack on Vietnamese communists had the support of Pope Pius XII. According to Malachi Martin, a former Jesuit priest who worked in the Vatican, the pope was alarmed by the communist takeover of China and the suppression of Christianity in Asia. "He turned to Spellman to encourage the American commitment to Vietnam," Martin said.

Kennedy and Mansfield were also instrumental in American support for Diem's army that in 1957 threatened the Hanoi leadership. For Ho, the time had come to liquidate Diem, who had become his worst enemy. "There are only two real leaders in Vietnam," said Hanoi general Vo Nguyen Giap. "One is Ho Chi Minh. The other is Ngo Dinh Diem. There is no room in the country for both." Ho's agents near Saigon selected a teenage commando, Ha Minh Tri, to do the deed. Tri stalked Diem on February 22, 1957, slipping through the crowd at the fairgrounds in the highland town of Ban Me Thuot. Wearing his white sharkskin business suit, the Saigon leader, short, paunchy, and duckfooted, was walking as always without armed guards. Members of the diplomatic corps, including David V. Anderson, the U.S. chargé, had accompanied the smiling, waving Diem on the excursion. Commando Tri was equipped with an automatic pistol that was improperly cleaned and checked. He got off one shaky shot that missed Diem and struck the minister of agriculture in the arm. An unflinching Diem coolly stared at the assassin. Tri brought the weapon to bear on Diem and pulled the trigger. Nothing. The weapon jammed. The crowd descended on Tri with kicks and punches. In a cable to the State Department, chargé Anderson saw it as "a striking example to the general public of Diem's strength of character.

"His calmness and courage also greatly impressed the many members of the diplomatic corps, including the undersigned, who witnessed the incident at close range," Anderson cabled. Instead of cutting him down in cold blood, Ho's bumbling attack burnished Diem's image to the point that the United States would elevate him to the pinnacle of American political celebrity. The event became icing on a cake of hyperbole baked by American journalism. Newspaper and magazine articles about Diem always seemed to contain the word "miracle" when describing Diem's ascendance to leadership in South Vietnam. "We rejoice that his life has been spared," said a *New York Times* editorial. "It would have been a major tragedy for Vietnam and an occasion for the gravest concern for all the free world had the assassin's bullet reached its mark. This was an act of sheer madness aimed not merely at a man but against a country and against the cause of liberty and progress." This was an understatement compared to *Time-Life* publisher Henry Luce's effusion. "President Ngo Dinh Diem is one of the greatest statesmen of Asia and of the world," said Luce, who twice chose to put Diem on *Time* magazine's cover. *Newsweek's* Ernest Lindley wrote: "Ngo Dinh Diem is living proof of what is often called a miracle." A *New York Herald Tribune* headline read: "Miracle-Maker from Asia—Diem of South Vietnam." And the *New York Journal-American's* William Randolph Hearst Jr. wondered, "How did the miracle of South Vietnam happen? The story is largely written in the ascetic personality of Ngo Dinh Diem."

All these accolades were not just the result of Diem's survival of Ho's death warrant. Commando Tri was just one hapless agent who misfired in an attempt to eliminate Diem. The U.S. State Department dispatched a series of ambassadors who sought to remove Diem.

And, like the young assassin, their fumbling served only to enhance Diem's reputation in the United States and—more important—in the White House. Most notable was Army General Joseph Collins, handpicked by President Eisenhower to evaluate and bolster Diem and his fledgling government in 1955. Collins, nicknamed "Lightning Joe" because of his World War II exploits, served under General Eisenhower and rose to be Army chief of staff.

On his arrival in Saigon, Collins stepped into the political minefield. The 1954 Geneva Conference produced turmoil in Saigon. While Ho headed a new communist government in Hanoi, the conference left France in charge of the newly created South Vietnam for at least two years. Although the French were defeated and out of money, they hung on in Saigon with a 140,000-man French expeditionary army, continued military aid from the United States, and control of Indochina's rice, rubber, and minerals. France's previous legal justification to rule in Saigon came from Emperor Bao Dai, who lived on the French Riviera. Paris underwrote his gambling losses and stable of women. Bao Dai was the last of a 143-year-old Vietnamese dynasty usurped by the French in 1820. The last emperor wound up serving any role assigned by the French in peace and war. Bao Dai got a cut of U.S. military aid—$4 million a year. He also shared with the French colonial government a slice of income—$516,000 a year—from the most celebrated whorehouse in Asia, the Hall of Mirrors. The brothel, the opium trade, river piracy, and the sprawling Grand Monde casino were all part of a criminal enterprise called the Binh Xuyen. The boss was Bay Vien, a former taxi driver and river pirate who was given control of the Saigon police department in exchange for payoffs to Bao Dai and the French governors. Bay Vien mixed with the rich Chinese, French rubber plantation owners, and Vietnamese at the roulette wheel, which continued spinning until six o'clock in the morning. Guests at Vien's riverside estate were permitted to feed his collection of tigers.

The corruption was also sanctioned by General Nguyen Van

Hinh, commander of the South Vietnamese National Army. Hinh was forever plotting coups against Diem, even riding his motor scooter onto the palace grounds and shouting insults against the premier. Palace troops deferred to the putt-putting general. General Collins embraced the oily enterprise after arrival in Saigon and quickly accepted the French view that Diem had to go. Collins was endorsing the written verdict of the resident U.S. ambassador, Donald Heath. "We must keep our eyes open for another leader," Heath cabled Washington. "[Diem's] lack of personality, his inability to win over people of opposite views, his stubbornness and intransigence, his general political ineptitude, and his slowness in decision and action" were just some reasons to seek a change. Heath's negative assessment came only two months after Diem was installed as premier in 1954. The coalition of American diplomats and the French in Saigon were greasing the slide for Diem.

In Washington, Kennedy signed on to Mansfield's warning that events had reached an "acute crisis." In a Senate Foreign Relations Committee report, Mansfield foresaw a military junta replacing the Diem government. "In the event that the Diem government falls, I believe that the United States should consider an immediate suspension of all aid to Vietnam and the French Union forces there," the Mansfield report said. Eisenhower and Dulles had handpicked Diem. But the turmoil reported by the U.S. embassy in Saigon upset the president, who had invested in Diem's anticommunist credentials. Ike dispatched Collins for a closer look.

Washington's pressure on the French was the big reason Bao Dai formally appointed Diem as premier of the newly created South Vietnam. Once before, in 1933, Bao Dai had made Diem minister of the interior—a job Diem quit in protest over French meddling after three months. This new appointment launched a relentless campaign by opponents to oust Diem or at least bring him under the domination of the French colonial government. That included enlisting American diplomats in Saigon and Paris to bring Diem under the French thumb. Collins became close to a fellow general, Paul Ely, who held France's title of commander in chief Indochina. Ely described Diem to Collins as a "losing game." The American envoy agreed that the French language and culture should be maintained in Vietnam and that the United States and France should build the Saigon military. Diem was not consulted on any of these bilateral agreements, which he bitterly opposed.

"Diem is a small, shy, diffident man with almost no personal magnetism," Collins cabled. "He evidently lacks confidence in himself and appears to have an inherent distaste for decisive action." It was a fundamental miscalculation by Collins. Although he carried the title of premier, Diem was powerless. The French controlled his military and American aid and the crooks controlled the police—all of them aligned against him. Despite the odds, Diem quietly plotted to finish off all of his enemies, including the detested French. First to go was General Hinh, who defied all direction from the presidential palace, the premier's office and residence. The South Vietnamese army commander was thrown into permanent exile in France after Eisenhower let Paris know that he personally endorsed Diem's order to expel Hinh. Next was the band of felons, the Binh Xuyen, that controlled the Saigon police, the Sûreté. Their leader, Bay Vien, had 40,000 men armed with automatic weapons and mortars supplied by the French.

Diem picked General Duong Van Minh to head the Vietnamese National Army and lead the military campaign. He was known as "Big" Minh to distinguish him from another but shorter army leader of same name. Still, at almost six feet, he was tall by Vietnamese standards, and his growing stature would make for a fateful appointment by Diem. Big Minh would play key roles in both the beginning and the end of Diem's political life. This soldier, initially an officer in the French colonial army, was known and admired in Saigon circles. Big Minh was tortured by Japanese occupiers during World War II. They extracted all but one of his front teeth. Big Minh's toothless smile became his badge of courage. His escape from a communist prison in Hanoi where he had been held as a military prisoner was also celebrated. Big Minh strangled one of his jailers before fleeing. Diem declared war in March of 1955 by refusing to extend the Binh Xuyen's criminal business license. At the same time, subsidies were ended for two religious sects that also maintained small armies— the Cao Dai and Hoa Hao. While the sects were effective in eliminating communist forces in their areas, they openly defied any Diem government direction. And Diem's crackdown resulted in the villains and the religious sects joining forces, creating the United Front.

Collins was under orders from Eisenhower and Secretary of State John Foster Dulles to do everything possible to support Diem. But Diem had consistently rejected Collins's advice, firmly refusing to include political opponents in the new government or implement other democratic reforms. "He is so completely uncompromising, ascetic and monastic that he cannot deal with the realities," Collins reported. As civil warfare simmered in the streets of Saigon, Collins wound up on the French side of the showdown. "I have done everything in my power to assist Diem." Collins cabled on April 7. "I must now say my judgment is that Diem does not have the capacity to achieve the necessary unity of purpose and action from his people which is essential to prevent this country from falling under communist control." Knowing turmoil was about to erupt in Saigon, Collins's verdict alarmed official Washington. Dulles awakened Eisenhower after midnight to read the cable. The president decided to summon Collins home for a first-person report. At a later White House meeting, Collins told Eisenhower of Diem's rejection of American advice and his micromanagement, such as his personally signing of exit visas. "The net of it is," Collins told the president, "this fellow is impossible." Reluctantly Eisenhower yielded. Dulles dispatched cables to Paris and Saigon saying representatives of both governments should inform Diem they "are no longer in position to prevent his removal from office."

Just what happened next is still classified by the Central Intelligence Agency. One unofficial version is that the brothers Dulles, both instrumental in putting Diem in power, rescued him at this crucial moment. CIA chief Allen Dulles alerted Diem to brother John Foster's cable terminating his leadership. Allen Dulles's agent in Saigon was Air Force Colonel Edward G. Lansdale. In turn, Lansdale informed Diem, who launched the Battle of Saigon. Lansdale flashed Diem's decision back to the CIA chief. Lansdale was a former advertising executive who had been in the spy business since World War II. Allen Dulles personally ordered Lansdale to Saigon to secretly advise and support Diem as he had other Asian leaders backed by the United States. From the moment Diem returned to Saigon, Lansdale, with his crew cut and brush mustache, was at his side, chain-smoking together sometimes into the wee hours.

Lansdale operated independently of the CIA station in Saigon, with a seemingly unlimited supply of cash, his own handpicked team of secret agents, and a communication line directly to the CIA boss. He was intricately involved with Diem in game-changing events in the spring of 1955. When John Foster Dulles's cable went out at 6:10 P.M. April 27, it was 6:10 A.M. April 28 in Saigon. Within hours, Diem had launched a full-scale assault on the criminal Binh Xuyen. The Battle of Saigon was under way. General Big Minh rolled out the howitzers and sent the river pirate's forces running. Diem's early military gains were relayed by Lansdale to Washington, where Eisenhower had second thoughts. By midnight Washington time, the secretary of state had canceled his edict dumping Diem and ordered both cables burned.

Still, Diem was far from victory. "It was a near thing," Diem said later. "A true nightmare." Artillery and mortar rounds thumped in the streets of Saigon. Machine gun fire rattled, some of it felling hundreds of civilian spectators. Whole neighborhoods went up in flames; a black smoke drifted everywhere. As the Binh Xuyen crumbled, Lansdale took care of the second part of the United Front, the Cao

Dai and the Hoa Hao sects. Lansdale targeted the military commanders of the religious organizations' armies for payoffs. Individuals got
$3 million each in covert CIA funds. Even so, some sect units skir-
mished as they retreated into swamps and jungles, some across the
border into Cambodia. Some units later joined Diem's army.

The shy and indecisive man dismissed by Lightning Joe now had
the upper hand in Saigon. Diem's victories brought citizens into the
streets of Saigon chanting for the downfall of the French puppet, Bao
Dai. Collins was recalled. A new American ambassador, G. Frederick Reinhardt, arrived and announced unequivocal backing of Diem
and an aid package of $300 million. By the fall of 1955, Diem called
for a nationwide vote between him and the absent emperor, Bao Dai.
A side benefit of the Geneva Convention enabled Diem to expand
his political base. The accord permitted an estimated 200,000 Catholics to leave North Vietnam and resettle in South Vietnam. Later
estimates were as high as 900,000. The CIA's Lansdale and his team
of secret agents were crucial in implementing the mass pilgrimage,
using U.S. Navy ships to transport thousands from north to south.

And Lansdale helped organize the 1955 election that gave Diem
a new legitimacy. The lopsided October vote ended Emperor Bai Dai's
position as head of state and sped the departure of the French colonial government. Diem was now president of the Republic of Vietnam. Lansdale made sure of the outcome. Bao Dai, for openers, was
prohibited from campaigning in South Vietnam. On Diem's behalf,
Lansdale implemented some of the worst techniques of the democratic process. Ballots cast for Bao Dai near Hue were simply thrown
in the trash, Chicago style. Or, as they did in Old New York, Diem
thugs would muscle supporters of the emperor. "The [Diem] agents
poured pepper sauce down their nostrils or forced water down their
throats," one voter told reporter Karnow.

No one was more delighted with the outcome of the October 23
vote—98.2 percent for Diem—than Eisenhower and the brothers
Dulles. The American secretary of state rebuffed final French de-

mands that Diem share power with pro-French opponents and otherwise broaden his government. "The U.S. cannot undertake to force upon him a government or policies which he does not like," Dulles cabled Paris. "He has a mind and will of his own and the fact that he survives proves he has virtues that are not easily replaced." It was the last time a senior American government official recognized that Diem knew more about running South Vietnam than the best brains in Foggy Bottom. A succession of American ambassadors to Saigon would ignore Dulles's sage insight in the coming years. Their cajoling, demanding, pressuring, intimidating, and even pleading failed to pry Diem's fingers from total control of South Vietnam. "I am not a puppet," Diem told more than one U.S. envoy. "I will not serve." For one reporter, Diem would imitate an American envoy waving a forefinger under the president's nose and demanding government reform that suited U.S. sensitivities.

To Diem, his government was formed in a crucible of mortars, howitzers, and machine guns. He was a wartime president with powerful enemies in Hanoi and a communist guerrilla force attacking his provinces. Democracy might be down the road, but in the meantime Diem forged a mandarinate with brother Ngo Dinh Nhu as chief counselor and brother Ngo Dinh Can as boss of central South Vietnam. His eldest brother, Bishop Ngo Dinh Thuc, was consulted on all family issues. The youngest brother, Ngo Dinh Luyen, served as ambassador to London and Paris. Outsiders joined the government only on the basis of unconditional loyalty to Diem. *Mandarin* stems from a word used by early Portuguese explorers in Asia and means to order or to command. Through study, dedication, and hard work, Diem's father, Ngo Dinh Kha, rose to be senior mandarin to the royal court in Hue, where Emperor Thanh Thai's decisions were implemented by the mandarin bureaucracy. The father instilled in his nine children the virtues of study, Catholicism, and service.

Diem's character was forged from a combination of Roman Catholicism and Confucianism. Both emphasized self-discipline, piety, and integrity. Mass and Holy Communion were a daily ritual for Diem. He dedicated a life of chastity to Jesus Christ. And his vow of chastity added to his image of incorruptibility. Sexual abstinence, a requirement for Buddhist monks, won Diem widespread admiration in both North and South Vietnam. Ho Chi Minh also claimed to be celibate, but many knew he was married—perhaps twice. Diem, who was baptized Jean Baptiste, briefly flirted with taking holy orders. "The discipline was too rigorous," Diem told reporter Stanley Karnow. Instead, he chose the mandarin's path to leadership in Saigon.

With the Saigon war over, General Big Minh finally captured Ba Cut, the fanatical guerrilla commander of the Hoa Hao sect in 1956. Diem marked the victory with a public execution of Ba Cut. When Ba Cut's head was placed on the block and the guillotine blade thudded home, it marked the growing stability of a government once viewed by Vietnamese and the West as having no chance of survival. An early priority was ousting communist political supporters and Viet Minh guerrillas. Hanoi's regular army units were withdrawn under the provisions of the Geneva Conference. Mobile courts and truck-mounted guillotines were used to eliminate residue throughout the country. Hundreds who avoided the blade wound up in cells of Con Son prison at Poulo Condore, the Asian version of France's Devil's Island. In some instances, Diem was as ruthless as Ho, who, after he assumed power, killed off thousands of opponents of communism in North Vietnam. Still, Hanoi maintained a secret network of communist supporters in South Vietnam, including the cell that selected Tri to gun down Diem in early 1957. The attempted assassination resulted in an important decision in the White House.

"Greatly shocked to hear of outrage at Ban-Me-Thout and relieved to know you are unharmed," Eisenhower cabled Diem. The American government had put aside Diem's request for a formal state visit to the United States in May. But shortly after the attempted assassination, Eisenhower approved the visit and even sent his personal airplane, the *Columbine III*, to pick up Diem in Honolulu. In Washington, Diem got the works—the president and the secretary of state at the bottom of the airplane steps to personally welcome him in as he descended to a twenty-one-gun salute. Diem was greeted by an estimated 50,000 federal workers and others who lined the streets, cheering and applauding as he and Eisenhower drove to Blair House. A white-tie state dinner was exquisite, with Long Island duckling, three great wines, and icy Pol Roger accompanying dessert. Guests including Francis Cardinal Spellman of New York applauded as the president of the United States toasted the president of South Vietnam. Pianist Arthur Rubinstein played Chopin.

Diem's five-foot-four stature and his potbelly seemed out of place to one American reporter. "Diem looks like a fat little teddy bear," said Andrew Tully of the *Washington Daily News*. But another, *New York Times* reporter Russell Baker, recognized the national genuflection to this bantam Asian. "Today only the best was good enough," Baker said. The last Washington event was the address to a joint session of Congress as Vice President Richard M. Nixon and Speaker Sam Rayburn looked on. Members stood frequently to applaud Diem as he repeatedly thanked them and the American people for helping to rebuild Vietnam out of chaos. He talked about the moral platform that was the basis for their diplomatic relationship. "It is on the same plane that your and our fight are one and the same," Diem told the assembly of cold war warriors. "We, too, will continue to fight communism." It got another standing ovation.

In New York, Diem met again with Cardinal Spellman, the prelate who five years earlier arranged a room for the exile at the Maryknoll Missionary Center in Ossining, New York. He visited old friends in Ossining, where he was known as a clumsy golfer, a dishwasher, and the first one in the pew for morning Mass. Seminarians in their black cassocks greeted him with "Hip hip hooray!"

"It was in this house that I had a clear vision of my plans to bring freedom to my people," he told the aspiring priests. Mayor Robert

Wagner, in presenting him with the key to the city, saw Diem's rise to power as a "miracle." Wagner said history would rate Diem "as one of the great figures of the twentieth century." In the whirl of introductions and congratulations, there were handshakes at the United Nations, including one from a man almost a foot taller—Henry Cabot Lodge Jr., the American ambassador to the UN. Both men would recall the encounter when they met again six years later in Saigon under very different circumstances. In 1963, Lodge was dispatched to Saigon by President Kennedy as U.S. ambassador empowered to decide if Diem would stay or go as head of the Saigon government.

On May 13, 1957, the world contained in the Big Apple was at Diem's feet. The day for Diem was akin to those in ancient Rome, when a triumph for heroes meant a chariot ride from the Servian Walls to the Circus Maximus amid cheering citizens and a rain of flowers, accompanied by a slave holding a golden laurel wreath over his head and whispering in the hero's ear how all glory was fleeting. In the United States, the celebration began at Bowling Green in lower Broadway and ended at Gracie Mansion, the office of Mayor Wagner. There were cheers and applause from more than 100,000 New Yorkers. A blizzard of torn office paper spilled from the canyons of the city to shower Ngo Dinh Diem. The ticker-tape parade featured bands and marching Army, Navy, and Marine Corps troops. There was no golden laurel wreath. Instead, *Times* reporter Robert Alden saw Diem being presented with a hat, a black homburg. Diem never wore hats. The homburg was strictly something to wave from the backseat of the open Cadillac limousine.

None of the passengers in the limo with the president of South Vietnam whispered that this American adulation was fleeting.

5

Head Butts

COPPER-JACKETED .50-CALIBER BULLETS SKIMMED THE bed of Ngo Dinh Diem. The fusillade would have ripped his short, plump body to shreds had not a headache in the night made him leave his bedroom in the palace for an aspirin from the bathroom medicine chest. "They meant to kill me," the president of South Vietnam said later. It was about three thirty in the morning and rebel troops with machine guns were raking the palace family quarters of the president of South Vietnam. These were paratroopers bent on removing Diem from power. The bullets—still the largest in the small arms inventory—were made in America. U.S. ammunition, tanks, and military training were provided to Saigon troops as a means of defending the Diem government in its battle with guerrillas backed by communist North Vietnam. Before dawn on November 11, 1960, Lieutenant Colonel Vuong Van Dong's airborne brigade shifted its aim from the Viet Cong to Diem's family-run mandarinate. After attending the Command and General Staff College at Fort Leavenworth, Kansas, Colonel Dong got a taste of American democracy—and political power. So his battle cry was for a more liberal, democratic government, with the emphasis on power sharing with a new military junta.

Word of the attack on Diem was a subject of the first intelligence briefings to the new president-elect Kennedy. He was in Palm Beach, recovering from the exhausting 1960 presidential campaign that produced victory on November 8. CIA Director Allen Dulles arrived and told Kennedy Diem was holed up in his Saigon palace surrounded by Colonel Dong's paratroopers. Both men saw it as a serious development. Dulles's CIA had played a key role in selecting Diem as the American-backed representative to confront communist forces in Vietnam. Along with his brother, Secretary of State John Foster Dulles, he had persuaded President Eisenhower to support Diem on this cold war battlefield. As a member of the Senate Foreign Relations Committee, Kennedy, too, had come to Diem's defense when French colonials conspired with American diplomats to oust the new Saigon leader. Kennedy had given the inaugural speech for a group of influential Americans, including a U.S. Roman Catholic cardinal, who supported the Roman Catholic president of South Vietnam. Until the November attack, most of Diem's serious opponents were in Paris, Hanoi, and the State Department in Washington. Now it seemed Diem was in trouble with his most powerful domestic constituency—the military. The main topic of Dulles's briefing in Palm Beach was preparations for the CIA-backed invasion of Cuba by opponents of Fidel Castro. Kennedy soon learned the coup attempt in Saigon had been encouraged by the American ambassador, Elbridge Durbrow.

Instead of supporting Diem's battle with the Viet Cong, Durbrow was directing an anti-Diem campaign while the communist guerrillas were making startling gains throughout the country. The often rude Durbrow, who resorted to curse words and other crude language in meetings with Diem, was also in open warfare with the CIA station in Saigon as well as with the American military adviser to Diem.

But a year would pass between the Palm Beach briefing and any semblance of a Kennedy policy for Vietnam. In between, Kennedy fended off relentless Pentagon demands to send U.S. combat troops to deal with the Viet Cong. What he finally approved was preceded by a noisy shouting match with Vice President Lyndon B. Johnson, who at first refused Kennedy's order to travel to Saigon and meet with Diem. Johnson, the reluctant diplomat, won Diem's approval for the foundation of America's military commitment to the Saigon government: American military advisers were imported to train South Vietnamese troops. Until his meeting with Johnson on May 12, 1961, Diem had rejected all U.S. proposals for American troops, either as advisers or for fighting the Viet Cong. At his final press conference in 1963, Kennedy said 25,000 Americans—Army, Navy, Marines, and Air Force—were supporting Saigon forces.

Kennedy inherited a badly divided U.S. team in Saigon. Until the arrival of Ambassador Durbrow, American diplomats had been under the firm direction of Secretary of State John Foster Dulles to leave the governing of South Vietnam to the man with the most knowledge and experience. The edict from Dulles meant a free and often autocratic hand for Diem. But as cancer slowed and eventually killed Dulles, Durbrow convinced the State Department of the need for a tougher line with Diem. Two goals were set by Durbrow: One was to win Diem's acceptance of a Washington-style democracy. The other was to kill a 500-pound Indochinese tiger. Durbrow's predecessor had bagged two. Instead of shooting from the back of an elephant or a tree stand, Vietnamese hunters dug a pit near a likely waterhole. The shooter and his guide jumped into the pit and it was covered with limbs and vines, leaving only a peephole. Then the exquisite cat was lured by the carcass of a buffalo. Durbrow and his guide waited silently in the pit for hours until the tiger walked almost on top of them. "I got two shots. Wounded one and goofed on the other," Durbrow recalled. "I didn't get my real spurs because I never got a tiger."

Durbrow wounded Diem, too. The seeds for the November 11 coup were planted by Durbrow six months earlier. It was nothing overt such as cash or planning. It was more filling the barracks and

Saigon cafés with the disenchantment with Diem at the American embassy. After a tour in a repressive Moscow, Durbrow arrived in Saigon as an apostle of the Four Freedoms—freedom of speech, freedom of worship, and freedom from fear and want. They were derived from a 1941 State of the Union address by President Franklin Delano Roosevelt and incorporated into the charter of the United Nations. Durbrow wanted open debate in a city where there was a real fear of prison for the politically outspoken. "You had to be careful," said Bui Diem, who managed to survive as a political critic in those days. Tran Kim Tuyen, chief of Diem's secret police, set the tone for dissidents. Tuyen was the tiniest man in the palace—under five feet and about seventy pounds. He would trace the list of the arrested with an elongated nail on his little finger. Tuyen, a physician by training, would free scores with a warning: Express your opinion, but don't try to overthrow the government.

Almost weekly, Durbrow pushed Diem to create such things as investigative oversight committees in the General Assembly. That elected body only bowed and rubber-stamped Diem's agenda. In addition to the other freedoms, Durbrow felt free to micromanage Diem's government. Instead of employing carefully nuanced language, Durbrow tried to persuade Diem with diplomatic head butts. "It was pretty damn tough on him," Durbrow said. "He didn't like a goddamned word I said." Lighting, puffing once, then dousing one cigarette after another, Diem would endure the speeches of the increasingly rude envoy. Diem ended these typical four-hour tirades with "I will think it over." Then nothing.

To Diem, his way was the right way. South Vietnam was flourishing. Diem had broken up 600,000 acres of large farms and redistributed them as 7-acre plots for 25,000 families mainly in the rice-rich Mekong Delta. Almost 900,000 refugees from the North—mainly Catholics—were resettled in new developments in the highlands of the South. He launched a plan to eradicate malaria within five years. American advisers offered advice on how to improve agriculture production with chemical fertilizers. Rubber exports were on the rise. Motorized fishing boats became common. Textile factories large and small sprung up everywhere. By Southeast Asian standards, Diem's South Vietnam was booming; the benefits were accruing to Vietnamese no longer under the yoke of French colonialism. This vibrant economic growth—a hallmark of successful Western democracies—seemed to mean little to Durbrow. The American ambassador was more intent on installing Diem's political opponents in the Saigon government. To Diem such a move was madness. Communist guerrillas were taking control in some provinces, so creating a politically divided government in Saigon was certain to lead to disaster.

Durbrow's open disdain for Diem was reflected by an embassy staff that saw the Saigon government as a threat to "success." Durbrow's team played down the much bigger threat of the growing attacks by the communist guerrillas. Diem's preference for running South Vietnam with brothers Ngo Dinh Nhu in the palace and Ngo Dinh Can in Hue had been approved by President Eisenhower. Following Dulles's advice, Ike had kept previous ambassadors from imposing American-style democracy in Saigon. To Eisenhower and Dulles, Diem was the best judge of the nation he ruled with Confucian social order and Roman Catholic justice. They preferred Diem's stability in the fight against communism. But Dulles died in 1959, and Durbrow boldly encouraged domestic opposition to Diem. To generate grassroots support, Durbrow selected George Carver to stimulate debate in Saigon over the need for political reform.

Although Carver was listed as a member of the embassy staff, he was in reality an undercover agent of the Central Intelligence Agency. He had the sort of sterling Ivy League background typical at the Agency. Carver was reared in Shanghai, where his father headed the English department at China's most elite university. At Yale, Carver was the debating champion, coxswain for the Yale crew, and graduated Phi Beta Kappa. At Oxford University, he earned a doctorate in philosophy and became the first American to cox the Oxford shell in the 97th Oxford-Cambridge race. At thirty-four, he had become a harsh judge of Diem. "I was absolutely convinced that to achieve American objectives in Vietnam, Diem had to be ousted," Carver said later. Following Durbrow's orders, Carver met with former Vietnamese officials in the French colonial government, wealthy landowners, and former members of the Diem government. Finally the group of eighteen men issued with great fanfare what became known as the Caravelle Manifesto, named for the new luxury high-rise hotel where they met with Carver. "Today the people want freedom," said the manifesto that criticized Diem, and called for civil rights and a democratic opposition safeguarded from the tiger cages of the Con Son prison on the offshore island of Poulo Condore. "We helped them write it a bit," Durbrow said with some pride. Durbrow and Carver also made sure the American, British, French, and Saigon journalists got the first copies of the document.

"Dictatorial Rule in Saigon Charged" was the page 1 headline in the *New York Times* on May 1, the day after the manifesto was made public. A week later in Washington, the document was used to undercut Diem with his most important benefactor—President Eisenhower. At a May 9, 1960, meeting of the National Security Council, the deputy director of the CIA told Eisenhower that the manifesto was proof that Diem's government was crumbling because of public opposition to his one-man rule. Eisenhower, who admired Diem's battle to overcome odds against his leadership in South Vietnam, rejected the move. Unlike Durbrow, Eisenhower had a history with Diem, who defied all the experts by emerging victorious from the Battle of Saigon. Eisenhower stopped plans to bully Diem with the threat to cut off U.S. aid unless he liberalized the Saigon government. "The U.S. ought to do everything possible to prevent the deterioration of the situation in South Vietnam," Eisenhower concluded.

Durbrow was forced to cool his evangelical ardor—temporarily. He found himself battling with not only Diem but two of the most senior members of the U.S. delegation: William Colby, who became CIA station chief in June of 1960, and Army Lieutenant General Samuel Williams, who directed military aid for the Saigon army. "We had some real knock-down, drag-out fights," Durbrow said of the general. "He and I just didn't get along. He had no respect for civilians." But Williams did have the respect of Diem, who twice requested Eisenhower to extend the general's tour in Vietnam. Willliams would later confide to friends that Durbrow was a self-important blowhard with no understanding of the people of Vietnam or of the reality of Diem's struggle. The ambassador's determination to pry Diem's fingers from the reins of government was opposed by Colby. To Colby, Durbrow's passion to install democracy ignored the reality of the need for central command in the face of increasing numbers of Viet Cong assaults in the countryside. Wartime leaders everywhere tend to crack down on the opposition. "I strongly disagreed with him," Colby said, describing Durbrow's proposals as irrelevant.

In Saigon, Durbrow mainly controlled State Department personnel. Colby was responsible to Director Allen Dulles of Central Intelligence. As head of the American military mission, Williams was just as independent. Colby and Williams teamed up to confront Durbrow's decision to halt U.S. funding for Saigon's army and civil guard unless Diem embraced democratic reforms. Colby and Williams praised Diem in official reports that countered Durbrow's critical cables to the State Department. Durbrow's block on military funding came just as Hanoi had launched a new guerrilla attack in 1959. The Viet Cong began systematic attacks on Saigon army outposts, killing soldiers and looting hundreds of rifles and ammunition. It was the start of Hanoi's plan to equip the Viet Cong with weapons and other supplies from the United States. The killing, maiming, and torturing of Diem government representatives outside Saigon became widespread. The Viet Cong halted Diem's malaria eradication program by killing off public health officials in the countryside. The turmoil in the countryside unnerved the elites of Saigon, bureaucrats, and business leaders who were still wedded to French colonial ways—the chattering classes, according to the CIA station chief. Both Colby and Williams saw the millions outside of Saigon as the foundation of Diem's government—not the denizens of Saigon cafés, who in conversations with journalists were quick to criticize Diem. Even so, their opinions were needed for government stability.

While Durbrow was staging angry confrontations with Diem, Colby was forging personal ties with Ngo Dinh Nhu, the president's brother and chief adviser, and Nhu's wife. Her birth name was Tran Le Xuan, or "Beautiful Spring," but the world came to know her as the fiery Madame Nhu. Colby arrived at the rear of the palace to be let in for a session with Madame Nhu. "Hair meticulously coiffed and stiffened, nails pointed and lacquered, fingers adorned with brilliant jewels, voice sharp and quick," Colby wrote, "she was the embodiment of real and mythical Oriental empresses." Her five-foot-two, eighty-pound body was in a sheath of silk, petite yet voluptuous. There was a hint of perfume as she clicked along in black French pumps to her seat at a gold-trimmed table. Too much eyebrow pencil and face powder, sniffed one American woman. What she wanted from Colby was legal advice. Before the CIA, Colby practiced briefly as a New York lawyer. Madame Nhu wanted a translation into English of a law she pushed through the National Assembly that radically changed the standing of women in Vietnamese society. It provided that the woman's property would remain hers after separation; divorce was prohibited; bastard children would no longer share a family inheritance. She wanted to circulate this breakthrough in women's rights to the rest of the world. It was just one of the life-changing regulations she got passed as an elected member of the National Assembly. She won passage of laws to outlaw prostitution, public dancing, contraceptives, abortion, prizefights, and the equivalent of the national pastime—cockfighting. She had been a Buddhist but converted to Catholicism. Many in Saigon saw themselves forced to abide by the tenets of a religion imported by the French—by a woman who flaunted her sexuality. Their anger focused on Diem, not just on the independent Madame Nhu.

Madame Nhu functioned as the nation's First Lady to the bachelor president. She could be vigorous, even explosive in family debates with Diem and Nhu. Angered by Diem's refusal to crack down on Buddhist demonstrators, she flung a bowl of chicken noodle soup at him. Another report had Beautiful Spring showing up in Diem's bedroom in a flimsy nightgown on the pretext of searching for something. Diem hollered for help and ordered her out. More often, at the end of a hard day, she would entertain Diem with gossip, humor, and the small talk that would distract him from his burdens. In Madame Nhu's forceful tone, Colby recognized her mother, the imperious Madame Chuong, wife of Tran Van Chuong, then serving as ambassador to the United States. Madame Chuong was a cousin of the last Vietnamese emperor, Bao Dai, and a rich and beautiful woman. According to Saigon gossip, Madame Chuong had had Ngo Dinh Nhu as a lover before Beautiful Spring seduced him away. Nhu was indeed handsome, judging by the heads he turned at the U.S. embassy, according to Colby. He would show up at the back gate of the palace for weekly meetings in Nhu's small office. It was more like the back room of a hunting cabin: tiger skins on the floor and animal heads on the wall. "Thin, dark and intense," Colby wrote of Nhu, who chain-smoked as he rifled through a desk covered with dossiers, reports, and files.

Colby's meetings were a continuation of a secret and separate channel of communication with the United States first begun by Edward Lansdale. It was also a channel of cash to Diem for such things as the creation of a praetorian guard of Vietnamese Special Forces. Millions of dollars never seen on any budget traveled from Washington to Saigon via the CIA. Usually Nhu ignored Colby's checklist for discussion and veered into conspiracies and the difficulty of erasing French-style corruption within the bureaucracy. "Nhu's comments and train of thought were invariably intelligent and

politically sophisticated," Colby wrote. "He was obviously fasci-
nated with intrigue." Nhu, the reigning intellectual in the palace,
was adept at flights of logical erudition based on the teachings of the
French philosopher René Descartes. As did his brother, Nhu first
tried but then quit the priesthood, He was then trained by the French
as a librarian and worked as chief archivist at the National Library.
When Diem fell into disfavor with the colonial government, so
did Nhu.

He was forced to find work in the mountain retreat, Da Lat.
When Diem established control in 1955, Nhu created the Can Lo, a
political party filled with government loyalists. It was an almost exact copy of the Communist Party's role in the leadership of the Hanoi government. Can Lo was Nhu's counter to the French-trained
elite who dominated the urban economic and social scene. To raise
money for the Can Lo, Nhu turned to the wealthy in Saigon. His
fund-raising along with the flow of CIA cash gave rise to endless
speculation that Nhu was an extortionist who was amassing millions in Swiss bank accounts. He was confronted with the rumors
by reporter Stanley Karnow.

"It's not true," Nhu said. "We have nothing. You can examine
our bank accounts. We are poor."

Karnow persisted: "But people think you are dishonest."

"I don't care what the people think," Nhu snapped.

Years later, his widow and children were in exile in Paris and then
Rome. They squeezed into apartments of relatives. U.S. diplomats
saw Madame Nhu as totally dependent on her relatives with no
sign of overflowing Swiss accounts. She was peddling herself to the
press for paid interviews. "Frail and broken," said one who knew the
fierce Madame Nhu at the peak of her power. Colby saw as his mission to understand, not debate, Nhu. But he frequently reminded
the counselor of the president of the importance of the Diem government's image to votes in the American Congress and even to the
support of the American people. "In general, however, I sympathized

with Nhu's insistence that Vietnam needed to discover and develop a new political identity, to counter the appeal of communism," Colby wrote.

With Nhu, the conversations were in French, a language Colby learned as a student in France and perfected as an American spy supporting the Maquis, the French underground, during World War II. But the talk was all in English when Colby met with Diem. Colby entered through the front door of the palace. Diem chain-smoked like his brother, but took only a puff of the cigarette before stubbing it out in an overflowing ashtray. There were no flights of theory and logical expositions. With Diem, it was his high-pitched staccato review of the building of roads, medical clinics, and schools and the infiltration routes of the Viet Cong. Diem oversaw almost every facet of his government, a burden he would not share. His knowledge of military matters impressed many American visitors. One conversation dealt with the destruction of an American Special Forces outpost by the Viet Cong and the loss of sixty native defenders. Roger Hilsman, then assistant secretary of state for intelligence and research, visited the ruined outpost before meeting with Diem. For the visitor, Diem detailed the camp's defenses and criticized the sloppy weapon placement. Diem noted the American camp commander was a West Pointer. "It made me squirm particularly when Diem recalled that I, too, was a West Pointer," Hilsman said later, impressed with Diem's military sagacity.

With most of the journalists in Saigon, Diem protected himself from probing questions with a monologue that routinely ran for four hours. Reporters were pumped full of tea and facts about the centuries of endless wars in Indochina as the Vietnamese expelled Chinese and Western conquerors. The veterans learned to inject a question just as Diem went silent long enough to light a new cigarette. To Colby, Diem lacked the warmth and charm exuded by many political leaders. And he fell victim to bad judgment in trying to establish new towns—agrovilles—in the Mekong Delta. Peasants were dragooned into building these villages and new roads. But the farmers wound up too far from their fields and abandoned the villages with their medical facilities and schools. A later version of this peasant consolidation called the Strategic Hamlet Program became a top priority of the Kennedy years. Overall, however, Colby admired Diem's integrity, dedication, and relentless pressure on outlying administrators to serve the population and combat the Viet Cong. Eighteen-hour days were the norm, with personal phone calls placed to handpicked province administrators. "This is my weapon," Diem said, flourishing a French-style telephone receiver.

By September 1960, Durbrow reopened his attack on Diem. In a cable to Washington, he called for the removal of Nhu and his wife, as well as that of the tiny secret police chief from Saigon, and a shift of power to new ministers of the interior and defense. The envoy also called for elimination of Diem's Can Lo political party. If Diem failed to follow these American directions, Durbrow said, "it may become necessary for the U.S. government to begin consideration of alternative course of actions and leaders in order to achieve our objective." At the same time, Durbrow peddled his disappointment with Diem to the entire diplomatic corps in Saigon.

Soon everyone knew that the American support for Diem was fading. Anti-Diem civilians, emboldened by the Caravelle Manifesto, soon conspired with Saigon army leaders to take on the government. When Colby was not meeting with Diem, Nhu, Madame Nhu, or their tiny secret police chief, he was keeping tabs on Diem's opponents. So when tracer gunfire banged into his bedroom a block from the palace on November 11, Colby alerted a network of agents via radio to find out what was going on. Agent Carver, who had helped organize the Caravelle Manifesto, went to the home of the civilian leader of the coup. Other agents pieced together the military details. A CIA man traveled to rebel headquarters set up at the joint military center near the airport. Instead of a full-scale revolt, the individual soldiers in the paratrooper units were told they came to the palace to rescue Diem, not to oust him. They soon found out the truth when the soldiers in the presidential guard cut down their ranks with automatic weapons. Civilian bystanders who came to watch the show were also caught in the cross fire. When it became clear that rebel airborne troops had reached a stalemate, Durbrow told Diem by telephone that he should negotiate with the commander of the paratroopers. Perhaps Durbrow was counting on the Fort Leavenworth–trained Colonel Dong to win concessions from Diem that had eluded the Americans. Durbrow refused to openly back the rebel soldiers. As long as Diem survived, Durbrow pledged U.S. support for his government.

But Carver, in touch with the civilian leaders, balked. He wanted the military to press the attack. "I was convinced that my orders were not in the rebels' interest and not in the U.S. interest," Carver said later. "I bitched and moaned why I thought my orders were stupid." At one point, he watched the rebel paratroopers milling about. "Every fiber of my being wanted to say, 'For Christ's sake, will you guys get off your ass and get this thing finished.'" Instead, Carver just watched as Diem outmaneuvered Colonel Dong and Ambassador Durbrow.

At one point, Diem appeared close to accepting rebel demands for more democratic change, even to stepping down. He was urged to quit by Brigadier General Nguyen Khanh, the army chief of staff. Khanh, while not part of the uprising, had agreed to be a mediator between the palace and the rebels. "It is the will of the population and all the armed forces," Khanh told Diem. The president and his brother seemed confused by Khanh's statement. Not Madame Nhu. She flew into a rage. "No, no, never," she shrieked at Diem. "You have to kill all the paratroopers." Khanh was stunned by her outburst. "All right, if you want to take my place, take command," Khanh told Madame Nhu. "I'm leaving now." Diem ordered Madame Nhu out of the meeting. To Khanh, Diem agreed to begin negotiations with the rebels. In the meantime, he secretly issued appeals by radio for help to military commanders outside Saigon. Elements of the 5th and 7th

Divisions, infantry closest to Saigon, arrived the next day, along with armored columns from other units. An angry Durbrow phoned Diem again when he learned of the rescue by loyal troops. Durbrow demanded negotiations to prevent open warfare in Saigon. Durbrow said he was "extremely perturbed." I will see what I can do, Diem said before hanging up. Both the American ambassador and the rebel leaders were foiled. Colonel Dong and other rebel officers realized the negotiations had been a ruse. They fled to the airport and a plane to exile in Cambodia. Diem ordered others arrested. A death warrant was issued for Carver. It was unsigned, but Colby figured it came from Counselor Nhu. Carver was sent home and Nhu did not mention the CIA rescue of a civilian leader in the revolt. Colby had him stuffed in an embassy mail sack and flown to safety. Despite claims of neutrality by Durbrow and Colby, their relations with the rebels gave Diem and Nhu a lasting suspicion of the Americans. Their view, not unlike many American politicians, was that you are either for or against me. There was no middle ground.

Diem's survival reinforced perceptions among the military and civilians that he was a shrewd manipulator of government power—even holding the U.S. embassy at bay. Still, the arrests made after the failed coup underlined the continuing disenchantment in Saigon circles. Imprisoned and tortured was Dr. Phan Quang Dan. He was a Harvard-trained physician who catered to the poor. Dr. Dan won an overwhelming vote a year earlier for a seat in the National Assembly. Diem refused to seat him, charging voter irregularities. In the midst of the 1960 revolt, Dan emerged as a spokesman for the rebel paratroopers. He called for Diem's resignation and a new, more liberal democratic government. The educated elite of Saigon sided with Dan and against the palace. Meanwhile, the Viet Cong were on the rise in the countryside, using terror and promises to win peasants away from the central government. "In the South Vietnamese spectrum, Diem and Nhu held a central position," Colby said. "But their strength was ebbing away on both sides."

At their 1961 summit in Vienna, Khrushchev warned Kennedy against deploying U.S. nuclear weapons in countries near the Soviet Union. But by August 1962, Kennedy deployed fifteen Jupiter missiles in Turkey with hydrogen warheads only fifteen minutes from Moscow. Within weeks of the start of Jupiter deployment, Khrushchev planned to slip nuclear weapons into Cuba. When Kennedy secretly agreed to get rid of the Jupiters in Turkey, Khrushchev pulled the Soviet missiles and sixty nuclear warheads out of Cuba. *(National Archives and Records Administration)*

The liquid-fueled Jupiters were considered obsolete by U.S. planners when deployed near Izmir, Turkey. But Russian generals saw the closeness of fifteen rockets, each carrying a 1.4-megaton warhead, as a "first strike" threat to Soviet forces as well as the Moscow command center. *(George Smith)*

In Cuba, the SS-4 Sandal rocket with a 1-megaton warhead had enough range to threaten Miami, New Orleans, Dallas, and other Southern and Southwestern cities. Khrushchev said the Cuba deployment was merely giving Kennedy a taste of his own medicine. *(U.S. Air Force)*

Kennedy feared General Curtis LeMay would leak the truth about the Cuban missile crisis during his 1964 presidential reelection campaign. The Air Force chief of staff was a close personal friend of Arizona senator Barry Goldwater, Kennedy's likely Republican opponent in 1964. LeMay was a table-pounding opponent of Kennedy's secret deal with Khrushchev. "We lost!" LeMay told Kennedy. LeMay gave Kennedy fits, according to one aide. *(John F. Kennedy Library)*

A 1959 photograph of revolutionary Rolando Cubela when he was wounded while fighting alongside Fidel Castro. But when Castro was made a target of assassination by the Kennedy White House, Cubela was recruited to kill Castro. For the job, Cubela was armed with a CIA poison pen on November 22, 1963—the day Kennedy was assassinated. Cubela was later jailed as a CIA spy. *(Corbis)*

Air Force Major General Edward Geary Lansdale was executive director of "Operation Mongoose," a secret White House project trying to overthrow the communist government in Havana with sabotage and the assassination of Fidel Castro. Kennedy's brother Bobby, the U.S. attorney general, was in charge of Mongoose. Lansdale also helped install Ngo Dinh Diem as president of South Vietnam. *(U.S. Air Force)*

Cuban premier Fidel Castro smoking a Cohiba, a cigar he personally designed. Dr. Edward Gunn of the CIA, who specialized in creating assassination devices, dusted fifty Cohibas with botulinum toxin. Castro needed only to put one in his mouth to be killed almost instantly by the lethal poison. But this plan to plant the cigar box on Castro's desk, like all other CIA schemes, fizzled. *(Associated Press)*

Reverend Martin Luther King Jr. and Adlai Stevenson both became targets for Kennedy White House smear campaigns. Despite Kennedy's demands, King refused to temper his 1963 campaign for civil rights. During the 1962 Cuban missile crisis, Kennedy and his aides leaked to reporters that Stevenson, then UN ambassador, sought a "Munich" style appeasement rather than confronting the Soviet Union. *(Associated Press)*

Malcolm Wilde Browne, Saigon bureau chief of the Associated Press, was the lone American photographer to capture the grisly death of Thich Quang Duc. The Buddhist monk was protesting President Ngo Dinh Diem's crackdown on Buddhist demonstrators in the spring of 1963. The June photograph created a worldwide shock and was a blow to Kennedy's policies in South Vietnam and his political standing as his reelection campaign loomed. "Once that photo was published, the Diem government was doomed," said William Colby of the CIA. *(Associated Press)*

This May 4, 1963, photograph of Birmingham police attacking school children protesting Alabama's racial segregation forced Kennedy to endorse King's civil rights campaign. Until Birmingham, Kennedy shunned King and sought to retain Southern voters who helped elect him president in 1960. But the photograph reprinted front page in *The New York Times* ignited demands by the nation's legal establishment and voters outraged by the use of police dogs. Browne's photograph from Saigon and Bill Hudson's photograph from Birmingham contributed to a steady decline in voter approval polls for Kennedy. *(Associated Press photograph by William Hudson)*

Lodge, wearing his World War II medals, presents his credentials to Diem. Two days before, Kennedy had approved the overthrow of Diem's government by a band of Saigon army generals. In their first meeting, Diem made clear to Lodge that the South Vietnamese president knew that Lodge was plotting against him. *(Associated Press)*

President Diem waved to a cheering New York City crowd during a ticker-tape parade in his honor in 1957. President Eisenhower, who had installed Diem in power in 1954, made the Saigon anticommunist leader something of a hero in the American press. Senator John F. Kennedy, who met with Diem while still an exile, defended him against French moves to oust him from power in Saigon. *(Getty Images)*

At a crucial August 15, 1963, White House meeting, Kennedy can be heard telling Lodge that it will be up to him as the new U.S. ambassador to Saigon to decide on the removal of President Ngo Dinh Diem. The manila envelope on the table contained Browne's photo of flaming Thich Quang Duc. Kennedy showed the photo to Lodge as an example of the American crisis in Saigon. The president said he retained the final decision but authorized Lodge to do whatever he wished in Saigon. The order led to the assassination of Diem, chaos in Saigon, and the eventual deployment of American combat troops to take on the communist forces of North Vietnam. *(National Archives and Records Administration)*

Rufus Phillips as a young U.S. Army officer working for the CIA in 1959 to bolster the Diem government. By 1963, Phillips had become the CIA liaison with Saigon generals staging a coup against the Diem government. Phillips later regretted his role in the coup, which he saw as a major mistake that pulled American troops into an Indochina war. *(Rufus Phillips)*

Lucien Conein in the uniform of a U.S. Army lieutenant colonel visiting Vietnam's Montagnard in 1962. The U.S. Army was a cover for Conein's role as an undercover agent dating back to World War II. His exploits behind Nazi lines in France and in North Vietnam are celebrated at the CIA. Following Lodge's orders, Conein along with Phillips secretly supplied American support for the Saigon army coup against Diem. *(Rufus Phillips)*

John Michael Dunn was Lodge's top aide in Saigon when Kennedy's new ambassador took over CIA operations against Diem. Under Lodge's direction, Dunn oversaw CIA agents Phillips and Lucien Conein in efforts to prod the reluctant Saigon army generals to move against Diem. Lodge said the generals lacked the troops and the guts to challenge Diem. *(Getty Images)*

After the first coup plan fizzled, Kennedy ordered Lodge to bribe Major General Ton That Dinh to lead the coup. Dinh commanded enough troops in the Saigon area to make the coup a success. The CIA later reported that Dinh was the key to the November 2, 1963, plot. Still, McGeorge Bundy, Kennedy's adviser on national security affairs, complained that Dinh had been paid too much. The exact amount is still unknown. *(Getty Images)*

Diem pleaded with Lodge to rescue him from angry Saigon army generals the day after he was overthrown. Dunn volunteered to pick up Diem from a secret destination and bring him to safety in the U.S. embassy, but Lodge refused. Two hours later, Diem and his brother were murdered in the back of an army personnel carrier on orders from the coup leader, Army General Big Minh. *(National Archives and Records Administration)*

President Eisenhower and Secretary of State John Foster Dulles personally greeted President Diem when he arrived for a state visit in Washington, D.C., in May 1957. Ike, Dulles, and Allen Dulles of the CIA handpicked Diem to lead South Vietnam's war against Hanoi's communist guerrillas in 1954. In retirement, Ike became outraged at Kennedy's "cold-blooded" killing of Diem, who had been the leader in the hot war against communism. *(National Archives and Records Administration)*

Both Bobby and McNamara wanted a bloody invasion of Cuba and the establishment of an American-backed government in Havana. The president overruled them and agreed to remove U.S. Jupiter rockets in Turkey as part of a secret missile swap with Soviet premier Khrushchev, who pulled the Russian missiles out of Cuba. The Soviets slipped the rockets into Cuba after Kennedy deployed fifteen Jupiters within striking distance of Moscow—a move Khrushchev warned Kennedy not to make during their Vienna summit in 1961. *(National Archives and Records Administration)*

In September 1963, Kennedy sent Defense Secretary Robert McNamara and Army General Maxwell Taylor to Saigon for what amounted to be an ultimatum for President Diem. They demanded that he remove his brother Counselor Ngo Dinh Nhu and silence Nhu's fiery wife and that the American press be given unhindered freedom in Saigon. Diem rejected these demands. When Diem refused, the American-backed coup was launched six weeks later. *(National Archives and Records Administration)*

Gains by the Viet Cong north and south of Saigon—one communist-controlled area was only forty miles from the capital—were the foundation of a January 28, 1961, report on Vietnam that alarmed the new American president. "The U.S. should recognize that Vietnam is in critical condition and should treat it as a combat area of the Cold War as an area requiring emergency treatment," said the report. Walt Whitman Rostow, a National Security Council deputy, insisted that the president read every word.

When he was finished, Kennedy looked up at Rostow. "This is going to be the worst one yet," Kennedy said. "I'll tell you something: Eisenhower never mentioned the word Vietnam to me."

Kennedy was impressed with the cogent and detailed account and the authoritative tone used by the author, Edward Lansdale. The longtime CIA operative's presentation was such a tour de force that Kennedy urged and the *Saturday Evening Post* agreed to print Lansdale's call to arms in defense of Diem and South Vietnam. Kennedy wanted Lansdale to replace Durbrow—a dismissal Lansdale recommended—in Saigon. Both the Secretaries of Defense and State had different ideas. McNamara and Rusk teamed up to blackball Lansdale and his CIA pedigree. He was neither a real Air Force officer nor a diplomat. Instead, he was assigned to direct the Operation Mongoose campaign of sabotage in Cuba and assassination of Fidel Castro. Still, Kennedy valued his expertise on Saigon and Diem. Lansdale was invited to key White House meetings and devised what became the foundation of American policy for the next thirteen years—send U.S. troops to Vietnam. He authored the 1961 recommendation in the White House Vietnam Task Force report used as a basis for Kennedy's May 11 formal finding: The United States would not permit communist domination of South Vietnam.

To the Joint Chiefs, this meant quickly dispatching American combat troops to turn back the Viet Cong. Opposed was the State Department. Undersecretary of State George Ball explained that even a small investment of American troops was "skin in the game," the start of what would be an open-ended commitment of U.S. forces to a war in a jungle where the French had been defeated. "If we went down that road we might have within five years 300,000 men in the rice paddies, impossible terrain, and we'd just never be able to find them," Ball told Kennedy.

"George," Kennedy replied, "you're just crazier than hell."

In the spring of 1961, Kennedy's foreign misadventures had produced a series of domestic political defeats. The Bay of Pigs fiasco made Fidel Castro an almost daily whipping boy for Republicans in Congress. Kennedy's escape from Laos was producing waves of panic among American allies and criticism from Eisenhower, the military establishment, and Republicans. In one speech, Eisenhower complained about Kennedy's "indecision and uncertainty," in Cuba and Vietnam. McNamara and Rusk joined in waving a political red flag. "The loss of Vietnam would stimulate bitter domestic controversies," the cabinet members told Kennedy. This "would be seized upon by extreme elements to divide the country and harass the administration." They were novices when it came to understanding a negative impact on Kennedy, the political pro.

"There are limits to the number of defeats I can defend in one twelve-month period," he told one adviser. "I've had the Bay of Pigs, pulling out of Laos, and I can't accept a third." Pulling out of Vietnam would haunt him, as the loss of China to communism undercut Democrats during the Truman years. He resolved to back Diem with a new ambassador to replace Durbrow. Frederick "Fritz" Nolting, the deputy chief of the U.S. mission to NATO in Paris, was chosen despite never serving in Asia. Kennedy pulled a newspaper clipping out of his pocket in his first meeting with Nolting. "The American embassy here is not terribly well regarded," Kennedy read to Nolting. "They all seem to stay in the embassy and not get out to meet all types of people." When he got to Saigon, Kennedy urged him to get out of the embassy. "Don't get deskbound," Kennedy told Nolting. The key to his job in Saigon would be Diem. "The outcome of your mission depends on what kind of man Diem is," Kennedy told Nolting. The new ambassador found flaws in Diem—besides being inept at public relations, he was a poor administrator with an inability to delegate, and he tried to do too much. Nolting also concluded that Diem's honesty and integrity and dedication to hard work were impressive. "I became convinced that the Diem regime was the best available to govern South Vietnam and that it could and would improve," Nolting told Washington.

While Nolting was delighted with his appointment to the hot spot, the next man Kennedy sent to Saigon was a far more reluctant diplomat. Lyndon Johnson objected to Kennedy's plan to emphasize the American commitment to Diem by sending the vice president to carry a personal message from Kennedy. Four times Johnson balked. "Mr. President, I don't want to embarrass you by getting my head blown off in Saigon," Johnson said. Not to worry, Kennedy said. "If anything happens to you, [House Speaker] Sam Rayburn and I will give you the biggest funeral Austin, Texas, has ever seen." Without Johnson's knowledge and consent, Kennedy announced the vice president's mission to Saigon at a White House news conference. Johnson's military aide, Air Force Colonel Howard Burris, recalled the vice president's anger when he heard Kennedy's decision on the radio. At the White House, Burris listened to a shouting match between the vice president and the president of the United States. "You're going tonight!" was Kennedy's final and loudest order. Johnson stormed out and got so drunk that he collapsed on his office couch. When he awoke, he was surrounded by State Department briefers. "There are more asses here than horses," Johnson told Burris before sending the briefers away. The hungover vice president threatened to throw Burris off their plane if he tried to brief him on the flight to Saigon.

Fear might have been one reason for Johnson's reluctance. Then again, fear that he—not Kennedy—might wind up holding the bag if Vietnam was a disaster. Two years later, Johnson was saddled with what proved one of the worst disasters in American history. American troops were at the top of Johnson's agenda, Kennedy told the May 11 news conference. Diem had repeatedly rejected U.S. offers of American soldiers, either for combat or as military advisers. He did not want another colonial force to replace the French—a certain propaganda attack by Hanoi. But Kennedy's flight from Laos changed attitudes in Saigon. In preparing his report for Kennedy, Lansdale met with Diem and convinced him of the surging threat of the Viet Cong. Prompted by the Joint Chiefs, Army Lieutenant General Lionel McGarr, the new head of the American military in Saigon, told Diem of the advantages of American forces in Vietnam.

By the time Johnson had arrived in Saigon, the stage had been set. McGarr, Colby, Nolting, and Burris sat in on Johnson's top secret exchange with Diem on May 13. Diem said the American retreat in Laos had forced him to increase his army—from 120,000 to 150,000. He wanted the United States to finance the entire increase. Johnson countered with an offer of American combat troops. "Diem replied that he did not want U.S. troops to fight in his country except in the case of overt aggression against South Vietnam; but he did want an increase in U.S. training personnel." Johnson's agreement to give Diem an almost unlimited increase in military and financial aid was angrily rejected by Kennedy. But the agreement to send advisers—McGarr set the expected total as 16,000—was implemented six months later.

Five months later, Diem would bend even further, agreeing to deployment of American combat troops on his border with North Vietnam as the Viet Cong increased their control in South Vietnam. Kennedy was firm: no combat troops. A secret war—secret from the American public and most of Congress—was under way. Shelved were State Department demands that Diem agree to democratic reforms. By November, a shipload of American combat helicopters was en route to Saigon. American fighter-bombers—flown by U.S. Air Force "volunteers"—followed along with armored personnel carriers that would repel the Viet Cong. The first block of advisers—500 Army officers and sergeants—were followed by a steady stream of thousands. Saigon troops were equipped with sophisticated American munitions and communication gear. Colby launched a massive counterintelligence program specifically ordered by Kennedy. Defoliants and herbicides sprayed by U.S. Air Force planes were used in a chemical warfare against Viet Cong ambush sites and cropland. American technology had gone to war in Vietnam.

With every increment of U.S. military and financial aid and the swelling number of Americans in Saigon, Diem began to wonder if his patron might one day set the real agenda for South Vietnam. "I found him in a suspicious mood," Ambassador Nolting said. Things were going badly in several provinces. The American press was attacking him. Would we, in a pinch, use the leverage of our aid to threaten or destroy his government in case of a disagreement? Diem wanted to know. "I consider it totally unfounded," Nolting answered Diem. The American pledged to use its aid only to support the constitutional government and never to impose final decisions. Diem asked if Nolting could get such a commitment in writing from Kennedy.

"Several days later a cable arrived," confirming what Nolting had promised Diem. "Signed by Rusk with the notation 'from highest authority,' meaning the president," Nolting said. "The U.S. government would work with him, not against him. Diem found this confirmation satisfactory."

President Kennedy had given his word.

6

Due Course

U-2 PLANES SPYING FROM THE edge of space, undercover agents, and countless analysts served as the eyes on the world for the president's daily intelligence briefing. President Kennedy greeted the briefing skeptically. The CIA was constantly predicting East Germany was on the verge of preempting West Germany as the dominant European economy. Then on August 17, 1961, the Soviet Union built the first of ninety-seven miles of wall around East Berlin. This act halted what had been the defection of 3.5 million disenchanted East Germans from what was supposed to be the vibrant heart of communist industry. In reality, East German industry produced inferior automobiles and inexportable consumer goods from a society robbed of its culture and corrupted by insidious informers. The Wall, designed to halt the German exodus to the West, was really a symbol of the failure of communism. It didn't play that way in the news reports of the day. Soviet premier Nikita Khrushchev's erection of the Berlin Wall was another knee in Kennedy's groin. It followed Khrushchev's demand at their Vienna summit that Kennedy withdraw U.S. troops from Berlin or face nuclear warfare. The Wall seemed an extension of the threat to prevent American, French, and British forces access to East Berlin. Kennedy was stunned by the threat to snatch what had been the allied prize in the war with Nazi Germany.

Kennedy's self-termed inept performance at Vienna in June followed the retreat from Laos in May and the fiasco at the Bay of Pigs in April. Newspaper columnists both hostile and friendly joined Republicans in Congress to lash the young chief executive for his incompetence. The CIA was surprised when the Wall was erected in secret at night and then announced to the world at sunrise. Blindsided, Kennedy had no response to the Soviet surprise. Another round of criticism washed over Kennedy at home and abroad. "Berlin expects more than words," said West Berlin mayor Willy Brandt. "It expects action." Kennedy, who hoped to increase his political capital through his expertise in foreign affairs, had a miserable first year. Reeling from these foreign policy losses, Kennedy grew to resent the CIA's miscalculation in Cuba and its continual surprise at Kremlin machinations. "Splinter the CIA in a thousand pieces and scatter it to the winds," he told one aide after the Bay of Pigs.

For Kennedy, newspapers and reporters were a far more reliable, accurate, and balanced source of world intelligence. "He always thought they knew what was really going on," said Jean Kennedy Smith, the president's sister. "Whenever we'd go to a strange city, he would say, 'Let's check in with the locals,' meaning the press." Kennedy's daily bible was the *New York Times*, but he perused other newspapers and magazines as well. The *Times* was often on the breakfast table or even spread on his bed, where he read in pajamas. Articles were clipped, peppered with question marks, and passed along to his staff. Or he would even make a quick, bureaucracy-rattling phone call. No one could elude the White House telephone operators. Sometimes Kennedy pulled the clipping from his pocket and read it aloud to an aide scrambling for a reply. Defense Secretary McNamara was confronted by Kennedy with a *Times* story saying there was rift in the U.S. embassy over the Strategic Hamlet Program. "How accurate is this story?" Kennedy demanded. "Is there a split?" Senior cabinet members as well some backwater diplomats were often forced to respond to something Kennedy clipped from his bible.

In the midst of the political setbacks from foreign misadventures, Kennedy got the first inkling of his most serious domestic political problem from a *Times* May 15, 1961, headline: "Biracial Buses Attacked, Riders Beaten in Alabama." Two Greyhound buses with both blacks and whites aboard were challenging Southern racial barriers. They became known as the Freedom Riders. Angry crowds ambushed and beat them in Anniston and Birmingham, Alabama. One bus was burned in Anniston and the mob outside tried to block the exits for the screaming Freedom Riders. These rides, nonviolent protests, were organized by the Congress of Racial Equality and its leader, James Farmer Jr. The goal was to eliminate barriers to washrooms, waiting rooms, and bus stop restaurants, restricted to whites only in the South's Bible Belt. Farmer, with his eye patch and operatic basso, relished goading Kennedy into the civil rights battlefield. "We put on pressure and create a crisis and then they react," Farmer said. As attorney general, Kennedy's brother Bobby was forced to send U.S. marshals to protect the Freedom Riders on their daring mission to New Orleans. But neither the president nor Bobby was sympathetic to the cause. "Stop them," the president told Harris Wofford, his special assistant on civil rights. "Get your goddamn friends off the buses." This was said, Wofford noted, without Kennedy's usual humor. To Wofford, Kennedy complained that Farmer and the Reverend Dr. Martin Luther King Jr. were out to embarrass the president—or to put Kennedy in a politically painful spot. The civil rights campaigns were inflaming passions against federal intervention by the Kennedy White House and the Justice Department. The movement was riling Kennedy's Southern political base. The South had produced seventy-three electoral votes in 1960 for Kennedy. Without them, Richard M. Nixon would have become president.

Since taking office, Kennedy seemed to forget his African-American supporters. He waited until after the 1962 congressional election to deliver on his 1960 campaign promise of an executive order denying federal guarantees of mortgages for whites-only housing. On the 1960 campaign trail, he accused Eisenhower of failing to end federal support of housing segregation with the mere "stroke of a pen." What about Kennedy's stroke of the pen? Farmer of CORE would ask in every television interview. The White House mailroom filled with hundreds of ballpoints labeled "Stroke of the Pen" from supporters of Farmer's demand for Kennedy's signature. It took Kennedy seventeen months to implement the attack on the nationwide practice of segregated housing and neighborhoods. He buried the announcement of the action in a news conference that dealt mainly with the aftermath of the 1962 Cuban missile crisis. Three months earlier, to the dismay of party liberals, Kennedy had proposed his first civil rights bill. Instead of banning literacy tests—a major roadblock to Negro voters in the South—he offered a compromise: Voters would have to demonstrate a sixth-grade education. Minnesota senator Hubert H. Humphrey urged for a more comprehensive attack on segregation. Unless the president acted, Humphrey warned that Republicans in New York would push civil rights to win over black voters. "When I feel that there's necessity for congressional action with a chance of getting that congressional action, then I will recommend it to Congress," Kennedy told Humphrey. It was a pragmatic approach that ducked Kennedy's responsibility to act as the nation's moral leader.

Kennedy also ignored civil rights leaders on judicial appointment in the South, where justice was brutal for blacks. Instead, the president and the attorney general deferred to Southern Democrats in the Senate who favored segregation. Kennedy installed four federal judges with records of racial prejudice on Southern benches; the most notorious was William Howard Cox, who was selected to preside in the Southern district of Mississippi in Jackson. He drew a bitter objection from Roy Wilkins, head of the National Association for the Advancement of Colored People.

"For 986,000 Mississippi Negroes, Judge Cox will be another

strand in their barbed-wire fence, another cross to bear," Wilkins said. He was right. In the first voting rights case before him, Cox characterized the plaintiffs as subhuman. "A bunch of niggers," Cox said, "acting like a bunch of chimpanzees."

While Kennedy risked loss of the white voters opposed to the civil rights movement, he was almost assured of the Negro vote in his reelection race in 1964—no matter the protests by King, Farmer, Roy Wilkins, and others. It was the old political axiom of the Democratic ward boss: Where else could they go? Republicans in Congress joined with conservative Southern Democrats to block civil rights legislation. In the 1960 presidential race, Nixon had gone on the stump and appeared in television commercials in an appeal to African-American voters. "This administration has made more progress on civil rights in the past eight years than in the preceding eighty years," Nixon said. "I want to continue and speed up that progress." The Republican position on civil rights stretched back to Abraham Lincoln. Even a small percentage of black votes in key states could swing things to Nixon. By contrast, Kennedy was muted on civil rights and depended on vice presidential candidate Johnson to curry the Southern vote.

Three weeks before the 1960 vote, Wofford advised Kennedy to intercede for King, who was arrested in Atlanta for protesting against segregation in department store restaurants. Using Georgia's Jim Crow laws, the court sentenced King to four months of hard labor on a chain gang. Fearing her husband would be killed on some hidden byway, King's wife, Coretta, called Wofford. Kennedy overruled Wofford, who pleaded for a campaign statement condemning the King sentence. But prodding by his brother-in-law Sargent Shriver produced a concession: Kennedy agreed to telephone Coretta.

"What the hell," Kennedy said. "That's the decent thing to do. Why not? Get her on the phone." Kennedy expressed concern and support, offering to do anything he could to help. The call lasted only two minutes. But word of the October 20 phone call—and Nixon's silence—spread widely through Negro communities. King himself did not endorse Kennedy, but his father did. "I had expected to vote against Senator Kennedy because of his religion," the Reverend Martin Luther King Sr. told his congregation at the Ebenezer Baptist Church "But now he can be my president, Catholic or whatever. It took courage to call my daughter-in-law at a time like this. He has the moral courage to stand up for what he knows is right," Daddy King said to cheers and applause. "I've got all my votes and I've got a suitcase and I'm going to take them up there and dump them in his lap." Two weeks later, Kennedy won 70 percent of the Negro vote, a 30 percent improvement from the previous presidential election. It certainly contributed to his narrow victory in Illinois. Kennedy won twenty-seven electoral votes by a razor-thin majority of 8,858 voters out of 4.7 million cast in Illinois. Kennedy also carried Georgia's twelve electoral votes, where the blacks and the whites combined to make 62 percent of the vote. Kennedy somehow forgot to invite King to the presidential inauguration.

As president, he became angry at efforts to desegregate public accommodations pushed by other than civil rights leaders. African diplomats driving between New York and Washington along Route 40 found themselves expelled from Maryland restaurants below the Mason-Dixon line. Complaints to the State Department found their way to the Oval Office. "Can't you tell these African ambassadors not to drive on Route 40?" Kennedy told Wofford. "It's a hell of a road. I used to drive it years ago, but why would anyone want to drive it today when you can fly? Tell these ambassadors I wouldn't think of driving from New York to Washington. Tell them to fly."

Wofford and the in-house historian, Arthur Schlesinger Jr., were sometimes dismayed by Kennedy's outlook. A "terrible ambivalence about civil rights," Schlesinger wrote in his official biography, *A Thousand Days*. While Kennedy eventually came around, it was "a long and difficult presidential journey," said Theodore Sorensen, Kennedy's liberal speechwriter and author of another in-house biography,

Kennedy. On civil rights, Kennedy was hard-nosed in 1961. The president had no interest in theories and was hardly the sort of intellectual that McGeorge Bundy knew as a Harvard dean before coming to the White House. "If you mean that he was a man with an uncommonly well-stocked mind and a high intelligence and a habit of believing that it was useful to apply intelligence to evidence—then he was that kind of man," said Bundy, Kennedy's national security affairs adviser. "He thought very much more concretely, and the word pragmatic is certainly right."

King would get a heavy dose of Kennedy's pragmatism. Wofford arranged for a ride up in the elevator to the family quarters. Such exclusive White House sessions were reserved to make the visitor feel very important. Wofford hoped to disarm King. "There was always a strain in his dealing with King, who came on with a moral tone that was not Kennedy's style and made him uncomfortable," Wofford said. The seduction ended when Kennedy laid it out for King: Banning federal mortgages for segregated housing would be delayed despite campaign promises. Civil rights legislation would be delayed so other priority proposals could get past Southern Democratic senators. Then there was the need to reelect Southern moderates and avoid the turmoil of desegregation. Kennedy was not about to expend political capital on King's priorities. "The president candidly explained how he felt limited by the federal system in what he could do to protect civil rights workers in the South." At the end of the session, Kennedy assured King of "his intention in due course to do most, if not all, of what King sought." Just what "due course" meant was left unsaid.

At dinner that night at the Wofford home, King made clear his disappointment. To King, candidate Kennedy had the brains, political skill, and moral fervor to change the world for American Negroes. As president, he had changed. "Now I'm convinced that he has the understanding and the political skill, but so far I'm afraid the moral passion is missing," King said. He was done waiting for "due course." King could go toe-to-toe with Kennedy with words, and his sermons in churches in Atlanta, Montgomery, and other Southern towns ignited a revolution among African-Americans. "There are three ways by which an oppressed people can respond to injustice," King preached. "One is by acquiescence, but that involves acceptance of evil. Another is by violence, but as Christians we should not obey the old law of an eye for an eye. The way we must rise up is through nonviolence."

By 1963, King had raised up the American conscience against Kennedy's "due course" civil rights policies and had shattered the president's political standing in both North and South. As with the Berlin Wall, Kennedy didn't see it coming.

7

Whoppers

Malcolm wilde browne submerged his lanky body in the muck of the rice paddy. Clawing the oozing mud, he pressed his face closer to the gray water of the flooded field. Only the stinking water, his buttons, and his gold belt buckle kept him from going deeper. Before his eyes, three-foot stalks of green rice were dancing to a tune played by Viet Cong machine gun fire. Browne was an American wire service reporter who had made a split-second decision to spend the day with a South Vietnam army unit. The H-21 Shawnee helicopter had unloaded the platoon in the paddy just outside a communist-guerrilla-controlled village. The American crew avoided an actual landing for fear of being glued to the rice paddy muck. As it hovered, Browne had to choose as the soldiers jumped from the *whup-whupping* banana-shaped troop carrier: Fly back to Saigon or join a platoon of the Army of the Republic of Vietnam (ARVN)? A bullet banged through the Shawnee, leaving a hole the size of a fifty-cent piece—proof that a firefight loomed with the Viet Cong insurgents. Browne jumped. If things went wrong and he was captured by the Viet Cong, his gold belt buckle might serve as ransom. He always wore it.

From the air, dazzling green rice paddies seemed to stretch from horizon to horizon. They were the breathtaking heart of Vietnam's beauty that captured Browne's heart and soul. Close up, however, the paddy reeked of excrement, human and animal. Farmers' toilets served as the primary source of fertilizer. As he walked with the soldiers toward the village, Browne was shin-deep in the paddy and the mud sucked at his boots with every step. His red socks, which he always wore, were drenched. He bought a bin of red socks from an army post exchange, so he never worried about one lost in the wash. He splashed down when the machine gun, likely a U.S. .30 caliber Browning, opened up from the village tree line. The Viet Cong armed itself with American weapons stolen from overrun South Vietnamese army bases.

The ARVN platoon leader was screaming at his cowering infantrymen. Attack! Advance! They would not move. The hip-high ripening rice hid them from mortars and the machine gun. Frustrated, the platoon leader sought to inspire his troops by an individual assault on the enemy position. He rose to his feet and yelled for his soldiers to follow. Through centuries of wars, the daring leader rallied his troops with just this maneuver. A massive statue portraying an infantry leader, mouth open and hand beckoning, stands at the U.S. Army Infantry School in Fort Benning, Georgia. Graduates of that school, American army officers and sergeants, had been training ARVN troops since 1961. Indeed, some of the ARVN officers were sent to Fort Benning for infantry training where the motto was: "Follow Me." Browne had witnessed the number of U.S. military advisers grow from 750 in 1961 to more than 16,000 in 1963. They were the sharp point of the spear brandished by President John Fitzgerald Kennedy. His million-a-day U.S. aid program was designed to defeat the Viet Cong, who were directed by a Hanoi government backed by Communist Russia and China. Vietnam was the hot spot in the cold war. Kennedy has placed big bets on a man he knew personally—Ngo Dinh Diem, the president of South Vietnam.

Browne watched the South Vietnamese lieutenant rally the ARVN platoon with his classic one-man charge. His bravery should have inspired his cringing troops to rise and follow, but they did not budge. After a few yards, the platoon leader's head exploded. The sudden halo of red burned into Browne's memory. *Brave but foolish,* Browne thought. He huddled with the soldiers until the Viet Cong guns were silenced hours later. Load after load of bombs and rockets from A-1 Skyraiders shattered the village and tree line where the Viet Cong were positioned.

The muscular, propeller-driven Skyraiders were flown by U.S. Air Force pilots, volunteers trained in the secret Jungle Jim program Kennedy created in 1961. These American pilots flew most of the combat missions as part of the also-secret Operation Farm Gate. Their role was a clear contradiction of President Kennedy's assurance that there were no American combat troops in Vietnam. At a January 15, 1962, White House news conference, a reporter asked, "Mr. President, are American troops now in combat in Vietnam?" The president answered no.

Browne exposed Kennedy's lie by loitering at the end of runways at Bien Hoa air base and clocking the Americans at the Skyraider controls. He was photographing the American pilots when the military police descended on him and ripped the film from his camera. Browne was arrested and held for a brief time; he detailed the event in an AP dispatch. He was the leader of a small but feisty band of reporters sending dispatches that sharply contradicted Kennedy, the American delegation in Saigon, and Diem and his family, who constituted the government in Saigon. Almost every Kennedy policy in South Vietnam was conducted in secrecy, a shadow war hidden from possible treaty violations but particularly from American voters. For example, in 1961 Kennedy personally approved Operation Ranch Hand, the most extensive use of chemical warfare since World War I. Over the next eight years, more than 20 million gallons of defoliants and herbicides were sprayed by U.S. Air Force planes over South Vietnam, Laos, and Cambodia. Ostensibly the chemicals were used to remove roadside and riverside jungle areas that were Viet Cong ambush locations. But in 1962 Kennedy also approved use of the herbicide Agent Orange to kill crops that might benefit the always-underfed communist guerrillas. There were concerns at the State Department that the killing of crops was a violation of a Geneva Convention prohibition against chemical weapons. Not known at the time was that dioxin, a toxic chemical compound in Agent Orange and the other herbicides being used, had a lethal and lasting effect on the Vietnamese and American troops. In addition to skin eruptions, cancer, heart disease, and diabetes, dioxin could last in the human bloodstream for months and years, causing birth defects. As many as 4.8 million Vietnamese were exposed to the American herbicides. Between 400,000 and 500,000 defects were reported in their children. Millions of American veterans became entitled to Veteran Administration payments because of Agent Orange.

While Browne reported on defoliation by U.S. Air Force crews—"Only You Can Prevent a Forest" was the unit's slogan—reporters in Saigon were unaware of the crop-killing program while Kennedy was president. Eventually, more than 8,000 acres of rice and other crops became so contaminated by Agent Orange that they were destroyed by the U.S. Air Force years later. As the results of U.S. programs filtered back to the White House, Kennedy had misgivings over the killings of the innocents caught up in the conflict. "We were killing lots of other people at the same time we were trying to kill the Viet Cong," said Michael Forrestal, a White House aide focused on the conflict. It bothered Kennedy, and the president sought to reduce the heavy use of herbicides, napalm, and land mines. The Pentagon objected to qualms from the commander in chief. "Our army supported all those activities and thought they were necessary and militarily justified," Forrestal said. Kennedy rolled over.

Thomas Hughes, head of the State Department's Bureau of Intelligence and Research, thought the president and his brother Bobby were obsessed with hiding U.S. involvement in Vietnam. Few in Congress had any idea of the costly infusion of American aircraft, heli-

copters, ships, supporting troops, and military advisers. Keeping
Congress and American voters ignorant avoided public criticism of
Kennedy's Operation Beef-up, as it was code named by the Pentagon.
"They had an interest in covert activities, in James Bond type of activity," Hughes said. "They saw it as a third way this side of military involvement and this side of diplomatic exclusiveness. They romanticized
about doing things in secret that could not be done openly, including
some very strenuous covert activity. They were very interested in it."
The secret buildup was a direct result of Kennedy's rejection of an all-
too-public introduction of American combat troops.

Since U.S. support for Diem began in 1954, American military
chiefs were urging U.S. combat troops to replace the inept and reluctant Saigon army in the fight with the Viet Cong. Kennedy, like
Eisenhower, said no.

When the first large contingent of combat helicopters arrived in
Saigon on December 11, 1961, reporter Stanley Karnow spotted them
on the flat top deck of the USS *Core*. Aboard were thirty-two Shawnee transport helicopters and four hundred men from Fort Lewis,
Washington, to man them. Karnow was having a drink with a U.S.
Army press officer on the roof of the Majestic Hotel when the *Core*
steamed into Saigon harbor. "I grabbed the officer's arm, shouting,
'Look at that carrier.'" The officer squinted at the massive ship. "I
don't see nothing," the officer said. Kennedy, McNamara, and Rusk
had taken elaborate measures to squelch press reports. "Supersedes
all previous messages," said a State Department cable before the *Core*'s
arrival. "Do not give other than routine cooperation to correspondents on coverage of current military activities in Vietnam. No com-
ment at all on classified activities." So when Karnow and other
journalists reported the terribly obvious arrival of the helicopter-
ladened *Core*, Kennedy erupted in a rage. Roger Hilsman at the State
Department recounted the president's early morning blast by using
"@2#34ljhf! 8!" instead of Kennedy's actual curses in a memo on the
telephone conversation.

Kennedy's personal prodding led the Central Intelligence Agency to launch Project Tiger, a secret counterintelligence program against Hanoi. Between 1961 and 1963, William Colby, then the CIA station chief, parachuted more than 250 South Vietnamese agents across the border. Of those, 217 perished. Few survived more than a week in North Vietnam. Those that did were assumed to be double agents for the Hanoi government. U.S. Navy ships conducted secret attacks on the North Vietnamese coastline and on islands controlled by Hanoi. These American naval operations were at the heart of the Gulf of Tonkin encounter in 1964. By contrast, Hanoi infiltrated spies into almost every branch of the Saigon government as well as into the American embassy, the military, the press corps, and other operations of interest to the communist north.

Browne of the AP would get wind of these secret efforts. The New York–born reporter was a supporter of war against the communists. However, Browne resented the U.S. duplicity in Saigon and Washington over the extent of American military involvement. Browne's reporting directly challenged the credibility of the president of the United States as well as that of the American civilian and military leadership in Saigon. But official Washington brushed off his accounts. Vietnam was a back-page story in a backwater country since Browne had arrived in 1961. Front pages were devoted to Soviet premier Nikita Khrushchev's policy of intimidation of the young American president. Berlin and Cuba were far more important. "Vietnam was peripheral," said George W. Ball, Kennedy's undersecretary of state.

Through secrecy, Kennedy hoped to keep it that way. In 1963, however, Vietnam was being elevated to center stage, and Browne would turn out to be the drama's leading reporter. Browne was the bureau chief for the Associated Press in Saigon. As boss, he could decide where and when to go, whether to stay or to leave. By 1963, after three years of combat trips, Browne felt that all of them blurred together. All seemed to end when he boarded a Shawnee for the trip back to Saigon. The American crew always tried to jump to at least

700 feet on takeoff. Even with a loss of power at that altitude, the big bird could be nosed over and flutter the big rotors to a safe landing.

On one memorable return trip, Browne watched the crew eating cookies as the Shawnee screeched for altitude. The smell of kerosene filled the cabin. About a foot above Browne's shoulder, a bullet sliced the transport's main hydraulic line. The Shawnee's two massive rotors quit. They were below 700 feet and the chopper plunged straight down into a rice paddy. Browne was knocked out by the crash. He was awakened by the crew chief's jostling. They were under fire. He was to grab a rifle and exit the wreck. Browne had served as a soldier with the U.S. Army and could handle most military weapons. Bloody and shaken, he scrambled out of the wreck and shot in the direction of the Viet Cong. It soon grew quiet. As the crew chief predicted, a rescue chopper arrived within an hour.

Dried mud and blood on Browne's torn shirt did not rate a second glance from the cab driver at Tan Son Nhat. All sorts came through the main airport for both civilian and military operations in Saigon. At his cramped office on rue Pasteur in the city center, Browne tried to bang out a report on the day's events on an old Underwood typewriter. A withered human hand hung on the wall, a grisly reminder of a grisly war. The bathroom, which doubled as photographer Horst Faas's darkroom, was full of a photo enlarger and film chemicals. Browne was too rattled to write anything decent. He chain-smoked, lighting, inhaling, stubbing out one cigarette after another, hoping the tobacco would inspire deft wording. A chemist before turning to journalism, Browne understood the effect of nicotine. Nothing came. Clumsy clichés helped end the dispatch.

As he finished, the phone rang. An intelligence agent with a diplomatic cover invited Browne to a black-tie cabaret at the Caravelle Hotel. Also attending were some senior Saigon army officers he had been trying to interview. And there were beautiful, exotic Vietnamese women. Millions of American men would become entranced by these women. Saigon "has the most stylish women in all Asia," Kennedy was told in a letter by John Kenneth Galbraith, who was then the American ambassador to India. The president had asked him to look around in Saigon in 1961. "They are tall with long legs, high breasts and wear white silk pajamas and a white silk robe split at the sides to the armpits to give the effect of a flat panel fore and aft. On a bicycle or scooter they look very compelling."

Browne would later wed a Saigon beauty. But he was single the night he accepted the cabaret invitation. He showered, bandaged his cuts, and donned a new tailor-made tuxedo. Saigon tailors whipped up all sorts of outfits for journalists at thirty dollars each. The Paris chanteuse Juliette Gréco was the star of the cabaret that evening. The sound of her sultry voice and cold drinks relaxed Browne. Through the hotel window he could see streams of red tracers from gunfire arching over the Saigon River. Yellow flashes marked shell impacts. Not too far beyond the river, past the rubber plantations, there were slinking tigers, screeching baboons, and trumpeting elephants. "Good-bye my heart," Juliette sang in French. This almost perfect day of adrenaline-drenched journalism ended in resentment. When Browne arrived at his apartment he found three radiotelegrams slipped under the door. They were callbacks, rockets from New York and Tokyo headquarters of the Associated Press, messages that wire service reporters detested. One implied he had missed the story that day: United Press International, the competing American wire service, reported three helicopters downed.

"Unipress has three choppers down but your crash has only one. If correct need matcher sappest, foreign." The AP foreign desk, using pidgin cablese, jargon to cut down cable charges for each individual word. The desk was demanding two more crashed helicopters in a new story as soon as possible. These rockets took different forms and delivered different messages. But most had an insulting undertone from desk editors, people who would never spit rice paddy water, much less survive a helicopter crash and come out shooting. Browne began making phone calls.

Browne was the dean of American reporters in Saigon in 1963, and his reports were the factual foundation of developments in South Vietnam. Almost every newspaper editor in the world reprinted his dispatches, which were delivered at sixty words per minute from a clacking teletype machine in their newsrooms. Almost all American newspapers were sharing the costs for members of the Associated Press cooperative. Most global news pages contained AP reports in the language in which the newspaper was published. Dispatches were also translated for foreign broadcasters. For U.S. television news editors without reporters in Saigon, Browne and the AP were the core of evening news shows, which in 1963 lasted only fifteen minutes. Newspapers of the period were still the most important source of information. Network news was brief and superficial and far from as influential as it is today.

For the editors of the two U.S. newspapers with reporters based in Saigon—the *New York Times* and the *Chicago Daily News*—the AP dispatches were the yardstick for their own reporter's accounts. Cabled questions from foreign news desks usually began by noting what Browne had reported that day. Or they would reference dispatches from United Press International, a feisty independent American wire service with a more limited circulation. It was the same for reporters with weekly news magazines, including *Time* and *Newsweek*. AP and UPI provided the daily yardstick and formed opinion around the globe. Because of the AP's relation with the American press and Browne's seniority, almost every new or visiting reporter made the rue Pasteur AP bureau the first stop in Saigon. To preserve time for his own work, Browne printed guidelines for new reporters. There was a list of what to take to the field, including combat boots. Browne stopped wearing canvas sneakers after a sharpened bamboo stake—a hidden punji stick—sliced through the rubber sole and deep into his foot. These simple Viet Cong booby traps would fell countless of Americans, including Army Captain Colin Powell, in later years. Mainly, Browne's guidelines were designed to help reporters find their way around the potholes of Saigon reporting.

"Don't believe any official report. Write only what you see. Don't trust information you get from anyone without checking in the best you can," Browne's AP booklet lectured. "This goes not only for Vietnamese and American officers, but from any source and for that matter, even your colleagues. You will find quickly that most 'facts' in Viet Nam are based at least in part on misinformation or misunderstandings.

"Beware in particular of any information at all you get from certain officials who can be counted on to tell bald-faced, 180-degree whoppers nearly every time. A list of these officials and their relative credibility indices is available at the AP office. Unfortunately, some of them are in high positions." By 1963, the top of the bald-faced whopper list included Nolting and the commander of American forces in Vietnam, General Paul Donal Harkins. They were in charge of implementing Kennedy's secret support of the Saigon government.

In 1963, U.S. secrecy and the hostility of President Ngo Dinh Diem's government had goaded the Western press corps into combat with the official line on the course of the conflict. With Browne leading the way, most reporters presented the American-backed South Vietnam government as fumbling, even losing the nine-year-old war with the communist government of North Vietnam. The source of this controversial assessment often came from American army officers sent to train ARVN troops. Captains, majors, lieutenant colonels, colonels, and a surprising number of generals were frustrated by their inability to create a fighting force. These American officers would recount their dismay to Browne and other reporters. Many ARVN soldiers would cower during firefights, refusing to fire their weapons, much less attack. Saigon commanders seemed determined to avoid battlefield confrontation with the Viet Cong. Losses could result in removal from command.

A big problem was President Diem. Even though Diem would

meet with reporters, they left most sessions at the palace with empty notebooks. Diem was portrayed as an out-of-touch mandarin more interested in diverting the military to deal with the many coups plotted by dissident generals. The president had dodged a full-bore attempt at overthrow in 1960 and a more modest effort in 1962 that was really more of an assassination attempt by aircraft. Diem, the American journalists reported, was cut off from reality by his ruthless brother Ngo Dinh Nhu and Nhu's wife, the beautiful and profane Madame Nhu. Brother Nhu used a secret police force to jail countless potential political opponents. His wife directed a morality crusade that generated hostility for Diem. As a Roman Catholic celibate who once aspired to the priesthood, Diem endorsed his sister-in-law's attempts to proselytize in a nation that preferred ancestor worship as a religion. Beneath the surface, the police state was boiling with public resentment in Saigon, U.S. readers were told. Nhu and his wife were widely hated in Saigon and this rubbed off on Diem.

Some policies were worse in parts of the countryside where 8.5 million tillers of the paddies were forced to live in one of 3,225 fortified hamlets. The peasants were often forced to witness the destruction of their own homes by fire and explosives. They were compelled to build housing in the Strategic Hamlets, which were far from their farms and the graves of their ancestors. Behind barbed wire and pointed stakes, they would supposedly be safe from Viet Cong intimidation. The hamlets were armed with outdated weapons and radios to call for help if the Viet Cong attacked. This program was a brainchild of the Central Intelligence Agency and was overseen by Counselor Nhu. By 1963, some of these forts had come to serve as supply depots for the Viet Cong. In the rice-rich Mekong Delta, scores of these hamlets had been overrun by the Viet Cong.

Browne's AP led the way in reporting the costly shortcomings of the program. One AP account likened them to World War II style concentration camps. Often the peasants defected back to their own farms. Still, the program disrupted the Viet Cong domination of villages, from which they got food and recruits. Hanoi saw it as a much more effective program than the American media did. Eventually, the Strategic Hamlet Program was abandoned. But for President Kennedy in 1963, the program remained a top priority. Almost 64 percent of the population was in these hamlets, Kennedy was told.

To visitors and official Washington, Ambassador Nolting insisted that President Diem's flaws could be corrected. Diem was the only leader suitable for this nine-year-old struggle against the Viet Cong and its sponsors in Hanoi. Counselor Nhu and his wife could be tamed. Kennedy sent Nolting to Saigon with orders to woo President Diem into following U.S. policy suggestions. Previous American ambassadors made blunt demands for democratic policies that Diem would simply ignore, but Nolting's change of approach did little to influence Diem toward a broader, more democratic government.

Number two on Browne's list of liars was Harkins. A polo-playing chum of General George S. Patton Jr., he wound up on the Patton staff during World War II. He was best known before Saigon for ousting the most talented members of the nationally ranked football team at the U.S. Military Academy. Harkins was the commandant at West Point in 1951 when he learned of a cheating ring there, and he forced cadets—they pledged never to lie, cheat, or steal or tolerate those who do—to snitch on other cheaters. Of the ninety cadets discharged, most were members of the Army football team, the Black Knights. Legendary coach Earl "Red" Blaik accused Harkins of bias. The scandal produced more intense but largely unvoiced emotion among graduates of West Point. The Black Knights of the Hudson were supposedly a symbol of unstinting military courage. This was a gutsy move by Harkins that riled the Army establishment. He was admired by Army General Maxwell Taylor, who recommended Harkins for the post in Saigon. Taylor was Kennedy's military adviser and later chairman of the Joint Chiefs of Staff.

Harkins, class of 1929 at West Point, had abandoned his cadet honor code in Saigon. Honesty was unacceptable at his headquarters. By 1963, his staff constantly rewrote, suppressed, or destroyed reports from U.S. advisers in the field with misgivings about the South Vietnamese army. The more senior advisers—colonels and generals— were ordered by Harkins to keep their doubts to themselves. Success and looming victory were the constants in Harkins's reports to Washington. "I am an optimist," Harkins told reporter Stanley Karnow. "I am not going to allow my staff to be pessimistic." Up the chain of command that ended in the Oval Office of the White House, Harkins reported an ill-nourished, ill-equipped, and poorly trained communist guerrilla army that would soon be vanquished. The communists would collapse in the face of what Harkins called an "explosion" by Saigon troops on North Vietnam's border. While he frequently touted this plan to Washington, it never actually came off.

American military tactics, artillery, and airpower provided to Diem's army were the key. This overwhelming American military technology would crush the hungry warriors wearing black pajamas favored by Vietnamese farmers, both north and south. "Raggedy-assed little bastards" was the description of the communist guerrillas favored at Harkins's headquarters. In Washington, success in crushing the Viet Cong trumped all other complaints against the Diem government. And in 1962, American training and supplies helped the Saigon army rout the Viet Cong guerrillas in a number of engagements. Diem concentrated his forces in the central highlands, long seen as the key to military control of South Vietnam. Years later, Hanoi would concede Diem's forces that year had gained the upper hand. It was a different story in the south, where Diem viewed the Mekong Delta as a less strategic battlefield. But as 1963 began, the delta hit the front pages of American newspapers as the place where the reality of the Saigon army's incompetence and the corruption of its leadership emerged dramatically. This all started with an American-designed planned assault by Saigon's best division on a Viet Cong stronghold spotted by sophisticated U.S. radio intercepts. The target was Ap Bac and an adjoining hamlet, farm villages surrounded by paddies, dikes, and canals in the Mekong Delta of South Vietnam.

Waves of American Shawnee helicopters whisked the ARVN 7th Division infantry to the battlefield. American pilots in Skyraiders pounded the village with napalm and rockets. Forward observers were landed to direct howitzer rounds on the enemy. Paratroopers came last, leaping from American transports to reinforce the infantry. U.S. Army Huey helicopters armed with machine guns and rockets flew low to strafe the Viet Cong as they fled the scene. A company of armored personnel carriers with .50 caliber machine guns in their turrets always terrorized the enemy. In the previous year, such combined assaults—particularly when the American M113 armored personnel carriers were used—had led to Viet Cong panic and slaughter. Running in the open made easy targets. Army lieutenant colonel John Paul Vann had worked out the tactics with his ARVN counterparts. He directed the operation from a plane flying over the battlefield. With each Saigon unit were U.S. Army officers and sergeants to advise and prod the ARVN troops. They were also in radio contact with the circling Colonel Vann.

As the tropical sun burned away the morning fog, the Viet Cong were braced for the assault, virtually hidden in tree lines along dikes. January 2 was the day the insurgents decided to stand and fight. Vietnamese who worked on the ammunition buildup for the Saigon attack alerted the commander of the 261st Main Force Battalion. Hanoi policy hides his name from history. The 261st was seasoned by twenty years of insurgency against foreign occupation. They had fought the Japanese during World War II, the French from 1945 to 1954, and now the Americans. They were armed with crates of stolen American ammunition for stolen M1 Garand rifles, Browning Automatic Rifles, Thompson submachine guns, and belt-fed machine guns. There was even a handful of U.S. 60mm mortars that would arc explosives at the attackers. This band of 320 men were also trained in basic infantry tactics used by American troops during World War II and the Korean War. They were taught how to aim ahead of helicopters and airplanes to compensate for their speed. Cardboard cutouts of the American aircraft were placed on poles. Runners carried them past soldiers being taught to lead or aim ahead. Interlocking fields of fire were laid out to catch the attackers in withering cross fires. American radios stolen from Strategic Hamlets enabled the 261st to monitor almost every move by ARVN attackers that day. The primary emphasis was on mass firing, where all weapons are brought to bear on a single target. Hundreds of soldiers all aiming at a single target—in the air or on the ground—created a wall of lead that had a devastating potential.

The sophistication of the 261st was instantly on display on that January 2 morning. All fourteen Shawnee helicopters were hit by the mass fire as they landed troops in waves on the Ap Bac battlefield. Most of them absorbed the gunfire and American crews flew them to safety. But as the battle unfolded, four of the Shawnee troop transports and a Huey Gunship were downed by disciplined Viet Cong gunfire. Saigon's 7th Division troops and civil guard units were pinned down in the paddies after they jumped from the Shawnees. Some were killed and many were wounded when they refused to shoot back or move from the rice paddies where they landed. The gray paddy water turned red. Eleven American crewmen aboard the downed Shawnees were also pinned down.

"Di, di, di!" yelled American Army Sergeant First Class Arnold Bowers, the Vietnamese phrase for "Come on." He was aboard one of the second wave of Shawnees crippled by ground fire. Bowers tried to get the cowering ARVN troops to attack. They would not budge. Bullets snapped and whizzed everywhere. Fear was in charge. Forward observers for air support and artillery were frozen into inaction. Napalm was dropped off target. Artillery rounds landed nowhere near the 261st and its invisible foxholes. Army Captain Kenneth Good, West Point class of 1952, tried to rally another ARVN unit burrowed into a paddy. Good, thirty-two, was wounded and bled to death when the ARVN unit commander failed to call for help. When the company of M113 personnel carriers arrived, they failed to inflict the terror of past battles. Instead, the Viet Cong fire-killed and wounded gunners on the armored vehicles, effectively silencing the powerful .50 caliber machine guns. Stymied by the massed gunfire, the M113s withdrew. The ARVN reserve force, the paratroopers, was dropped in the late afternoon by Americans flying the lumbering C-123 Providers. A mistake in targeting the jump zone landed many too close to the Viet Cong guns. A total of nineteen were killed and thirty-eight wounded, including two American advisers who jumped along with the unit.

Initial accounts of the emerging disaster appeared in American newspapers published on January 3. The day's competition belonged to Browne of the AP and his staff, including Peter Arnett. "Vietcong Downs Five U.S. Helicopters, Hits Nine Others," said the *New York Times* headline. The subhead read: "Defeat Worst Since the Buildup Began, Three Americans Are Killed in Vietnam."

Arnett of the AP confronted the senior American adviser to the defeated ARVN forces the next day. Colonel Vann had spent hours screaming at South Vietnamese commanders over the radio from his airborne command post. Vann landed at one point to accuse the senior 7th Division commander of avoiding combat and deliberately letting the Viet Cong slip away in the night. Vann was at the end of his rope when Arnett asked him what had happened. "A miserable damned performance, just like always," Vann snapped. The quote became headline material, but Vann was not identified as the source. Neil Sheehan, the lone UPI reporter, wound up with the most comprehensive account of the Ap Bac fiasco later in the week. He was flown to the battlefield where ARVN bodies were beginning to bloat in the sun. The village itself was an empty, smoldering ruin.

The 261st had slipped away during the night with its dead and wounded. They lost eighteen killed and thirty-nine wounded, Sheehan would learn decades later. Saigon forces had eighty killed and more than a hundred wounded. Sheehan was walking the battlefield with U.S. Army Brigadier General Robert York. "What happened here?" Sheehan asked. "What the hell's it look like," York snapped. "They got away. That's what happened."

General Harkins rarely visited the front line of the guerrilla war. But he arrived at the ARVN command post the day after the world learned that United States was up against something more than "raggedy-ass little bastards." Harkins sought to salvage the disaster with the most feeble form of spin. "We've got them in a trap," Harkins told reporters, "and we're going to spring it in half an hour."

That was what Malcolm Browne would call a bald-faced, 180-degree whopper.

8

A Nail in the Coffin

MICHAEL JOSEPH MANSFIELD'S PRIZED DECORATION was like himself—quiet and unpretentious. Few at the White House meeting noticed his tie clip that bore the Marine Corps insignia. He wore it every day. It was a reminder of an escape from an unhappy boyhood. At fourteen, he fled his Montana home, enlisted in the U.S. Navy with a forged birth certificate, and served at sea during World War I. When superiors discovered his real age, he was kicked out. He then enlisted in the U.S. Army, but only for a year. His best memory was his next enlistment—two years in the Marine Corps, including a stint on the China station. It gave Mansfield an abiding interest in Asian affairs and, in 1963, an instrumental role in American intervention in South Vietnam.

At sixty, Mansfield was Senate majority leader and probably Kennedy's closest friend in the Cabinet Room on January 8, 1963. In terms of influence on Vietnam policy, he could control the Senate and its leadership in congressional foreign policy. Mansfield—Mike to many—was also the best prepared for the briefing on Vietnam. He had just returned from his fifth visit to Saigon since 1953. But in the Cabinet Room that day, he packed his pipe with Prince Albert and sat back and listened.

The session was staged for both Democratic and Republican

leaders of Congress. Kennedy rolled out the big guns: Secretary of State Dean Rusk, Defense Secretary Robert McNamara, Director John McCone of Central Intelligence, and Vice President Lyndon Johnson, the man Mansfield had succeeded as Senate Democratic leader. Front-page newspaper reports on the debacle at Ap Bac showed Kennedy was floundering in Vietnam along with Diem's army. It could quickly become a running political sore unless he could reassure the Republican leadership. Except for Mansfield, Kennedy knew he could count on the Democrats in Congress. Kennedy sat at the center of the assembly in the Cabinet Room. The president leaned forward in his leather chair and imperceptibly flipped a switch hidden beneath the long mahogany table in front of his chair. That activated a microphone hidden in the nearby wall lamp.

"Say something about this fight last week," the microphone recorded Kennedy as saying. Most of fifteen leaders already had an idea about the "fight." Breakfast in the nation's capital usually included coffee and the *Washington Post and Times-Herald*. Yesterday's edition had a front-page account of the Battle of Ap Bac by Neil Sheehan of UPI. "It was a miserable damn performance," said an American military man in the dispatch. Sheehan starkly recounted the whipping of Saigon troops paid with congressional appropriations. The unnamed American military adviser concluded: "These people won't listen—they make the same mistakes over and over again in the same way." McNamara, who had displaced Rusk as chief policy adviser on Vietnam, took Kennedy's cue to explain what happened at Ap Bac. To many who understood Saigon best, making South Vietnam a military instead of a political issue was a fundamental miscalculation by Kennedy. At the Pentagon, every problem was seen as a nail; every solution, a hammer. Rusk had meekly surrendered the issue to the defense chief two years earlier. Now he watched McNamara squirm.

"There are many questions still unanswered," McNamara told the congressional leaders. He quickly twisted the facts: fifteen helicopters involved, of which five were shot *at*, instead of five shot *down*.

He also dodged the fact that fifteen were shot at and fourteen Shawnees sustained bullet holes. "On balance it was successful," McNamara said. "In the sense that Viet Cong casualties counted far exceeded Vietnam casualties." While the ARVN losses—68 killed and 100 wounded—were correct at the time, no one knew the true Viet Cong total. Sheehan of the UPI, who walked the battlefield, knew most of their dead and wounded were carried away. The actual body count—eighteen killed and thirty-nine wounded—would not surface until years later. McNamara manufactured the Viet Cong death toll to offset Sheehan's account of a lopsided defeat. McNamara admitted the operation was poorly executed. But he distorted the reasons, saying there was no air support, ignoring the reality of Huey Gunship bullets and rockets, repeated Skyraider bomb sorties, and even a bomb load by an ancient American B-26 Marauder. "It lacked airpower," he said—more misinformation. But these were the men who controlled McNamara's budget. He was fumbling to put Ap Bac in a better light. "As I say," the defense chief concluded, "on balance it was successful. The newspaper reports were incomplete partially because of ignorance, partially because of information that was supplied to newspaper reporters."

Puzzled by McNamara's account was Senator Leverett Saltonstall. The Massachusetts Republican had served as an Army infantry officer in World War I. The Boston Brahmin had been on the receiving end of General Harkins's version of the ill-equipped Viet Cong. So he was surprised by the Ap Bac pasting presented by UPI's Sheehan in the *Washington Post*, who said the communists were outnumbered ten to one. "Is that evidence of new weapons in the hands of the communists?" Saltonstall asked. "No, on the contrary," McNamara replied. "There was evidence in the newspapers of such new weapons, but we have no evidence of new weapons. They haven't received any weapons in quantity." Although he knew in great detail of the Viet Cong's organized theft of American weapons, he made no mention of it to Saltonstall.

Senator Richard B. Russell was disturbed by Sheehan's quoting of an unnamed American military adviser who deplored the ARVN performance. "Any American personnel give a version of the fighting that was contrary of what you said?" asked Russell. The Georgia Democrat oversaw the U.S. military as chairman of the Senate armed services committee. He was one of the most influential members of the Senate. Most members voted his way because they deferred to his experience and insight. "Don't go letting American personnel give their version of any engagement," Russell lectured McNamara. "We've queried General Harkins about that," McNamara responded. "We let them give their version, if it's truthful. General Harkins reported that in this particular instance, the newspaper reports were substantially in error; particularly the initial reports were not true."

Aware of Russell's influence and thirty years of military oversight, Kennedy quickly jumped in. He was concerned that the report on Ap Bac reflected badly on administration goals in Vietnam and might jeopardize congressional support. "First, we have to see if the situation in the last six months is going better or see if the situation is deteriorating," Kennedy said. "We've done pretty well under worse conditions." Then he acknowledged the downside of the criticism of Saigon troops by anonymous American military advisers. "It looks bad for us to be attacking them," Kennedy said. "It seems unfair." Everett McKinley Dirksen, the Senate Republican leader, also wondered how the Viet Cong staged the defeat Sheehan had described. "Are they using larger caliber weapons?" Dirksen asked in his breathy basso profundo. "Generally, no," McNamara said. "We have anticipated much larger weapons and much larger units. But they are still small units."

After the briefing, the congressional leaders would amplify the Kennedy message in the public mind. Of the thirteen Senate and House leaders, twelve would brief Capitol Hill journalists as well as their constituents that—on balance—the Battle of Ap Bac was a success. Those young reporters in Saigon were ignorant and misinformed. Fighting communism in Vietnam was still a bipartisan rallying cry in early 1963. Support for whatever Kennedy was doing in Vietnam was a constant of newspaper editorials and columnists. The disaster at Ap Bac did not dent the conventional wisdom of the day and the start of Kennedy's reelection planning.

Speaker John McCormack of Massachusetts briefed a large contingent of reporters before the start of the House sessions. "Dugout chatter" was his name for these daily House and Senate leadership meetings with the press. Usually in attendance with AP, UPI, the *New York Times*, the *Washington Post*, the *Chicago Tribune*, the *Chicago Daily News*, the *Los Angeles Times*, and representatives for other major city newspapers. In addition, radio and television reporters represented the ABC, CBS, NBC, and Mutual networks. Often *Time* and *Newsweek* reporters attended. Together these journalists accounted for from 30 to 80 percent of national and international news published daily. And they reflected their primary sources fresh from the White House briefing by Kennedy and his senior Cabinet members. At the Defense Department, reporters specializing in military matters also echoed McNamara and the administration line.

There was rarely a hint of media doubt, much less criticism. On balance, Ap Bac was a success, and this became the accepted wisdom. Truth was that at the White House, the Pentagon, the State Department, and the Capitol, there was little journalistic interest in this small country almost nine thousand miles away. Ap Bac quickly vanished from the American radar. Once more Vietnam faded into the background. Kennedy had effectively contained any worry that his Vietnam policies were in difficulty. The ringer in all this unanimity was Mansfield. He doubted McNamara's version of Ap Bac as well as the defense chief's upbeat analysis of the Saigon situation. "There are a number of indications that the government forces of South Vietnam are getting stronger," McNamara said at the outset of the briefing for congressional leaders. Mansfield clenched his pipe.

Mansfield was just back from Vietnam after his third visit with Ngo Dinh Diem since he took power in 1954. Mansfield was sent by Kennedy for an unvarnished view. In a sometimes stormy private meeting three weeks before the White House session, the Senate leader told the president he must reconsider the U.S. commitment to the Saigon government and its leader, President Diem. Time had come, Mansfield told Kennedy, to begin a phased withdrawal of U.S. troops. Combined forces from the Army, Navy, Air Force, and Marines totaled 25,000 in 1963, including 16,000 military advisers.

Mansfield's verdict on Diem was particularly shocking to Kennedy. As senators, Mansfield and Kennedy repeatedly came to Diem's rescue when American representatives in Saigon urged removal of a defiant Diem. Now Mansfield told Kennedy that an exhausted Diem and a stumbling Saigon government could drag American soldiers into jungle warfare. In his last session, every question Mansfield addressed to Diem was answered by his brother, Counselor Nhu. "I didn't ask you," Mansfield said sharply. "I asked the president." Diem was using a cane. Perhaps nine years of eighteen-hour days had caught up with him. Mansfield's written report told the president that virtually nothing had changed since 1955 despite billions of dollars in American aid. "We are once again at the beginning of the beginning," Mansfield wrote. The Viet Cong still controlled the countryside at night and held sway over the peasant population through intimidation or the promises of a tax-free land ownership.

Viet Cong strength was estimated at 20,000—"the highest number I have ever encountered since the Geneva Accords of 1954," Mansfield said. It was a reference to international conference that divided Vietnam into North and South following the defeat of French forces by Ho Chi Minh. The centerpiece of Kennedy's new approach—the Strategic Hamlet Program—would require a massive social engineering budget far beyond what was being spent—and beyond the capabilities of the Diem government to implement. "The real test has yet to come," Mansfield said, describing reports from Saigon as "extremely optimistic."

To Mansfield, all this incompetence was leading in a dangerous direction. "It is difficult to conceive of alternatives with the possible exception of a truly massive commitment of American military personnel and other resources—in short, going to war fully. Ourselves against the guerrillas. And establishing some form of neocolonial rule in South Vietnam," Mansfield said. "That is an alternative which I most emphatically do not recommend."

In even harsher terms, Mansfield laid out a looming nightmare of jungle warfare for American soldiers during a meeting with Kennedy the day after Christmas, December 26, 1962. The gist of his written report to the president was published by the Senate Foreign Relations Committee a week earlier. In a series of interviews during and after his Senate career, Mansfield recalled the post-Christmas session dampened the president's holiday cheer. "I was much more forceful with him," Mansfield recalled.

A Secret Service speedboat raced Mansfield and his wife, Maureen, to the presidential yacht, the *Honey Fitz*, on Boxing Day. It was floating on Clear Lake, not far from the Palm Beach home of the president's father. Aboard were the president's wife, Jacqueline, their daughter, Caroline, family friends, and two dogs. Kennedy wore a blue shirt and white slacks. They moved to chairs on the fantail. Smoking his pipe, Mansfield watched as Kennedy grew increasingly agitated as he read the Vietnam report. The meeting was eight days before the Ap Bac fiasco. "You could see the blood rise up through his neck," Mansfield recalled. "He became angry. Said I was too pessimistic. I said, 'Well, you asked me to do it.'"

Many of Mansfield's findings were based on meetings with Browne of the AP and other Saigon journalists. The U.S. embassy in Saigon cabled dismay over the fact that the Senate leader met with journalists instead of listening only to American political and military experts. Mansfield was spooning bitter medicine down Kennedy's throat. It challenged almost every aspect of State and Defense Department reports of political stability and military victory. "This is not what my advisers are telling me," Kennedy growled. Despite the

$1.5 million a day in U.S. aid, Saigon's army was no match for that of the communists, which included more regular troops from Hanoi supporting the Viet Cong guerrillas. President Diem himself looked older and worn by the strain of his years in office, Mansfield said. While Diem's integrity and honesty was beyond reproach, Mansfield saw that Nhu was financing his secret political society through extortion. And Nhu was mismanaging Kennedy's top-priority Strategic Hamlet Program. The enterprise was bound to fail, Mansfield told Kennedy. To avoid shifting the war to American combat troops, Kennedy must now transfer the primary burden of defending South Vietnam to the government of Ngo Dinh Diem. "Our role is and must remain secondary," Mansfield said. "It is their country, their future, which is most at stake—not ours."

The Saigon government was neither vital nor essential to American national security, Mansfield said, challenging the view prevailing among Kennedy's top policy advisers. While Kennedy should not suddenly withdraw American support, he must now halt the buildup of American forces and begin a gradual reduction. "We may well discover that it is in our interests to do less rather than more than we are now doing," Mansfield concluded. Kennedy was both angered and alarmed by Mansfield's call for a withdrawal. "I got angry at Mike for disagreeing with our policy so completely," Kennedy would later tell an aide. "And I got angry with myself because I found myself agreeing with him."

It was particularly painful for Kennedy to hear this downbeat assessment from Mansfield. When it came to Vietnam, Kennedy and Mansfield had a special bond with President Ngo Dinh Diem. It began in the spring of 1953, when they were both freshly minted senators. They had become friends while both served in the House of Representatives. Both Mansfield and Kennedy were elected to the Senate in 1952. They shared an Irish-American heritage, wit, laughter, a quick intellect, and the Roman Catholic faith. Immigrant roots aside, their lives could not have been more different.

While Kennedy was born to wealth, Mansfield's life began in poverty in New York City, where a widowed father sent his children to be raised by family in Great Falls, Montana. Mansfield became defiant and rebellious in his new surroundings, which led to a nine-month stay in a public orphanage. He finally escaped into the Navy in 1918 by forging his date of birth on his baptismal certificate. At fourteen, he was rated an apprentice seaman. After World War I, the wiry Mansfield drilled, shoveled, hauled, and smelted copper ore from the mines of Butte, Montana. He sweated alongside once-powerful miners who choked to death, lungs ruined by copper dust. He feared the same fate awaited him until he met a high school teacher, Maureen Hayes. His future wife guided the grade-school dropout from the mines of Butte and into the classrooms of what is now the University of Montana in Missoula. He emerged with a Ph.D. and a post as an assistant professor of Far Eastern history. In 1943 Mansfield was elected to the House. The miner-turned-professor was the platform that launched the beginning of a thirty-four-year career in Congress. Kennedy joined him there in 1947. Both men swam against the Republican tide to Senate victories in 1952, the year General Dwight D. Eisenhower rode a nationwide tsunami into the White House. Together, they wound up with seats on the Foreign Relations Committee.

Mansfield's life took on a new direction when Kennedy telephoned on a spring day in 1953. "Kennedy called and said there was someone he wanted me to meet," Mansfield said. The occasion was a May 7 reception in honor of Ngo Dinh Diem, in exile from Vietnam since 1950. While Mansfield was knowledgeable about China, Japan, and Korea, he knew little of Indochina at the time. For Mansfield, Kennedy's invitation also opened the door to the stratosphere of American society, where wealth created a network of powerful connections. The exile's reception was arranged by Supreme Court Justice William O. Douglas. The liberal jurist had heard of Diem while traveling through Asia. In a later book, Douglas would tout Diem as a heroic figure who had defied both the French colonial government in Saigon and the communist leader Ho Chi Minh in Hanoi. Diem's reputation arose from his record as the incorruptible minister of the interior who quit because of French meddling.

As a young lawyer, Douglas worked for Joseph P. Kennedy during FDR's New Deal. They became close friends for a lifetime. And Douglas had known Joseph's son Jack since he was fourteen. As an adult, Douglas viewed Kennedy as a listless legislator, bored with public office and devoting his energies to an endless number of stunning women. "I remember I'd see him at Palm Beach and Hyannis and Washington, and he never seemed to get into the midstream of any tremendous political thought or political action or any idea of promoting this or reforming that—nothing," Douglas recalled. "He didn't seem to be caught up in anything like that and he was sort of drifting. And when he started drifting, then I think he became more of a playboy." Kennedy had been elected to the House in 1946 in a campaign financed by his father.

Douglas had urged Kennedy to run for the Senate in 1952. As part of that campaign, Kennedy burnished his foreign policy credentials with an around-the-world trip in the fall of 1951. It included a stop in Indochina, where the 262,000 French colonial troops were in bloody battles with the communist Viet Minh, a nationalist movement led by Ho Chi Minh. Seeing the war firsthand, Kennedy became even more opposed to France's determination to cling to its colonial empire. Raw rubber and the phenomenal rice harvest of the Mekong Delta made Vietnam one of France's richest possessions since 1867. President Roosevelt vowed to end Europe's colonies after World War II, but the promise fizzled under pressure from America's wartime allies. At the time of Kennedy's visit, President Truman had made the U.S. government the largest supplier of arms to the French forces in Vietnam to battle the communists of Hanoi. In a movie newsreel and a radio address after he returned, Kennedy said French arms alone would not halt the spread of communism. "The task is to build strong native noncommunist sentiment within these areas and rely on that as a spearhead of defense," Kennedy told a nationwide audience on Mutual Broadcasting. Kennedy continued his criticism of American policy after President Dwight D. Eisenhower continued to arm the French in Saigon.

To Justice Douglas, Kennedy's trip and criticism of American government support of the French was one reason he invited the senator to the 1953 reception for Ngo Dinh Diem. At last Joe Kennedy's boy was getting involved. In Douglas's chambers, Kennedy asked questions and Mansfield took notes. "Diem was very impressive," Mansfield said. "His English was not fluent, but it was good enough." He was short, about five-foot-four, with a high-pitched voice. Black hair set off his ivory skin. Diem's black eyes sparkled with intensity and there was passion in his voice. To the men assembled in Douglas's rooms, Diem proclaimed himself a nationalist who vehemently opposed French colonialism as well as Ho's communism. He recounted the Hanoi leader's offer to join the communist government as a senior official—minister of the interior. Diem rejected the offer, telling Ho to his face that he was a criminal responsible for the death and destruction committed by his Viet Minh forces.

In response to Kennedy's questions, Diem said he could rally political support for a nationalist movement without ties to the communists or the French. But, Diem said, he would need American help. Kennedy and Mansfield were both Roman Catholics, and Diem's Catholic faith was also part of his presentation. He had spent the last two years living in seminaries of the Maryknoll Missionaries, visits arranged by Francis Cardinal Spellman of New York. Spellman was introduced to Diem by his brother, Ngo Dinh Thuc, a Catholic bishop in Vietnam. Thuc had been a classmate of Spellman's when both studied as young priests in Rome.

At the time Spellman was the most politically active churchman in the history of the United States. He had lines into Congress, the White House, the FBI, and the State Department and world capitals.

He also had close ties with Joseph Kennedy. Spellman first rose to power in Boston as an auxiliary bishop. Spellman and Joseph Kennedy had worked together on a number of Boston projects. In 1953, they were leaders in the national crusade against communism.

Diem's performance would have a profound and lasting effect on Kennedy and Mansfield. "He had this deep conviction and confidence that he could be the choice between the French and the communists," Mansfield recalled. "But you had to wonder how he could do it when he was an outlaw in Hanoi and Saigon."

Diem's rise to power came with the fall of French forces a year later at the battle of Dien Bien Phu. Despite American military aid and modern weapons, Ho Chi Minh's forces destroyed the French redoubt. The loss toppled the government in Paris and led to a 1954 Swiss conference and Geneva Accords on Vietnam. Vietnam was divided into North and South by the conference; present were representatives from China, the Soviet Union, France, and the United States. While Ho Chi Minh was the victor and certain leader of the North, the United States led Western delegates to Geneva in the search for a suitable leader for the South. But who? Once again, Justice Douglas had just the right man for the job. Diem's name rose to the top of the American list during a chance meeting between Douglas and a Kennedy classmate from Harvard University, Robert Amory Jr., then the deputy director of central intelligence.

They converged at the familiar haunt of Washington power brokers: the Georgetown cocktail party. The Supreme Court justice lobbied the number two man at the CIA. "I was at an after-theater party in [talk show host] Martin Agronsky's house," recalled Amory. "Pleasant, a couple of scotches and canapés. Got off in the corner with [Supreme Court Justice] Mr. Douglas. Douglas said, 'Do you know who's the guy to fix up Vietnam? He's here in this country and that's Ngo Dinh Diem.'" Douglas used the correct pronunciation: *Zee-em*. "Well, I wrote it down in my notebook on the way out—you know, Z-I-M," Amory said. But at the CIA the next day, research analysts were perplexed. "We ain't got anything on this guy," Amory quoted his staff. But one aide, Frank Wisner, finally figured *Zim* was Diem. Amory took the name to Director Allen Dulles of Central Intelligence. "The next morning I said to Allen Dulles, 'A suggestion out of the blue,'" Amory said.

Allen Dulles passed along Diem's name to his brother, Secretary of State John Foster Dulles, who then sought Eisenhower's approval. John Foster became an early booster and brushed aside complaints in Paris that Diem lacked the courage or the skill to be leader. "This guy, I think, has the guts to do it," Dulles told aide John Hanes, "and we're going to back him."

Diem's Catholicism was also a factor in his final selection by the White House. "My recollection is that Secretary Dulles had talked to Cardinal Spellman before making the proposal," recalled retired General Andrew J. Goodpaster, Eisenhower's staff secretary at the White House. Diem's ascension in official Washington was certainly pushed by Justice Douglas, who would later boast that he had the most influence in promoting the impassioned exile. "I think perhaps if there is any one individual who is more responsible than any other, it was myself," Douglas would write later. Amory agreed. "And that's how Ngo Din Zim [*sic*] became our man in Indochina," Amory said. "The long hand of Mr. Justice Douglas." Once installed in power in 1954, Diem would receive CIA advice, money, and manpower to build a stable South Vietnam.

By the start of 1963, the rout at Ap Bac showed Diem's government was still shaky. Kennedy and Mansfield were two of the oldest and most important supporters of Ngo Dinh Diem in Washington in 1963. And now Mansfield had jumped ship. Mike wanted Jack to join him before the Vietnam conflict engulfed the American army. The U.S. ambassador to Saigon, Frederick "Fritz" Nolting, read Mansfield's negative appraisal published by the Senate Foreign

Relations Committee and cabled by the State Department. Knowing Mansfield's history of support, Nolting realized it was a seismic shift.

"I think it was the first nail in Diem's coffin," Nolting would write later.

9

Ratholes

RATHOLE WATCHING, AS REPORTERS CALLED it, was the solemn duty of news wire services. Every U.S. embassy announcement, all reports from the American military, statements by Gia Long Palace—the daily run of the predictable had to be checked out by the wire services, usually with marginal results. It tied up the limited manpower of the Associated Press, United Press International, and Reuters, the British wire service. The specials—the correspondent for the *New York Times*, for instance—could ignore predictable events and race off to the Mekong Delta to follow hunches and play angles on the main story. If the unpredictable occurred, well, leave it to the wires. Or the newspaper correspondent could fold the wire service story into a dispatch with the special's byline. Plagiarism was a hallowed tradition. After all, newspapers paid for the wire service reports. The most fabled example came from a Fleet Street reporter's message to the London editor: "I looked in horror as . . . Pick Up Reuters."

That practice contributed to Malcolm Browne's decision to reject David Halberstam. The *New York Times* reporter wanted to set up his office in the Associated Press's Saigon bureau. No, said Browne. Perhaps the main reason was lack of space in the cramped office at 158 rue Pasteur. But Browne, the AP bureau chief, was a competitive reporter, and the competition for news in Saigon had suddenly become intense by the summer of 1963. With a desk in the AP, Halberstam would be able to pick and choose from Browne's daily report, and overhear talk about exclusive or investigative dispatches that he and his staff worked hard to produce. Besides, they were different cats. Halberstam was big and noisy and craved company after work. His dispatches ran on and on. Browne was cool and reserved. He holed up in the apartment above the bureau and delighted in vinyl records of Richard Wagner's *Tristan und Isolde*. Browne harped sharply, cablese pidgin for writing tautly, the hallmark of the wire service copy. Halberstam had already become a pain for Browne. The *New York Times* reporter used his boundless energy and his newspaper's influence to gather information that AP did not have. That would produce rockets from New York and Tokyo demanding Browne match Halberstam's efforts. Browne loathed these callbacks, as they were known. They implied the AP bureau was falling down on the job.

In fact, Browne was on top of the story that would put Saigon at center stage. It began May 9, with an innocuous announcement from the Gia Long Palace rathole: There would be a press conference to discuss the May 8 killing of eight Buddhists by the Viet Cong in Hue. Halberstam got the palace alert but kissed it off and left Saigon for a monthlong vacation. Leave it to the wires. Halberstam then missed the beginning of the end of President Ngo Dinh Diem. Events in Hue, four hundred miles north of Saigon, united his enemies—in Saigon and Washington—who wanted to end his rule.

It started with a dispute between Buddhists and Catholics, something familiar on the banks of the Perfume River in the old capital of Hue. Diem had been born there, one of six sons of Ngo Dinh Kha. Religious persecution had almost killed Diem's father. By chance, Kha was studying abroad when rampaging Buddhists herded more than a hundred members of the Ngo clan into a church and set it afire. It was part of an anti-Catholic, anti-French movement that the royal government initiated as Paris increased control of Indochina at the close of the nineteenth century. As the French colonial masters were despised, so was its imported religion. Buddhism, its adherents argued, was the rightful and traditional belief of Vietnam.

Diem was sensitive to religious preferences. Although a devout Roman Catholic, Diem also had a streak of Confucian beliefs. Along with most in South Vietnam, Diem adhered to Confucius's dedication to religious tolerance. His government was generous with funds to construct Buddhist pagodas throughout South Vietnam. He appointed Buddhists to key government positions. But his government was top-heavy with Catholics. One reason was education. The French legacy of Catholic schools in Vietnamese cities meant Catholics were the best educated, the best qualified. While the schools were open to everyone, Catholic children were most likely to end up in universities in Saigon and Paris.

A week before the Buddhist uproar, Diem could almost see it coming. He was in Hue for ceremonies honoring his brother, Ngo Dinh Thuc, the archbishop of Hue. As the oldest living brother, Thuc by tradition dictated to Diem on family and religious matters. Also attending was another brother, Ngo Dinh Can, the governor of Hue and the region. Can lived with their mother in the old family home in Hue. Can and Thuc had lined the streets of Hue with the gold-and-white banners of the Catholic church. It was a violation of a rarely enforced law, and Diem became irritated. He knew it could inflame old wounds. Flags were permitted in the church or on pagoda grounds but not outside. Diem complained to Can and said the religious flags should be limited in the future. A week later, to celebrate Buddha's 2,587th birthday, Hue's Buddhists planned to outdo Archbishop Thuc with their own multicolored banners. When the police said no, the passive, peace-loving Buddhists turned into a mob angry over the double standard. They defied water cannons used at one demonstration. Another protest by 3,000 Buddhist supporters at the Hue radio station demanded their local leader, Thich (the Reverend) Tri Quang, be permitted to broadcast his objections.

Tri Quang was a leader in the New Buddhism movement that began in 1950. The World Buddhist fellowship wanted monks to be more socially and politically active instead of restricting their lives to incense and chanting in the pagoda. To Tri Quang, that meant removing the Roman Catholic president in favor of a Buddhist and Buddhism as the national religion.

Police and army soldiers confronted the protestors. It was never certain what happened next. But police gunfire and explosions killed one woman and six children. A seventh child was run over by an armored vehicle. In Saigon the next day, Diem's spokesman blamed Viet Cong agents. Another demonstration in Hue sent fifty-four Buddhists to the hospital. Brothers Can and Thuc clearly lost control in Hue. A month later, Diem lost control in Saigon.

In their saffron robes Buddhists from all over the country swarmed into the capital to protest Diem's policies in Hue. The Western press considered this a case of religious persecution of the country's Buddhist religion by a dictator who was a member of the Catholic religion. *New York Times* reporter Halberstam and other Western journalists reported—erroneously—that Buddhists accounted for 70 to 80 percent of the population. That off-repeated "fact" meant that Diem was conducting a nationwide crackdown on almost everyone in South Vietnam. At his post in Paris, ex-ambassador Durbrow was outraged by Halberstam's reporting, even though he had no love for Diem. Durbrow saw Diem as dedicated to equal treatment to all religions. "Vietnam is not a Buddhist country, never has been a Buddhist country, and can't be unless they boot a bunch of them in," Durbrow said. "About 10 percent were Buddhists. About 10 percent were Catholic. Most of the population, about 40 percent, was a mixture of Confucianism, Taoism, and very few tenets of Buddhism. We had this dirty, mean old Catholic Diem persecuting these nice poor Buddhist people. It was the best bunch of propaganda and undermining operation you can think of." He complained to the *Times* bureau in Paris.

In fact, the Vietnamese worshipped ancestors, trees, rocks, and other inanimate objects that might contain spirits. Of the 14 million people in South Vietnam, only about 4 million were practicing Buddhists. Still, throughout the crisis, the *New York Times* portrayed the Buddhists as accounting for 70 percent of the population. News dispatches from both the AP and the *New York Times* tempered their accounts with "alleged" and other qualifiers. But in the "he said, she said" reporting for the next month, Diem and his government clearly lost out to Tri Quang. The tiny band of American reporters, resentful of policies by Diem and the American government establishment supporting him, colored their reporting to bolster the Buddhist claims. Public relations were Diem's weakest suit, and he never did mount a coherent explanation of dedication to religious freedom.

Initially, Tri Quang demanded—and Diem refused—reparations for the families of those killed in Hue and an investigation of soldiers and police under brother Can's control to single out the culprits. Can wanted a compromise, but Archbishop Thuc told Diem to crack down hard and the Buddhists would come crawling. Tri Quang was a junior member of the General Association of Vietnamese Buddhists. He baffled one American diplomat who approached him in Hue with U.S. concerns. Tri Quang listened and replied, "The sky is blue, but clouds drift across it." Diem reached out to Buddhist leaders other than Tri Quang. In a previous statement, Diem had pronounced the demonstrators "damn fools," a view underlined by an official palace statement using the same language. Then the palace issued a call to respect religious freedom.

Where Diem appeared a clumsy and intemperate autocrat, Tri Quang peddled Buddhist persecution with a slick—by Saigon standards—public relations campaign. His base of operations was set up in the heart of Saigon in the Xa Loi Pagoda. The changing banners out in front—in English—all had the same theme. "Down with the Government," or, the next week, "Destroy the Government." Nolting, the American ambassador, became convinced that the Viet Cong had infiltrated the ranks of the Buddhists. After all, anyone could shave his head and become a monk. To Nolting, the Buddhists were intent on toppling the Diem government. In fact, in later interviews with U.S. officials, Tri Quang would admit to that goal. Ho Chi Minh had the same goal. To Nolting, religious persecution was overstated, particularly by Halberstam in the *New York Times*. The press was being manipulated. "They never gave Diem a break," Nolting said.

Xa Loi Pagoda became a daily stop for newsmen, like police headquarters back home. Inside, the Buddhist nuns wore white. The bonzes were in bright orange. Children shrieked. The smell of boiling cabbage mixed with incense filled the nose. The chanting was backed by gongs and tinkling chimes. It was a step inside the mysterious East. Tri Quang's press representative was twenty-four, frail, with an ever-present smile. At one point, he did a stint at Yale Divinity School. "Boola, boola" was his greeting to every American reporter. His name was Thich (the Reverend) Duc Nghiep. Western tongues simplified it to Tic Tac Toe. He struggled with English as well. But he was dedicated in alerting by telephone or messenger all reporters, who were filing almost daily dispatches. His promise to writers and photographers was that a monk would soon disembowel himself or set himself on fire to protest Diem's persecution. One way or another, the press was promised a public suicide. A decade earlier, some Buddhists had immolated themselves to protest French rule, and Buddhists had done the same in China and, more recently, in Tibet. But the idea was new to Saigon reporters. Soon the story started to fade at Xa Loi. Most days were spent following Buddhist marchers chanting as they marched through the inner city. Despite the promises, a suicide was never staged. Some reporters grew weary of Duc Nghiep and his "boola, boola."

Not Malcolm Browne. He delighted in the delicious vegetarian dishes served to him at Xa Loi. The pagoda was a pleasant rathole compared to the palace or the U.S. embassy, where the occupants were in a constant lather over press treatment of the Buddhist protests. The AP bureau chief was the only American reporter to take seriously Duc Nghiep's call that something very special and important was going to happen at Xa Loi on the morning of June 11. "He sent the same message to half a dozen other American correspondents, but they all ignored it," Browne said. "I did not."

At 7:45 A.M., Browne arrived with his Petri 35mm, a Japanese camera supplied by the AP. The news photographers carried Nikons, Canons, or Leicas, but Browne was a writer, not a shooter, so he had to make do with AP's second line, the Petri. It was not the digital point-and-shoot so familiar today, with its crisp color and perfect, computerized exposure. Browne had to focus to make sure the subject was not blurred. The lens opening had to be correct; otherwise the picture would be too dark or too light. Setting the speed of the shutter was crucial for picture sharpness. So much could go wrong. After each picture, Browne had to flick the speed winder to advance the film. It was loaded with Kodak Tri-X, a high-speed black-and-white film. Browne had eight extra rolls. The film needed to be immersed in three chemical baths before negative images could be examined in a dark room.

At Xa Loi, almost five hundred Buddhists had assembled. The heat was suffocating. Incense smoke filled the air. Browne sat next to a large gilded statue of Buddha. Buddhist nuns in tears served Browne tea. The chanting became intense. Duc Nghiep hurried over. "I advise you," he told Browne, "to stay until the very end." At eight A.M., a column of marchers formed behind a British-made two-tone Austin sedan that was leading the way. Inside were five monks in saffron robes. At the intersection of two busy streets—Le Van Duyet and Phan Dinh Phung—the Austin stopped. The marchers formed a circle around the car, effectively blocking the intersection. The chanting was hypnotic as it grew louder, faster. The sounds were rising to a crescendo, similar to a moment in one of his favorite operas, *Götterdämmerung*.

Three monks got out of the Austin. One was old and feeble from fasting. He was assisted to the center of the intersection by two younger monks. They placed a cushion in the center of the street and the old man sat down on it. It was the seventy-three-year-old Thich (the Reverend) Quang Duc. From Duc Nghiep's earlier promises, Browne had an idea what was going to happen. "A horror show was at hand, I realized, and the sweat started from my brow and I cocked my camera," Browne said. His watch read 9:20 A.M. From the Austin, two monks lugged a five-gallon plastic container. Browne learned later that it contained gasoline mixed with kerosene to ensure a lasting conflagration. They sloshed a pink fluid over Quang Duc, soaking his face, his body, his orange robes, and the cushion. His legs and arms were folded in the lotus position for meditation.

"I saw Quang Duc strike a match in his lap and let it fall," Browne said. "Instantly he was enveloped in a column of smoky yellow flame. As the breeze whipped the flames from his face, I could see that although his eyes were closed, his features were contorted with agony." He was looking at the scene through the viewfinder of his Petri. "Numb with shock, I shot roll after roll, focusing and adjusting exposures mechanically and unconsciously," Browne said. "Trying hard not to perceive what I was witnessing, I found myself thinking: 'The sun is bright and the subject is self-illuminated, so f16 and 125th of a second should be right.'"

White-belted police who had been struggling to hold back a sea of orange monks turned to watch the human inferno. More and more monks prostrated themselves before burning Quang Duc. Browne kept shooting and tried to ignore the stench of burning flesh. "But I couldn't close out the smell." Chanting gave way to screams and wailing. A banner was unfurled: "A Buddhist Priest Burns for Buddhist Demands," it said in English.

"It took him eight to ten minutes to die," Browne said. The flames died away. Smoke and the reek of burning flesh hung over the intersection. Quang Duc pitched over. His legs twitched. Then he was still, his body smoldering. A wood coffin was produced, but his contorted arms and legs would not fit and were sticking out as the coffin was carried away. Browne raced on foot to the AP bureau. The photos would never get past the Saigon censors. He decided to send the unprocessed rolls of exposed film by "pigeon," meaning a passenger on a regular flight whom you have persuaded to carry a package for you. "The whole trick was to get it to some transmission point," Browne said. "We used a pigeon to get it as far as Manila. And in Manila, they had apparatus to send it by radio."

Once on the AP network, Browne's photos made the world's jaw drop. Pictures of the blazing Quang Duc were sent to every newspaper, every magazine, every television station everywhere on the globe. Words exchanged between Gia Long Palace and the Xa Loi Pagoda gave way to images of a human who had sacrificed himself. Browne made the dying Quang Duc immortal, an icon of the turmoil that raged on June 11 just as it had in Indochina for centuries. Not everyone realized the import of the moment. But President Ngo Dinh Diem instantly recognized the depth of the wound Quang Duc inflicted. "An undeserved death that made me very sorry," the president of South Vietnam said in a radio broadcast later that day. There was no scheme to crush Buddhism, Diem said, and noted the constitutional guarantee of religious freedom—a law he promised to enforce by himself.

Few were reassured. Within a week, Diem reversed himself and granted compensation to the families killed in Hue, where the death toll had risen to nine. There were more Diem meetings with Buddhist leaders but not with those from Xa Loi Pagoda. More than ten thousand protestors showed up in Saigon for Quang Duc's funeral. Younger monks battled briefly with police and fire hoses. The dead bonze's other robes were sliced into thousands of orange swatches that suddenly could be seen pinned to countless sympathizers all over Saigon. Police officers began ripping off the bits of cloth but quickly gave up trying to suppress the silent protest.

In Washington, the photo of Quang Duc's immolation outraged

Harriman after he saw it on July 11 in the *Washington Post and Times Herald*. It was time to slap down the defiant president of South Vietnam. Without consulting Kennedy or Rusk, Harriman fired off a cable demanding that Diem accept the Buddhists' demands. "If Diem does not take prompt and effective steps to reestablish Buddhist confidence in him, we will have to reexamine our entire relationship," Harriman said in a cable drafted by Roger Hilsman, the assistant secretary of state for the Far East.

Details of the cable were quickly leaked—probably by Harriman—to *New York Times* reporter Max Frankel. His June 14 dispatch was the first Kennedy knew of the damaging ultimatum to Diem. It was the president's turn to be angry at Harriman's usurpation of Kennedy's prerogatives. "The president was upset that Diem has been threatened with a formal statement of disassociation," said a White House memo. "He wants to be sure that no further threats are made and no formal statement is made without his own personal approval."

Kennedy had personally ordered Ambassador Nolting to support Diem without interfering in domestic matters or using threats of cutting off aid. But Nolting was in Greece on vacation. He was confident that conflict with the Buddhists had simmered down enough to permit a long-postponed holiday with his children. He left Saigon on May 23. "I could not have made a worse mistake," Nolting said.

William Trueheart, his deputy, was left with instructions to contact him if a crisis developed. Nolting checked daily with the U.S. embassy and the CIA station in Athens. There was nothing from Trueheart. Had he been alerted, Nolting was convinced he could have mediated the dispute between Saigon and Washington. Trueheart was listening to Harriman and Hilsman, who has replaced Harriman as assistant secretary of state for the Far East. After a stop in Washington, Nolting finally returned to Saigon on July 10. Trueheart apologized but said he was just too busy to call. Besides, Trueheart said he had become convinced that the war against the communists could not be won with Diem in power.

To Nolting, his deputy's betrayal was more a case of "drifting with the winds from Washington." The new American ultimatum to Diem, Nolting knew, came from Harriman, now number three at State. And Nolting believed Harriman ordered Trueheart not to contact him in Greece. Earlier in the year, Harriman sent Nolting a letter saying it was "time to be cultivating the opposition" to Diem. The very same wording was used by others under Harriman's control. Nolting rebuffed Harriman at the time, noting Kennedy's orders to create a friendly atmosphere of support for Diem. Now Browne's photos gave Harriman a new opening.

To Nolting, Harriman was getting back at Diem for his refusal to sign the Laos treaty in 1961. "No doubt I underestimated Harriman's influence, tenacity, and vindictiveness," Nolting said, tracing it back to Diem's confrontation with Harriman two years earlier. "I never envisioned that he would carry his grudge against Diem to the extent he did. Nor did I think that he would develop a grudge against those of us who supported [Diem] as the best available leader."

The American military commander in Saigon, General Harkins, summed up the change in policy for Nolting. "It looks like the State Department thinks Diem is the enemy rather than the Viet Cong," Harkins told Nolting.

Halberstam's report about a possible coup against Diem seemed colored by his own animosity toward the president of South Vietnam. Rumors of coups were a Saigon constant. Halberstam faced some hostile questioning while a guest at the U.S. embassy Fourth of July reception. When it came time for the traditional toast to Diem as the leader of the host nation, Halberstam refused.

"I'd never drink to that son of a bitch," Halberstam announced loudly. He had inherited his dislike for Diem from his predecessor, Homer Bigart. The celebrated war-horse detested Diem, Saigon, the weather, and the secrecy. "I almost went nuts," Bigart said of his six-month stint. He was much more comfortable on the battlefields of World War II and Korea. Bigart was a shoe-leather reporter. He would not have missed the burning of Quang Duc. Halberstam slept in on the day in happened. About nine A.M. he and a UPI reporter who was staying at the *Times*'s Saigon villa were rousted. They ran to the intersection, but the action was pretty much over. Browne, the rathole watcher, was leaving just as they arrived. Neither had a camera.

Next day the *Times* ran a Halberstam dispatch that led with Diem's apology. It mentioned Quang Duc's death lower in the report, but it had none of the horror and drama of that landmark moment. Even so, Long Island University cited his "eyewitness" report on Quang Duc's death in giving him the 1963 George Polk Award for Foreign Reporting. Browne's photo lost out to another AP colleague, Roger Asnong, who captured Jack Ruby's shooting of Lee Harvey Oswald.

The June 11, 1963, edition of the *Times* also lived up to its nickname of the Grey Lady, a paper that prefers columns of black ink to pictures. The editors refused to run Browne's picture of Quang Duc. "They said it was not suitable for its breakfast audience," Browne said. The photo did finally appear in the *Times* and again in the *Washington Post* when a group of ministers used Browne's picture for a full page ad. The ad's text reflected recurring errors in both papers, saying that Buddhists accounted for 79 percent of the population and that the protest was strictly about religious persecution—not the overthrow of the Diem government.

But the June 27 ads with Browne's picture were a deep political wound for President Kennedy, the most important supporter of President Ngo Dinh Diem. To William Colby, then overseeing Vietnam at the CIA, Browne's photograph greased the skids for Diem. "Once the picture appeared, it was all over for the Diem government," Colby said.

10

Hard Condition

JUST AS MALCOLM BROWNE'S PHOTO of the flaming Quang Duc brought attention to President Kennedy's policy in Vietnam, another powerful news photo underscored his feeble support of the civil rights movement. The editors of the *New York Times* published it on the front page, spread across three columns above the fold. It showed one of Commissioner Eugene "Bull" Connor's police dogs sinking its fangs into the stomach of a Birmingham high school senior. Associated Press photographer Bill Hudson caught the ferocity of Alabama's opposition to equality for African-Americans. The picture of the German shepherd's attack on seventeen-year-old Walter Gadsen symbolized the hatred of segregation that was dividing the nation just as slavery and the Civil War did a century earlier. The AP photo permitted a detailed look at what first was viewed in American living rooms as video broadcast by the three major networks. Such footage tarnished the image of America around the world. Schoolchildren as young as eight were sent tumbling by high-pressure fire hoses, were arrested, and were jailed eighty-eight to a cell designed for three prisoners. Placed in the same Birmingham jail was the Reverend Martin Luther King Jr., leader of 2,500 elementary and high school students who were charging the racial barriers in one of the most segregated cities of the South. In giving the picture such dramatic display, the Grey Lady of newspapers overcame its distaste for tabloid-style shockers. The front page of the *Times* on May 4, 1963, called on the establishment to rise up against segregation. It also spotlighted Kennedy's failure of moral leadership in the battle against racism in the United States.

As president, Kennedy was a reluctant emancipator. Despite his campaign promises, Kennedy shelved demands by King and other civil rights leaders while yielding to conservative Southern senators who controlled Congress and promoted segregation. The New Frontier, said the NAACP's Clarence Mitchell Jr., looked "suspiciously like a dude ranch with [Mississippi] Senator James O. Eastland as the general manager." On the day the *Times* showed the chaos in Birmingham, the Americans for Democratic Action—representing the most liberal wing of the Democrats—showed up in the Oval Office for a testy session with the defensive president.

"I think it's a terrible picture in the paper," Kennedy said. "There's nothing we can do. I mean, what law can you pass to do anything about police power in the community of Birmingham? And as I say, Birmingham is the worst city in the South. They have done nothing for the Negroes in that community, so it is an intolerable situation."

He would again portray himself as helpless at a nationally televised news conference. Asked by a reporter if he was using all the powers of the presidency to quell the turmoil in Birmingham, Kennedy said federal law did not apply to civil rights marches. "There isn't any federal statute that was involved in the last few days in Birmingham," Kennedy replied. It was a feeble performance by Kennedy, who was still straddling the political divide of civil rights. The South's seventy-three electoral votes had made Kennedy president in 1960 just as African-American voters in Illinois made the difference in a razor-thin win in that crucial state. Birmingham made clear to everyone except Kennedy that he could no longer win both of these constituencies. The country was in flames and Kennedy was still fiddling with the electorate. Birmingham also marked the end of what

Kennedy's closest aides called a "terrible ambivalence" on civil rights and a "painful journey" to the front of the moral crusade.

In Alabama, Mississippi, Georgia, Virginia, and Maryland, peaceful Negro protestors were met with spit, beatings, murder, and bombings. Yet King and other leaders refused to step back. "Ain't gonna let nobody turn me around," sang Fannie Lou Hamer in the South and Pete Seeger in the North. From jail, King wrote an epistle to the world on the plight of 20 million black brothers and sisters turned away from restaurants, motels, voting booths, and jobs in a flourishing economy. King described the humiliation of explaining to black children why "your first name becomes 'nigger' and your middle name becomes 'boy' however old you are." To King, the events in Birmingham marked the end of black acceptance of segregation. "There comes a time when the cup of endurance runs over and men are no longer willing to be plunged into an abyss of injustice where they experience the bleakness of corroding despair," King wrote. "I am not criticizing the president, but we are going to have to help him," King later told a church congregation. "The hour has come for the federal government to take a forthright stand on segregation in the United States." It was a taunt delivered by the nation's media to the White House.

In public, Kennedy's brother Bobby seemed more sympathetic. The attorney general was using members of the Justice Department's civil rights division to be present at racial hot spots in the South and to protect buses full of black and white Freedom Riders through Mississippi and Louisiana. In private, however, Bobby complained to his brother that a number of protests was getting out of hand. "You could make a pretty strong argument that we should end those and get them off the front page," Bobby said at a White House strategy meeting with the president. "It's bad for the country and bad for the world." The chaos was also bad for his brother's reelection campaign, which Bobby planned to direct in 1964.

Kennedy's argument that he was helpless in the face of growing civil rights violence was soon challenged by religious leaders and other members of the moral and legal establishment. The deans of the law schools at Yale and Harvard delivered a devastating rejoinder. "It seems clear to me that he hasn't even started to use the powers that are available," said Erwin Griswold of Harvard Law. His remarks were quickly endorsed by Eugene Rostow of Yale Law. King brushed aside the need for some relevant statute in the federal code to deal with the denial of voting rights, equal housing, education, jobs, and justice for Negroes. "I feel there have been blatant violations of basic constitutional principles," King told reporters. The U.S. Commission on Civil Rights, of which Griswold was a member, voted to cut off all federal funds for Mississippi because of its segregationist policies.

In a background session with reporters, Kennedy called the commission vote a mistake. "I wouldn't have issued that report," Kennedy said. "It doesn't do any good. It just makes people mad." The chairman of the commission, the Reverend Theodore Hesburgh, saw Kennedy's bobbing and weaving as craven politics. "Kennedy is afraid if he does more than he has about Negroes, he can forget about being president for eight years," said Father Hesburgh, who was president of Notre Dame University.

Under mounting establishment pressure, Kennedy buckled. "I think Birmingham did it," King said later. "Birmingham created such a crisis in race relations that it could no longer be ignored. No matter what the polls revealed, he had to take a strong stand on the issue." A month after the violence erupted in Birmingham, he decided to lead the nation toward the abolition of segregation with a package of new civil rights laws. A nationwide television address followed the federal showdown with Alabama governor George C. Wallace over the admission of black students to the University of Alabama. Wallace had vowed to stand in the doorway of the Tuscaloosa University to block their entrance, despite an order for integration issued by the federal courts. Kennedy was still in his pajamas in bed, going over the June 11 morning papers, when he called his brother, the attorney general. Bobby was explaining the federal choreography with Wallace in the doorway when the president interrupted.

"Jesus Christ!" Kennedy exclaimed. The president had just seen Malcolm Browne's photo of the immolation of Quang Duc. It was just as shocking as Bull Connor's police dog attacking the Birmingham high schooler. These two iconic photographs were to become an indictment of his policies and an undertow for his administration. They, in effect, acted to force his hand to act against the oppression of a black minority at home and to end support for suppression of Buddhist rights abroad. For Kennedy, violence in the avenues of America had intersected with turmoil in the streets of Saigon. For the next five months Kennedy would tack back and forth between his most burning domestic issue and his most crucial foreign policy initiative. Both crises defied solution, and both sapped his political standing and his morale.

Evelyn Lincoln, the president's personal secretary, said that during this period Kennedy became discouraged. "He felt like packing his bags and leaving," Lincoln said. At times like these, a morose Kennedy would talk of a situation in which it seemed everything was turning against him. McGeorge Bundy, his adviser on national security affairs, noticed Kennedy's frequent lament during his final months of office. "I was actually rather surprised to find that just at the end of his life he was quite familiar with and constantly had in his thoughts that famous speech in *Henry V* in which the king describes how everything came back to him," Bundy recalled. Bundy was talking about a scene in Shakespeare's play where Henry in disguise visits his troops the day before the Battle of Agincourt. In Act IV, Scene 1, the soldiers bitterly complain how the king's warring could lead to their death and leave their wives and children with debts and poverty. Stung by their candor, Henry returns to his tent and broods.

> *Upon the King! Let us our lives, our souls, our debts,*
> *our careful wives, our children, and our sins,*
> *lay on the King!*
> *We must bear all. O hard condition.*

Vietnam and civil rights underscored the weakness of his administration. Although there were Democratic majorities in both the House and Senate, Kennedy was unable to forge support for civil rights, just as he failed to win approval of health care for the elderly, federal aid to education, or income tax reform. An inept congressional liaison staff, headed by Larry O'Brien, combined with Kennedy's lack of interest in domestic issues, meant few victories on Capitol Hill. Southern Democrats, angered by Kennedy's ambivalence on civil rights, took it out on other administration programs. Representative Carl Albert of Oklahoma, the House majority leader, explained the chemistry to Kennedy in a phone call. "Civil rights," Albert said. "It's overwhelming the whole program. This is going to affect mass transit, there's no question about that. It's gonna kill these farm bills."

When Kennedy finally decided to embrace the civil rights movement, he was following in the footsteps of Vice President Lyndon B. Johnson. Two weeks after King's arrest in Birmingham, Johnson became the first in the administration to acknowledge the legitimacy of King's crusade. "One hundred years ago, the slave was freed," Johnson said at a Gettysburg ceremony marking the hundredth anniversary of that bloody Civil War battle. "One hundred years later, the Negro remains in bondage to the color of his skin. For years now I have heard the word 'Wait!' It rings in the ear of every Negro with piercing familiarity. This 'Wait' has almost always meant 'Never.' We must come to see, with one of our distinguished jurists, that 'justice too long delayed is justice denied.'"

In large White House strategy sessions on civil rights, Johnson contributed little. As did Secretary of State Dean Rusk, Johnson preferred imparting his advice to others in private. There is no record of what Johnson told Kennedy when others were not around. But Johnson did outline the script Kennedy used in a landmark television address to claim moral leadership of the civil rights movement. Johnson spelled out his ideas on what the president should do in a telephone conversation with Kennedy's speechwriter, Theodore Sorensen. Kennedy could no longer delay becoming the leader on what was a moral issue, Johnson told Sorensen. It was time to forget about Southern political votes in 1964. "I know the risks are great and it might cost us the South," Johnson said. "But those sort of states may be lost anyway." Kennedy must appeal for fairness. "We got a little popgun and I want to pull out the cannon," Johnson said. "The president is the cannon. You let him be on all the TV networks just speaking from his conscience." Kennedy's backdrop should be a military honor guard of black and white soldiers holding American flags, Johnson said. "Then let him reach over and point and say, 'I have to order these boys into battle in foxholes carrying the flag. And I don't ask them what their name is, whether it's Gomez or Smith, or what color they got, what religion. If I can order them into battle, I've got to make it possible for them to eat and sleep in this country.'"

Kennedy's nationwide address on June 11 had no multiracial honor guard. A draped Old Glory was the only backdrop. He asked the nation to examine its conscience. "We are confronted primarily with a moral issue," Kennedy said. "It is as old as the scriptures and is as clear as the American Constitution." The president reminded viewers that the nation was engaged in a global struggle on behalf of freedom around the world. "When Americans are sent to Vietnam or West Berlin, we do not ask for whites only," Kennedy said. "It ought to be possible therefore for American students of any color to attend a public institution they select without having to be backed up by troops."

It was another magnificent Kennedy speech that left the nation with a lump in its throat. But it did little to stem a rising tide of violence, particularly in the South. A few hours after the speech, a sniper murdered Medgar Evers, who was leading the fight against school segregation in Mississippi. In Dixie, the president's approval rating in one poll had plummeted to 33 percent. "I can kiss the South good-bye," Kennedy told Pittsburgh mayor David Lawrence during a campaign swing later that year. Lawrence also recounted the president telling a racist joke that reflected concerns about blacks moving into all-white neighborhoods. "Knock, knock," the president said.

"Who's there?"

"Izya," Kennedy said.

"Izya who?"

"Izya new neighbor."

Unlike Johnson and Humphrey, Kennedy was unaware of the poverty that gripped the throat of black Americans. To King, Kennedy lacked an emotional commitment to civil rights because of his ignorance of the plight of African-Americans. "He didn't know too many Negroes personally," King said. "He never really had the personal experience of knowing the deep groans and the passionate yearnings of the Negroes for freedom because he didn't know Negroes generally." Growing up rich, Kennedy saw blacks only in menial positions. While Kennedy was in the service in the U.S. Navy, African-Americans were restricted to servant duties as shipboard stewards. Kennedy shared a streak of racism with his predecessors. President Franklin Delano Roosevelt rejected an appeal from civil rights leaders to open all naval duties to 139,000 black stewards. Instead, Roosevelt suggested elevating Negros to shipboard bands.

"There's no reason why we shouldn't have a colored band on some of these ships because they're darn good at it," FDR told the leaders in a session recorded in the Oval Office on September 27, 1940. "That's something we should look into. You know, if it'll increase the opportunity—that's what we're after. They may develop a leader of the band."

FDR's view of African-Americans through his pince-nez was not as blunt as that of Missouri farmer Harry S. Truman. During his presidency and afterward, Truman privately spoke of blacks as "niggers." He had a solid white supremacist view of mankind that meant he used ethnic slurs for Negroes, Jews, Chinese, and our wartime enemies, the Japanese and the Germans. Even so, Truman delivered the first telling blow to segregation when he ordered the integration of all U.S. military forces. His July 26, 1948, executive order did not really take effect until the 1950 Korean conflict. The killed and wounded white soldiers in Korea were replaced by African-Americans. For the next twenty years, the draft put millions of white and black soldiers in the same barracks, an eye-opening experience for both races.

Kennedy's legislative proposals put forth in the summer of 1963 would have eliminated discrimination at the voting booth and in hotels and other public facilities, the workplace, and public schools. They would have required a cutoff of federal funding for segregationist programs. It would fall to Lyndon Johnson when he became president in 1964 to break the congressional logjam and win passage for the landmark laws. In 1963, however, Kennedy was hitting a congressional stone wall. In the summer of 1963, Kennedy dealt with civil rights and Vietnam at the same time, with every twist and turn of both issues weighing heavily on his reelection chances in 1964. There were striking similarities between the two. Both dealt with civil rights. Kennedy had no control over the two key players in both situations—King in the South and Ngo Dinh Diem in Saigon. Both defied Kennedy's efforts to curtail their single-minded dedication to their life's work.

As Birmingham erupted, Kennedy was estranged from King instead of treating him as one of his most influential supporters. As King took the leadership of what *Time* magazine termed in its headline "The Negro Revolt," Kennedy became increasingly cool to the thirty-four-year-old Baptist minister. He rejected at least four requests by King for a meeting. The attorney general, his brother Bobby, planned a meeting of civil rights leaders in the White House after the chaos in Birmingham. The president specifically told Bobby not to invite King, although he later relented.

"King is so hot these days that it's like having [Karl] Marx coming to the White House," the president told Bobby. Kennedy may have been alluding to King's ties to Stanley Levison, a one-time contributor to the Communist Party USA. Levison had become one of the earliest and most important advisers to the civil rights leader. Bobby gave FBI director J. Edgar Hoover the attorney general's approval to intercept Levison's telephone calls on March 6, 1962. Some of Levison's phone conversations with King ended up as transcripts for the brothers Kennedy. Levison was a wealthy New York Jew who contributed to liberal causes. He was active in supporting opponents of Wisconsin senator Joseph McCarthy, notorious for his unfounded allegations about communists in the federal government. The brothers Kennedy were devoted to the red-baiting McCarthy. Bobby had worked for McCarthy's Republican staff. Senator Kennedy sat on McCarthy's panel during his infamous hearings. Kennedy refused to vote for McCarthy's censure, a decision that won the undying disgust of Eleanor Roosevelt and other liberal Democrats.

Hoover's records, since made public by Freedom of Information requests, show Communist Party members informing the FBI of Levison's involvement in financial affairs from 1952 until reports fell off sharply in 1955. As a result, the FBI stopped tracking Levison for a number of years until 1962, when agents learned of his close association with King. Despite years of digging, the FBI never turned up solid evidence that Levison was a card-carrying member of the Communist Party. Although the FBI knew from party informants that Levison had severed ties seven years earlier, Hoover told the attorney general and the president that Levison was "a secret member of the Communist Party." Hoover probably sparked a Senate investigation of Levison a month after Bobby Kennedy approved the FBI wiretap. Mississippi senator Eastland, chairman of the internal security subcommittee, subpoenaed Levison April 25, 1963. At a secret hearing, Levison, after being sworn, led off with a statement: "I am a loyal American and I am not now and never have been a member of the Communist Party." After that, he refused to answer any questions on constitutional grounds against self-incrimination.

Hoover also told the Kennedy brothers that at Levison's recommendation, King had hired Hunter "Jack" O'Dell to administer the New York office of the Southern Christian Leadership Conference—the civil rights leader's political organization. Levison warned King of O'Dell's past connections with American communists, but King brushed them off. "No matter what a man was," King told Levison, "if he could stand up now and say he is not connected, then as far as I am concerned, he is eligible to work for me." When the attorney general's office was alerted to the fact that King's senior adviser had a communist connection, Bobby ordered Justice officials to give King a series of warnings. In most cases, King thanked them for their concern but said little. But when Harris Wofford, Kennedy's adviser on civil rights, alerted King, the civil rights leader expressed doubt about the FBI's facts.

The threat of exposure of a political opponent is a staple dirty trick in American politics. The brothers Kennedy were masters of hardball tactics. If the warnings were also designed to rattle King, even slow the pace of demonstrations, this didn't work, even after the president himself applied the pressure. At the June 22 White House meeting with civil rights leaders, Kennedy took King into the Rose Garden for a private chat. "I assume you know you're under very close surveillance," Kennedy said, putting his hand on King's shoulder. Then he told King that Levison and O'Dell were communists and were under the control of the Soviet Union. "You've got to get rid of them," Kennedy said. The president argued that Levison and O'Dell were still active in Communist Party affairs. Disclosure of their communist ties could weaken chances for civil rights legislation, Kennedy said. "If they shoot you down, they'll shoot us down, too," the president said. Bobby Kennedy later recalled it was a harsh exchange.

"The president was very firm and strong with him," Bobby said.

King was dismissive. "He sort of laughs about a lot of these things. Makes fun of it," Bobby said. King challenged the president's facts about O'Dell's communist activities. "I don't know he's got to do all that—he's got two jobs with me," King shot back. Besides, King said there was no proof that Levison was a communist agent. King's defiance clearly upset Kennedy. At one point, the president's face turned red and he shook with anger, according to King.

After the exchange in the Rose Garden, the two rejoined the other leaders to discuss plans for an August 28 March on Washington. More than 250,000 Americans showed up to hear King's "I Have a Dream" speech, now considered one of the finest speeches of the twentieth century. Portions are broadcast every year to mark Martin Luther King Day, a national holiday. But on June 22, 1963, Kennedy was opposed to the mass demonstration planned for August 28 in the nation's capital just as Congress was starting hearings on civil rights legislation.

"It seemed to me a great mistake to announce a march on Washington before the bill was even in committee," Kennedy told the leaders. "We want success in Congress, not just a big show at the Capitol." Opponents would call the march a gun to the head of Congress. Many other administration programs would be lost. "I may lose the next election because of this," Kennedy said to stress his commitment. "I don't care."

King admitted that the schedule for the march might be awkward. "But frankly, I have never engaged in any direct action movement which did not seem ill timed," King said. "Some people thought Birmingham was ill timed." Despite the president's demands, a defiant King continued to organize the March on Washington. And he continued to consult Levison and have contacts with O'Dell. Bobby learned of the contacts through new FBI wiretaps on the telephone of King's lawyer, Clarence Jones. For all the intercepts over a nineteen-month period, the FBI failed to produce any hint that King was part of a Moscow-controlled Communist conspiracy.

David Garrow, a Pulitzer Prize–winning historian, combed 17,000 FBI files for evidence against Levison. "The case against Levison is in legal terms so weak as to be virtually worthless," Garrow concluded. Many of the FBI files of that era are filled with hearsay, the sort of nudge nudge (wink wink) gossip aimed at smearing suspected targets of Hoover's obsessions. Despite the FBI's dry hole, Bobby authorized a third program of tapping and bugging, this time of King himself. The attorney general signed two orders: October 10 for King's home and October 21 for the office of the SCLC. Bobby would later say these wiretaps were justified based on the fear that public exposure of the communist connections of King's advisers might derail the civil rights bill in Congress. "This is also the reason that President Kennedy and I and the Justice Department were so reserved about him," Bobby Kennedy said.

There was another, more sinister reason as well. The attorney general spelled it out to *New York Times* columnist Anthony Lewis while preparing an oral history for the Kennedy Library in March of 1964. "King was in a very vulnerable position," Bobby told Lewis. "First, because of his association with members of the Communist Party, about whom he had been warned." Also, "to see what other activities he was involved in. I think there were rumors." With nothing new on the communist front from the intercepts, Bobby trolled for personal information that would provide leverage on King. The "rumors" were verified two month before Bobby met with Lewis. The telephone tap on Jones revealed King planned to spend two nights at the Willard Hotel in Washington, D.C., starting January 5, 1964. The FBI planted a listening device in the room before King arrived. The bug recorded the Baptist minister participating in what sounded like a sex orgy with two women. Other bugs in other hotel rooms would also record King's extramarital relations.

To Lewis, Bobby expressed his disapproval of King's hotel room behavior, but his exact criticisms were sealed from public view by the Kennedy Library. In giving approval for the invasion of King's privacy,

Bobby lifted his foot off the neck of J. Edgar Hoover. The FBI director was a racist with a deep-seated hatred of King. Three days after these recordings were made, Hoover had launched the most elaborate smear campaign by the federal government in the history of the United States. When Hoover heard the Willard recordings on January 10, he was elated. "They will destroy the burr head," Hoover told his deputy, William Sullivan.

Transcripts from the recordings at the Willard along with copies of the tapes were prepared for wide distribution within the government, including to the new president at the White House. Johnson found them more entertaining than shocking. As did his predecessor, Johnson had a long list of liaisons outside his marriage to Lady Bird. The FBI offered transcripts to newsmen, but many refused to take them and none published accounts of King's sexual activities. Sexual antics by political leaders were taboo topics for the media in those days. In closed-door testimony on January 29, Hoover laid out the details of the King tapes, which spread rapidly to right-wing congressmen and segregationists. Representative Howard Smith, a Virginia Democrat, planned a floor speech on the subject. But Smith was waved off by the FBI. "Despite our desire to see the scoundrel exposed," Deke DeLoach of the FBI told Smith, the exposure might disrupt other operations. FBI agents bugged almost every hotel room King used in 1964. Neither Bobby, still the attorney general until December 1964, nor the new president, Lyndon Johnson, did anything to disrupt the FBI's smear campaign, even though they knew what Hoover was doing.

When Hoover learned King planned to meet with Pope Paul VI, the FBI contacted New York's Francis Cardinal Spellman and urged him to warn the Vatican about King's extramarital behavior. FBI records indicate Spellman alerted Rome, but the pope went ahead with the King meeting. When King was named winner of the 1964 Nobel Peace Prize, Hoover was outraged. Federal agencies participating in the awards ceremony as well as U.S. embassies were supplied with the FBI dirt on King. One package of the recordings was sent to King, where it was opened by his wife, Coretta. It contained a note written by a Hoover deputy to King. "King there is only one thing left for you to do," said the unsigned note. "There is but one way out for you. You better take it before your filthy fraudulent self is bared to the nation."

President Kennedy had been dead for two months when the Willard Hotel recordings were made. Some apologists said Bobby was a grief-stricken attorney general unable to focus on Hoover's smearing of King. But Bobby was just as bad as Hoover when it came to demeaning King's image with the president's widow, Jacqueline Kennedy. In a June 4, 1964, interview, Mrs. Kennedy at first said it was her husband but later said it was Bobby who told her about King, "how he was calling up all these girls and arranging for a party of men and women. I mean, sort of an orgy in the hotel and everything. Bobby told me of the tapes of these orgies.

"I just can't see a picture of Martin Luther King without thinking, you know, that man's terrible," Jackie said.

11

The Proconsul

T HE WHITE HOUSE, THE INNER sanctum of American power, reminded Henry Cabot Lodge Jr. of his boyhood. When Lodge was still of an age to be sitting on laps, his grandfather, Senator Henry Cabot Lodge Sr., took him to meet President Theodore Roosevelt. The senior Lodge and Roosevelt were the closest of friends. Teddy beamed at little Cabot and gave him a bronze lion. Through his family connections, then as a newspaper reporter, a congressman, a U.S. senator, and a soldier, Lodge knew the next six presidents personally. The seventh—Dwight D. Eisenhower—had been recruited for his job by Lodge, the Republican kingmaker. The eighth was the first one younger than he was. Lodge was sixty-two. John F. Kennedy was forty-six.

On August 15, 1963, the 35th president of the United States rose to greet Lodge in the Oval Office. "Cabot," Kennedy said brightly, "it is so good to see you." He shook the visitor's hand with the warmth reserved for friends. They were old opponents but hardly enemies. Kennedy and Lodge were much alike. They were born to wealth and position that eased their passage to the pinnacle of American power. Both were handsome and had an eye for the ladies. Lodge was two inches taller and far more fastidious about his appearance. They attended Harvard and tried newspaper writing before entering public life. They fought heroically in World War II, Kennedy in a PT boat in the Pacific, Lodge in a tank in Egypt. When they competed in the 1952 campaign for the U.S. Senate in Massachusetts, Lodge accepted his defeat with sincere congratulations to Kennedy. Lodge was effusive with well-wishes when the Kennedy-Johnson ticket defeated the Nixon-Lodge ticket in 1960. "I always liked Jack Kennedy," Lodge said. He was a moderate, progressive Republican, a species now almost extinct. Lodge and Kennedy saw most of the world through the same lens.

In the Oval Office, Lodge sat on the couch. Kennedy pulled up his rocker and took from a manila envelope a glossy copy of the AP wirephoto by Malcolm Browne. It showed a wreath of fire enveloping the Reverend Quang Duc, his face contorted with pain. He handed it to Lodge.

"Look at what they are doing to me," Kennedy said. He could have meant Browne or the Saigon press corps in general. Or perhaps he was referring to the Reverend Tri Quang and his public relations operation out of Xa Loi Pagoda, as well.

Lodge chuckled to himself. Quang Duc's pain had seeped into the president's political bloodstream. Both men knew the photo was a political nightmare for Kennedy. The president's polls had been declining steadily because of the civil rights movement, and now Vietnam was turning ugly. By appointing Lodge as ambassador to South Vietnam, Kennedy hoped to save his political bacon. The president offered Lodge the post June 12, the day after the AP photo of Quang Duc's immolation shocked the world.

Republican colleagues were in an uproar because Lodge accepted. If events turned sour in Saigon, Lodge, and by default the GOP, could take the fall. The party faithful saw one of their stars becoming a Kennedy dupe. "I don't trust anyone in this administration," warned Congresswoman Frances P. Bolton, a Cleveland Republican, in a note to Lodge. "I think they are perfectly capable of using a possible defeat in Southeast Asia to ruin the Republican Party." When Lodge broke the news to Eisenhower, the former president was dismayed by Kennedy's ability to get top Republicans in the Democratic government. "I marvel how . . . he gets the men who are needed to arouse the country to the evils of this administration and gives them these nasty, mean jobs to do," Eisenhower told Lodge. It was clear that Kennedy was setting Lodge up for his diplomatic dirty work. The conversation in the Oval Office quickly turned to the assassination of Ngo Dinh Diem, the president of South Vietnam, his brother Ngo Dinh Nhu, and his fiery wife, Madame Nhu.

"They all will be assassinated," Lodge says, recounting his conversation with Madame Nhu's mother, the wife of Tran Van Chuong, Saigon's ambassador to Washington. According to Lodge, Madame Chuong said the only hope for her relatives was exile.

"She didn't think they can be saved, is that it?" Kennedy replies.

It was close to the view of some of his top advisers. Averell Harriman, number three at the State Department, spelled out for the president on how they should organize a coup to oust Diem. It came during a Fourth of July briefing on Browne's picture of Quang Duc. The president was assured that the bonze set himself on fire. "He dropped the match. I think it was a willing act," the president was told by Roger Hilsman, the assistant secretary of state for the Far East. The photograph magnified the missteps of Diem, who was clinging to power because of Kennedy's support. To Harriman, it was time to get rid of Diem, who was now viewed as one more impediment to Kennedy's looming reelection campaign. "I think we have just got to get him out," Harriman told Kennedy. "If we can get the vice president [Nguyen Van Thieu] to take the front job, we could get a few of the better generals to get together and have a junta." Hilsman said it was uncertain what would happen after the ouster of Diem. "If there is a coup and Diem is killed, it is hard to say whether there will be a smooth transition or chaos," Hilsman told Kennedy. Harriman challenged assessments that Diem's overthrow would trigger political chaos and would disrupt the fight against the Viet Cong.

"I am a little more optimistic that this thing will not fall apart if something happens to Diem," Harriman told Kennedy.

Political chaos that would hamstring the war or smooth sailing with a new crew in Saigon? Predicting the aftermath of Diem's ouster preoccupied Kennedy over the next four months. Of all his close advisers, only Senator Mike Mansfield warned Kennedy that Diem's exit would draw America into an all-out war in the jungles of Vietnam. To Mansfield, only a gradual but total withdrawal of American troops would avoid the costly missteps of the French in Indochina.

When he met with Lodge on August 15, Kennedy appeared to be inching closer to Harriman's viewpoint. Although twenty minutes of the recording are still secret fifty years later, their exchange offers a rare glimpse of the relaxed ruthlessness of presidential decisions. Kennedy offers an ominous instruction to Lodge that Lodge must find just the right person to skillfully remove Diem if and when the time comes. Kennedy makes it clear that while Lodge will make the recommendation about Diem's fate, Kennedy himself will make the final decision. In giving Lodge his marching orders, Kennedy says he is still uncertain about choosing a successor to Diem.

"I wanted to be sure that there is somebody who would be better than this fellow," Kennedy tells Lodge. "After all, he has sustained himself against the French, the Viet Cong, and he did it for ten years. That's a pretty good record. I don't like to see us just decide on someone just because we are getting heat from the press." As senator, Kennedy had supported Diem while he was in exile and when others in the State Department wanted his head. There was a personal relationship, fleeting perhaps, but Kennedy remembered the small man with intense black eyes from ten years earlier.

Kennedy told Lodge he would be the chief adviser on Diem's fate, bypassing more senior members of his cabinet. But Kennedy reserved the final decision to the president.

"I will leave it almost completely in your hands and your judgment," Kennedy tells Lodge. "I don't know whether we would be better off with the alternatives. I think we want to take a good look before I come to that conclusion. We don't want to get carried away until you get a good chance to look at it." Even so, Kennedy maintains that the outlook is not great.

"The time may come where we are just going to have to try to do something about Diem," Kennedy says. "I think that is going to be an awfully critical period. I don't know how well prepared you are in finding who we are going to support. That's going to be your key problem. Maybe this woman's right. I don't see how we can go on without the situation disintegrating further. It may be he—they—ought to go. It's just a question of how skillfully that's done and you get the right fellow . . ." The president's voice trails off without finishing the thought. Lodge understood.

Kennedy digresses to give Lodge the historical context of Diem and South Vietnam as one more U.S. client state that lost American support because of attacks by the press. "There is a great temptation to do what we did to Chiang Kai-shek, the military ruler of the Nationalist government of China. Washington abandoned Chiang because of his persecution of political opponents after he was defeated by the Communist Chinese in 1949. "Chiang was so pasted by the American reporters, American public opinion was formed—it was hopeless," Kennedy says. It was the same thing in South Korea with President Syngman Rhee in 1960. "All of our people always seem to get pasted," Kennedy tells Lodge. "Everybody we are for is always a son of a bitch."

Kennedy maintains that a big part of the problem is the press. "They are antigovernment wherever they are," Kennedy tells Lodge. "The press is instinctively liberal. They are against any military regime. I don't know. I assume this fellow [Diem] is probably in an impossible situation to save. I just want to be sure our policy [is not] caused by a couple of smart young reporters. The press out there, you know how they can get in those places. They feel they are carrying out a job of political action to get rid of Diem. They would argue it's the only way they can win." Even so, Kennedy argues that the press's record of predictions is not great. "They're a lot of fellows without much experience. They are not first line. You're going to have a difficult time maintaining a satisfactory relationship with them."

Lodge spent more time than Kennedy as a journalist. He was a reporter for the *Boston Evening Transcript* and the Washington bureau of the *New York Herald Tribune*. Lodge understood the use of flattery to tame the beast. In his conversation with Kennedy, Lodge says his chief concern is stroking the daily reporters of the Associated Press, United Press International, and the *New York Times*. "They have been frightened by the Vietnamese police—really physically," Lodge says. "They've been lied to. They have been condescended to socially." Starting on his first day, he would invite the top reporters to lunch one by one. "I'm going to ask [them] for advice. Try to get a human frame of mind. At least I'm not going to lie to them. They always can come in and see me. And anything they are entitled to get, I'll see that they get it."

When Lodge mentions Madame Chuong's comments about her daughter, Kennedy presses for gossipy details. Kennedy's curiosity about and dislike for Madame Nhu had intensified after her televised comments two weeks earlier about Quang Duc's self-immolation. "What have they done but barbecue one of their monks," she said, fluttering a fan while she spoke. Her view gave editors reason to run Browne's photo of Quang Duc once again. "What about Madame Nhu?" Kennedy asks. "Is she a lesbian or what? She's awful masculine." While she was a girl living in Washington, her mother found her a handful, Lodge says. "I think she was very promiscuous, a nymphomaniac. When she was here in Washington a couple of years ago she took an overdose of sleeping pills and they had to pump her stomach." Kennedy sought—without success—to silence her through repeated diplomatic messages to Diem and Nhu. She would drive him into fits of anger in the coming weeks. "That bitch" was his frequent refrain. While the embassy in Saigon and the State Department identified Counselor Nhu as the problem, to Kennedy it was the Dragon Lady of Saigon.

Lodge's fastidiousness came up when Kennedy asks about his departure to Saigon. Lodge had become celebrated during the 1960 campaign when he insisted on a daily nap to remain sharp on the hustings. "He got in his jammies every day after lunch," recalled Bob Healy of the *Boston Globe*, who covered Lodge's vice-presidential campaign. Candidates, including Kennedy, often went from before dawn until midnight when votes were at stake. But Lodge maintained that a candidate should not look tired and irascible. After his nap, he appeared wrinkle-free and immaculate before a frazzled press corps. He was not about to let jet lag weaken him by traveling direct to Saigon. Instead, he tells Kennedy, he will stop over in Honolulu, Tokyo, and Hong Kong. "I want to feel fresh when I get there," Lodge says to the president. "The day I arrive on a thing like this is always a big day. People trying to embarrass you are out in full force."

In vetting Lodge for the job, the State Department told Kennedy that Lodge would take the bit in his teeth in Saigon. As ambassador to the United Nations under Eisenhower, Lodge often ignored State Department direction and made his own foreign policy in New York. On an important vote on North Korea, Lodge was instructed to vote yes, on behalf of the United States. Lodge voted no instead. When Undersecretary of State Robert Murphy called to find out why, he learned Lodge was not under Foggy Bottom's thumb. "I am not bound by instructions from the State Department," Lodge said, according to Murphy. As UN ambassador, he had cabinet rank and took instructions only from Eisenhower.

Murphy was rocked. "I was flabbergasted," he recalled. He took Lodge's defiance to Secretary of State John Foster Dulles. The next time, Dulles told Murphy, "just tell me and I will take care of it." While he was at the UN, Lodge's power base was in the White House, where Eisenhower granted him almost every wish. Lodge made one of the first overtures to Ike to consider running for the presidency.

Lodge beat back conservative forces at the 1952 GOP Convention to engineer Ike's nomination and then managed his victorious campaign.

Kennedy was not about to exercise his authority to curb Lodge. On the contrary, the president granted his new envoy almost complete leeway in Saigon—a decision he would later regret. In effect, it was part of the deal. Lodge would provide political cover in Saigon; in return he would require, and Kennedy would grant him, freedom of action. But that very freedom was insurance for the president that Lodge, the Republican star, would be fully complicit, whatever the outcome.

While a portion of Kennedy's marching orders remains secret, Lodge would recall a specific presidential instruction in his unpublished Vietnam memoir. Kennedy told Lodge to keep close contact with the apostolic delegate in Saigon. Lodge thought Kennedy was anticipating a Roman Catholic voter backlash with the American Catholic president taking on the Saigon Catholic president. Informing the Vatican's representative was an attempt to assure Vatican support, Lodge said.

Now, at the conclusion of what would be their last meeting, Lodge mentions weeding out undesirables from the American contingent in Saigon.

"People who blab too much," Lodge says. "Will I have authority to remove them?"

There is a pause on the tape recording.

"You have authority to do anything you like," Kennedy says.

12

The Guy Next to the Guy

SAIGON

JOHN MICHAEL DUNN'S 201 FILE showed he was a combat soldier with miraculous survival skills. His army record listed two Purple Hearts. A Mauser Maschinengewehr 34 had shredded his body with eleven bullets during the Nazi counterattack in the Ardennes in 1944. In Korea in 1950, Dunn took a bullet to his skull after trading nighttime sniper fire. Lieutenant Colonel Dunn's brain was undamaged. And brains were what Lieutenant General Barksdale Hamlett Jr., the Army vice chief of staff, was looking for in 1961. Dunn had intellect plus Irish charm, graduating from Harvard and eventually winning advanced degrees from Yale and Princeton. With coal black hair, bright blue eyes, and a wide smile, with large white and even teeth, Dunn lit up a conversation with his wit and deft use of language. Hamlett summoned Dunn to the Pentagon for a touchy mission. You see, explained Hamlett, Henry Cabot Lodge Jr. was meddling in army affairs. Lodge, who resigned his Senate seat to command tanks during World War II, had gone on active duty at the Pentagon as a reserve army major general in 1961. It was something to do after losing with Richard M. Nixon to John F. Kennedy. Now Lodge was using his experience as a senator, UN ambassador, and political kingmaker to meddle in army affairs.

"I want you to keep Lodge out of my hair," Hamlett told Dunn.

Dunn's family in Boston had been voting against Lodge for decades. Dunns were Democrats, and men such as Lodge were viewed as stuffed shirts with too much money, too little humor, and an imperial outlook—the Back Bay Brahmin. Instead, Dunn found Lodge perceptive, smart, and full of the laughter that life afforded. For months, Dunn provided an insightful, "mostly honest," and always entertaining tour of U.S. military bases. It was a life-changing assignment. Impressed by the street-smart Boston Irishman, Lodge picked the thirty-six-year-old junior army artillery officer to be his chief assistant at the U.S. embassy in Saigon. With a wave of his hand, Lodge transferred Dunn from the army to the U.S. Foreign Service. The moved insulated Dunn from the powerful military bureaucracy in South Vietnam. Lodge's other deputy was Frederick Flott, a Foreign Service officer and friend of his son, George. But Flott's loyalty and career belonged to the State Department. To Lodge, Dunn was his man alone.

"I needed someone I could trust," Lodge said.

As Lodge's right-hand man, Dunn became the second most powerful American in Saigon. He was elevated to an inside role during President Kennedy's fateful change in American policy in South Vietnam. Dunn became close to Ngo Dinh Diem and, at the end, held the president's life in his hands. "If you want to deal with the top guy in that part of the world, you connect with the guy next to him," Dunn explained. "In Saigon, I was the guy next to Henry Cabot Lodge." His experience in Saigon was bittersweet. "It was a fun place to be, aside from the human tragedy and the monumental mistakes," Dunn said, looking back. Dunn gave up the howitzers at Fort Sill, Oklahoma, for the big guns in Washington. Take the night in Tokyo where Lodge was very slowly heading to his new assignment. On the phone was the undersecretary of state, an agitated George Ball, yelling at a still-groggy Dunn. All hell had broken loose in Saigon, Ball said. The president wanted Lodge in Saigon—today!

Diem had declared martial law and was arresting thousands of protesting students and Buddhists in Saigon, Hue, and other cities. It was a sudden and dramatic end to Diem's promise of conciliation with the protesting Buddhists after the immolation of Quang Duc. Frederick Nolting, the departing ambassador, had assured Lodge earlier that week in Honolulu that Diem was committed to compromise. Now Dunn heard the chaos in Ball's voice. University students, high school students, and even children from elementary school took to the streets in support of the Buddhists. The elite of Saigon, including senior military officers, had to come to the crowded prisons to seek the release of their children. Ball had been unable to get through Lodge's order that he not be disturbed. Lodge's obsession with being fresh and alert after a night of uninterrupted sleep meant the junior army officer would spend many hours with very senior Kennedy people.

When Lodge finally arose, Dunn described the alarm in Washington, the president's order, and developments in Saigon. They would have to scrap the stopover in Hong Kong and fly straight to Saigon. Nine hours on an aging Lockheed Constellation, a four-engine propeller plane Dunn rustled up from the Air Force. Lodge grimaced. He detested long flights. He did not complain. He made only one request. "Please find me some coffee, a croissant, and some strawberry jam," Lodge said. If he was rattled by the presidential urgency, Dunn didn't see it.

It was a steamy night in Saigon when Lodge's plane rolled to a stop at 9:30 P.M. in front Tan Son Nhat airport terminal. Lodge bypassed the official welcoming party and headed for a band of forty journalists standing in the drizzle. They were a forlorn bunch. Diem had cut off their communications, blocking their reports on the big story about mass arrests, deaths, and frequent brutality. Death threats led some reporters to arm themselves. Malcolm Browne, the AP bureau chief, brandished a German submachine gun to deal with a late-night visit by Diem's secret police. David Halberstam of the *New York Times* and Neil Sheehan of UPI had fled their homes for safer quarters with an American diplomat.

To the reporters, Lodge apologized for having nothing of substance to reveal. Then he spent five minutes planting a big wet kiss. He noted their vital role in a democracy and offered to personally help them to do their jobs. "This was the nicest thing anyone except the Buddhists had said to them in a long while," said John Mecklin, an ex-*Time* magazine reporter now in charge of media relations at the U.S. Information Agency in Saigon. "This was the first glimpse of Lodge's masterful way with newsmen," Mecklin would write later. Mecklin had watched Lodge's predecessor, Nolting, in testy debates with reporters. At one point the courtly Virginian threw Halberstam, whom he found both obnoxious and insulting, from his office. Watching Lodge in the aiport rain, Mecklin knew his press problems were over. "I liked him immediately," said Malcolm Browne of the AP, the dean of American reporters in Saigon. "Lodge spoke bluntly and honestly and newsmen rarely if ever felt they were being misled by him."

Next morning, Lodge took charge with a vengeance. He cleared everyone from the top floor of the embassy, using the space for his office and for offices for Dunn and the deputy chief of mission, William Trueheart. Other senior staff members were ordered to halt all ongoing programs with the South Vietnamese government. He froze American relations with the Diem government. The chief of the military mission, General Paul Harkins, had been a friend of Lodge's since before World War II. But Lodge quickly cut Harkins off all cables between the ambassador, the president, and the State Department. It was the shake-up Lodge intended. "Lodge was truly formidable when he wanted to be," Dunn said.

The American mission in Saigon was divided over supporting or removing the embattled Diem. The political section at the embassy, led by Trueheart, saw the South Vietnamese leader as being at the end of the road. Harkins, most of the twenty-two American generals, and the military advisory staff overseeing 16,000 U.S. advisers to the Saigon army insisted on sticking with Diem, as the war against the Viet Cong was going well. "Harkins was an unmitigated disaster," Dunn said. Harkins gave his undiluted support to whoever was in power. It was the conservative bent of the military mind, Dunn said. "He was totally insensitive to all the political considerations."

More difficult to assess was the Company, as the Central Intelligence Agency was known in 1963. John Richardson, the CIA station chief, remained close to Diem and his brother Nhu. It was Richardson who revealed to Washington that top Saigon generals had urged Diem to impose martial law and crack down on the Buddhist demonstrations, which were undercutting the fight against the communists. Although the generals met with Nhu, Richardson noted that Diem was still making the final decisions. Other CIA agents had penetrated the U.S. Information Agency and the Agency for International Development. Army officers who had been in and out of the CIA were suspect to Dunn. Most notable to Dunn were Rufus Phillips and Lucien Conein. Air Force Brigadier General Edward Lansdale, who originally helped install Diem to power, told Dunn that these two were the best informed and best connected Americans in Saigon.

Phillips came to the CIA from genteel Virginia stock by way of a prep school, Yale, and a bloodless stint in the U.S. Army in Korea. Lucien Conein was expert at slitting throats and snapping necks while the CIA was still known as the Office of Strategic Services (OSS). He parachuted behind Nazi lines in France and trained the Maquis, the French resistance, in killing and sabotage. Conein, known as Luigi to many, was scary. "A dangerous man, a kind of John Dillinger on our side," Phillips recalled. "There was a hint of barely restrained violence about him." The short temper and blustery manner were accented by blue eyes and bushy eyebrows. As an Army major along with one sergeant, Conein had parachuted into Vietnam at the end of World War II to seize the Hanoi airport from the Japanese army. Phillips arrived by plane from Korea in 1954. While they were both working together to bolster Ngo Dinh Diem's fledgling government,

Phillips sometimes found Conein unnerving. There was the night Phillips walked into the kitchen of the CIA apartment in Saigon. Conein was cutting yellow blocks of C-3 explosive into five-inch slices. He was muttering curse words in French and English as he wrapped each plastic slice with orange Primacord—a detonating cord—inserted a blasting cap, and wrapped them with fuse wire.

When an astonished Phillips asked what he was doing, Conein snapped, "None of your goddamn business. What the hell does it look like?" Phillips volunteered to help. When all the small bombs were assembled, Conein told him to get out. "You didn't see any of this," he said. After midnight, Conein triggered the bombs in the yards of the French ambassador and French military targets. This was done in reprisal for the French bombing of the American library and U.S. automobiles. Ostensibly, the French and Americans were part of a joint task force helping the new South Vietnamese government. But in Saigon, it was often difficult to sort friend from foe. In summer 1963, after nine years of dedication to Diem's success, Conein and Phillips wanted to end his reign. Shortly after Lodge arrived, they invited Dunn to a reception. "Phillips had a very elegant house," Dunn said. "There were a lot of meetings that took place there. They told me how magnificent it would be to have new and strong leaders. They were a group of cheerleaders. They were advocates of a political move."

So was Patrick J. Honey, a University of London professor who for years had spent several weeks in Saigon annually to study Vietnamese culture. After an initial meeting, Dunn arranged for Honey to brief Lodge. "Honey was a rare man—a highly intelligent Westerner who had thoroughly mastered the Vietnamese language and could discuss abstruse subjects in Vietnamese," Lodge recalled. Following Kennedy's instructions, Lodge immediately contacted the Vatican's man in Saigon, apostolic delegate Salvatore Asta. It was a renewal of an old acquaintance. Lodge knew Monsignor Asta from his United Nations days.

Dunn's reports and briefings by Honey and others in Saigon complemented the view Lodge had gotten from Averell Harriman and George Ball before leaving Washington. "Conversations with these men confirmed my impression that although President Diem had been an effective leader in the past, his rule was entering its terminal phase," Lodge said. While still unpacking, Lodge was under pressure by Washington for an assessment of the suppression of the Buddhists and a possible course of action. The CIA station chief, John Richardson, already warned against overthrowing Diem. "Diem is the only figure who holds the armed forces together and if he died, there would be anarchy," Richardson said, citing the views of senior Saigon army officers. According to Richardson, army leaders pressured Diem to crack down on the Buddhists out of fear that Hanoi could capitalize on the crisis. The real threat to Diem would be his refusal of Saigon army leader demands that the Buddhists be silenced. "However, if he retreats on the Buddhist question, if he vacillates and compromises weakly, the generals will end up killing him as well as the Buddhist leaders," Richardson reported to Washington.

Lodge would soon fire Richardson, the leading U.S. supporter of Diem in Saigon.

Instead of leaving Richardson as the only input for Kennedy's consideration, Lodge ordered Dunn to produce intelligence independent of CIA station boss. In turn, Dunn recruited Rufus Phillips and Lucien Conein. All three reports were dispatched to Washington on August 23, the day before Kennedy's fateful decision.

Still, Lodge wanted to move cautiously. But the new ambassador quickly lost the initiative to Rufus Phillips and Lucien Conein.

To Dunn, Phillips was an intelligent and talented operator with close ties to senior members of Diem's government and the military. Conein seemed a coarser agent, but he had seventeen years of friendship with Saigon generals who were French colonial army sergeants when they first met. Dunn ordered them both to prepare reports for Lodge of any Saigon meetings that would offer insights into the Diem crisis. "Dunn asked me to write up the meetings as 'Eyes Only' memos for Lodge and classify them 'Secret' or higher," Phillips said. He immediately contacted General Le Van Kim, an old personal friend with the reputation as the smartest member of the army general staff. Phillips arranged a second meeting with Diem's secretary of state, Nguyen Dinh Thuan. Both men sharply contradicted the CIA report by Richardson, the station chief, that the generals supported the raids and arrests of Buddhist demonstrators on August 20. And both portrayed Nhu as replacing Diem in decisions of State. Kim told Phillips the generals were tricked by Nhu. "The army knew nothing of plans to raid Xa Loi [Pagoda, Buddhist headquarters in Saigon]," Phillips quoted Kim as saying. The raids were carried out by the police and Special Forces, a palace guard financed by the CIA and controlled by Nhu. As a precaution against a coup, Nhu split control of the military among the three generals seen as most loyal to Diem.

Meanwhile, Conein got a different version. Operating undercover as a U.S. Army lieutenant colonel, Conein met with the army chief of staff, General Tran Van Don. In an August 20 meeting with Diem, Don said the president approved the arrests of the Buddhist monks at Xa Loi Pagoda but stressed they should not be harmed. The crackdown was proposed by the generals without encouragement from Nhu, Don told Conein. He stressed that Diem was still in charge, with Nhu implementing presidential decisions and acting as his brother's "thinker." Although this was not in Conein's report to Lodge, when Conein and Don met at a Saigon nightclub July 4, Don said he was plotting a coup against Diem.

According to Conein, Don and the other generals wanted to keep Diem in power for the foreseeable future. That included the generals with actual control of the troops needed for any coup. Replacing Diem would be difficult. No one in the general's rank was qualified to replace Diem, Don said.

Phillips heard just the opposite from General Kim. According to Kim, the military was ready to move against the Diem government. "The key question is, Where does the U.S. stand?" Kim told

Phillips. "If the U.S. takes a clear stand against the Nhus and in support of army action to remove them from government, the army . . . will unite in support of such action and will be able to carry it out."

Kim's focus on Nhu was a recurring but dubious distinction by army plotters. Everyone, including Lodge, knew Diem and Nhu were the inseparable foundation of the Saigon government. Conein and Phillips gave their conflicting reports to Dunn on Saturday morning. It was four days after the attack on the Buddhist demonstrators and three days after Lodge's arrival. "I figured Lodge would read them and call me in for a talk," Phillips said. Instead, the differing messages from Conein and Phillips were fired off to Washington without further discussion. They were followed by a red flag from Lodge. While General Kim said the coup would be launched once Washington gave the green light, General Don noted the generals controlling troops needed for such an action were loyal to Diem, who was very much involved in the mass arrests on August 20.

"Suggestion has been made that U.S. has only to indicate to the 'Generals' that it would be happy to see Diem and/or Nhus go and the deed would be done," Lodge cabled. "Situation is not so simple in our view. Action on our part in these circumstances would be a shot in the dark. Situation at this time does not call for that, in my judgment, and I believe we should bide our time, continuing to watch situation closely."

The Saigon cables arrived in Washington at dawn, where Averell Harriman dismissed Lodge's caution. Instead, he singled out General Kim's request for Kennedy administration approval for the army to move against Diem.

It was just what the Crocodile was waiting for.

13

End Run

Few in Washington would risk taunting Averell Harriman, the undersecretary of state for political affairs. His slashing personal attacks and long memory for insults made him an opponent to be feared. In one 1963 Oval Office meeting, Harriman was telling President Kennedy that Henry Luce's publications—*Time* and *Life* magazines—were accusing the Kennedy administration of undercutting the president of South Vietnam. "They are pushing the idea that we are trying to undermine Diem," Harriman told Kennedy.

"In other words," Michael Forrestal said, "they've got you figured out, Ave."

There was smothered laughter. Forrestal, thirty-five, could get away with wisecracks at Harriman's expense. He was like a son to his eminence. In 1946, when Forrestal was eighteen, Ambassador Harriman made him assistant naval attaché at the U.S. embassy in Moscow. Forrestal's father, James, was defense secretary in the Truman administration and engineered a U.S. Navy commission for his son. Harriman extracted the prep school graduate from a troubled home. Michael's mother suffered from alcoholism and emotional problems. His father's manic behavior led to his dismissal from the Pentagon and a controversial leap from the psychiatric wing of

Bethesda Naval Hospital. Forrestal remained under Harriman's wing through Princeton, Harvard Law, and a partnership at a Wall Street law firm. Kennedy personally invited Forrestal to join his White House team. He was the National Security Council's specialist on Far Eastern affairs. The more important role, Kennedy said, was to serve as "emissary to the sovereignty, Averell Harriman." As Harriman became Kennedy's top disarmament negotiator, he took Forrestal with him to Moscow. In a meeting with Nikita Khrushchev, Harriman was going to present new documents. But he fumbled and dropped the key to his briefcase. Forrestal dropped to the Kremlin floor to search for it. He was joined by the Soviet premier. They found the key in the cuff of Harriman's pants.

Forrestal lived at Harriman's N Street home in Georgetown, an assembly point for American opponents of Ngo Dinh Diem. John Kenneth Galbraith stayed there while on leave from his post as ambassador to India. In a series of letters to Kennedy, his former undergraduate student at Harvard, Galbraith was the first to urge removal of the president of South Vietnam because of his refusal to include Western political values in his Asian government. "Without doubt Diem was a significant figure in his day," Galbraith wrote on October 9, 1961. "But he has run his course. He cannot be rehabilitated. It is a cliché that there is no alternative to Diem's regime. It is a better rule that nothing succeeds like successors." In agreement at Harriman's dinner table was George Ball, undersecretary of state for administration, who always viewed Diem as a "third-rate dictator" and identified himself as an "anti-Diem activist."

All this was background grumbling in the foreign policy ranks until Quang Duc dropped the match on the mixture of gasoline and kerosene. One of Diem's key supporters, Ambassador Frederick "Fritz" Nolting, saw the move against the president of South Vietnam as a matter of political expediency. "Harriman actually thought a coup would be a quick way to bring the Vietnam struggle to a successful conclusion," Nolting said. "They were fed up with Diem; they were tired of the criticism by the media, they were impatient with the slow progress of pacification—and the 1964 presidential election was approaching."

Forrestal and Roger Hilsman, head of the State Department's Bureau of Intelligence and Research, visited South Vietnam in early 1963. They had then endorsed Diem and the view that his army was winning the war in a report to the president. But when Hilsman replaced Harriman as assistant secretary of state for the Far East, Hilsman converted to the anti-Diem church. So did Forrestal. It would fall to Forrestal, as Harriman's cat's-paw, to dupe Kennedy into approving an army coup against Diem. When the humiliated Forrestal realized what he had done, he submitted his resignation to the president. Unwittingly, perhaps, Forrestal became the middleman in a byzantine ploy by Harriman to win presidential approval for the overthrow of Diem while Diem's most important administration supporters, including the president, were escaping the awful August weather of Washington.

Kennedy was at sea off Hyannis Port, where his family owned a collection of homes and boats. Kennedy enjoyed H. Upmann Petit Coronas even though the cigar had become contraband under the trade embargo with Fidel Castro. The day before he signed the 1961 ban on Cuban goods, press secretary Pierre Salinger purchased 1,200 of the little Upmanns for the president. White smoke drifted in the sea air while Kennedy read the newspapers. No matter where, Kennedy could not escape WHCA—the White House Communications Agency. It was part of the long tail of Air Force One, helicopters, military aides, machines, and staff. A flotilla of reporters watched him through binoculars.

His first document of the day was Forrestal's compilation of the president's intelligence checklist for Vietnam. U.S. intelligence remained uncertain about Saigon government control. "We cannot determine as yet who is calling the shots—Diem or the Nhus," the checklist said. According to one source, Diem was making the decisions, although Nhu was credited with the Buddhist crackdown and imposition of martial law. Lodge believed division within the military would produce fighting between competing factions in the event of a coup. "General Don tends to confirm this," the checklist said. Forrestal, in a second cable, gave Kennedy the complete cables from Phillips, Conein, and Lodge. General Kim's offer to move against the Diem government—if Washington approved—was emphasized. Conein's report that Diem was still in charge and had approved the Buddhist crackdown was not discussed. "It is now quite certain that Brother Nhu is the mastermind behind the whole operation against the Buddhists and is calling the shots," Forrestal cabled Kennedy. Harriman, Hilsman, and Forrestal now agreed that Washington could not tolerate Nhu in a dominant position in Saigon, Forrestal said. It was not "quite certain" by any means, but Forrestal slanted it to Harriman's opinion. "Averell and Roger now agree we must move before the situation in Saigon freezes," Forrestal told Kennedy. "Lodge recommends wait and see," Forrestal cabled Kennedy at 4:50 P.M. "Harriman and I favor taking action now."

It was Kennedy's first inkling that an urgent and crucial decision was looming. They wanted presidential approval for a go-ahead on a coup against the Diem government. It was finally spelled out in a cable to Lodge that had been drafted by Hilsman. Things seem to be roaring along. He had just talked to Lodge in the Oval Office nine days earlier. Lodge had been in Saigon for only three days. What was supposed to be a painstaking assessment of Diem's situation had apparently been shelved. In State Department lore, the August 24 draft became known as the infamous Cable 243—a number arbitrarily assigned by the telex operator. It instructed Lodge to demand concessions from Diem, including the exile of his brother Nhu and Nhu's bombastic wife.

"If, in spite of all your efforts, Diem remains obdurate, then we are prepared to accept the obvious implication that we can no longer support Diem," the cable said. "You may also tell appropriate military commanders we will give them direct support in any interim period of breakdown central government mechanism." In case Lodge felt he was being set up to take responsibility for some disaster, Harriman added a spine-stiffening promise. "You will understand we cannot from Washington give you detailed instructions as to how this operation should proceed," the cable said, "but you will also know we will back you to the hilt on actions you take to achieve our objectives."

Forrestal called Kennedy in Hyannis and read him the cable draft after a copy was sent to the president. "The only people who had functioned on [approved] it were the Department of State," Forrestal said.

"Can't we wait until Monday when everybody is back [to work in Washington]?" Kennedy said.

"Averell and Roger," Forrestal replied, "really want to get this thing over right away."

"Well," Kennedy said, "go and see what you can do to get it cleared." Specifically, Kennedy told Forrestal to get McCone's views.

Diem's most important defender, Defense Secretary Robert S. McNamara, was out of reach, hiking somewhere in the Grand Teton Mountains of Wyoming. The Pentagon view was later offered by Army General Maxwell Taylor, chairman of the Joint Chiefs of Staff. By law, military approval was not required. Politically appointed civilians control the American military. Taylor found out Saturday night about Cable 243 only after it was sent. "Our position was that Diem is certainly not ideal. He is a terrible pain in the neck in many ways. But he is an honest man. He is devoted to his country. And we are for him until we can find someone better—looking under the bushes for George Washington, as I used to call it," Taylor said.

Forrestal had become positively slippery as he pushed Harriman's plan through the bureaucracy. He got Defense Department approval of Cable 243 by deception. He duped Deputy Defense Secretary Roswell Gilpatric, who was at his farm on Maryland's Eastern Shore. According to Forrestal, the draft was "favored" by Kennedy, Rusk, and Harriman already. Although Gilpatric had reservations, he was not about to buck his leaders. He viewed it as strictly a State Department matter, he said later. Taylor's view was very close to the position of Director John McCone of Central Intelligence. McCone's was similar to that of William Colby, the CIA Far Eastern chief, who foresaw Diem's departure as the start of endless and dangerous turmoil in South Vietnam. But with McCone out of town, approval was up to Deputy Director Richard Helms. "It's about time we bit the bullet," Helms wrote in approving the draft.

Cable 243 needed the approval of Secretary of State Dean Rusk. But he was in New York watching New York Yankee pitcher Whitey Ford blank the Chicago White Sox, 3–0. Acting in Rusk's place was the number two man at State, George Ball, another opponent of Diem. Harriman and Hilsman tracked Ball down on Falls Road Golf Course in Montgomery County, Maryland. Ball called Kennedy in Hyannis. This would be Kennedy's approval for a coup against Diem, Ball concluded. "He knew what it meant," Ball said. "The president on the whole seemed favorable to our proposed message, although he recognized the risk that if the coup occurred, we might not like Diem's successor any better than Diem himself." Then again, a Diem successor would not be responsible for Quang Duc's suicide, the suppression of religion for 70 percent of the population, and a Saigon press corps that was eroding Kennedy's political standing with American voters.

Despite the misgivings, Kennedy approved with two provisos. "If Rusk and Gilpatric agree, George, then go ahead," Kennedy said, according to Ball. Rusk left Yankee Stadium and traveled to the American ambassador's office at the United Nations, where he read Cable 243. Rusk saw the draft as a fait accompli. He was not about to buck the system. "If Ball, Harriman, and President Kennedy were going to send it out, I wasn't going to raise any questions," Rusk said.

Forrestal called Kennedy. Everybody was onboard, he told the president. That was untrue. Neither McNamara nor McCone approved. Rusk acted only after he assumed Kennedy approved Cable 243. Harriman had eluded Diem's supporters by playing the system with a virtuoso's flair.

"Send it out," Kennedy said.

Ball signed the cable. But in the corner reserved for the identity of the communicator, there was the neat signature of Averell Harriman. It was sent at 9:36 P.M. Saturday night—9:36 A.M. Sunday in Saigon. By that evening, Lodge had requested a change in his instructions. "Believe chances of Diem's meeting our demands are virtually nil," Lodge said. "Therefore, propose we go straight to the generals with our demands without informing Diem." Lodge had yet to talk with Diem, let alone explain he was doomed unless Diem accepted the new demands from Washington. The most important recommendation he was empowered to make by Kennedy ten days earlier was complete: Diem must go. Harriman quickly approved Lodge's request.

On Monday morning at the White House, McNamara and McCone were livid. Bobby Kennedy was also upset when he had been left out of the Saturday deliberations. The attorney general was aligned with McNamara and McCone in supporting Diem. "An end run" was the way Taylor described Harriman's machinations. When everyone calmed down at the National Security Council meeting, Kennedy went around the room asking his most senior advisers if Cable 243 should be rescinded or recalled. The president said there was still time, even if the Saigon generals had gotten Lodge's approval for a coup. "The president polled the meeting, going the rounds one by one. Was there anyone who favored backing off?" Hilsman said. "There was not."

After the meeting Kennedy angrily criticized Forrestal. The president had specifically told him to get McCone's approval. Without it, Kennedy said Forrestal should have held Cable 243 until Monday. Kennedy rejected Forrestal's offer to resign. "You're not worth firing," Kennedy told Forrestal. "You owe me something, so you stick around." Kennedy would later blame himself and Harriman for the chain of events triggered by Cable 243 over the next three months. "I should not have given my consent to it without a roundtable conference at which McNamara and Taylor could have presented their views," Kennedy said. Diem's overthrow began "with our cable of August in which we suggested the coup. In my judgment, that wire was badly drafted. It should never have been sent on a Saturday."

During the ensuing three months of Saigon turmoil, Kennedy's resentment about Cable 243 deepened.

"The fact of the matter is that Averell was wrong on the coup," he told Undersecretary of State Ball. "We fucked that up."

14

Perfidy

AMBASSADOR HENRY CABOT LODGE PRESENTED a profile in perfidy between August 26 and November 2, 1963, a perfect example of treachery in pursuit of diplomatic goals. With President Kennedy's approval, Lodge on August 25 gave the green light to a band of generals willing to overthrow Ngo Dinh Diem. Lodge had been in the country only four days. "They were asking me to overthrow a government I hadn't even presented my credentials to," Lodge said.

The very next day, Lodge and Diem would come face-to-face. Lodge was rattled. As he prepared to present his credentials to the president of South Vietnam, he ordered General Paul Harkins, the U.S. military commander in Saigon, to stay away from the Gia Long Palace ceremony August 26. "In case they try something funny," Lodge told Harkins. American treachery might result in Vietnamese treachery. Since his arrival in Saigon, Lodge was the target of a stream of death threats intercepted by the Central Intelligence Agency station. His worry increased the closer he got to the coup d'etat that Kennedy approved on August 24. Lodge kept a pistol on his desk and carried a hidden .357 Magnum when traveling outside the embassy.

Impeccable as usual, Lodge had decorated his blazing white

sharkskin with his army medals. This man with the bluest of American blood—a soldier and a statesman from the top rank of U.S. politics—bowed to Diem as etiquette demanded. Even bent at the waist, the six-foot-two Lodge seemed taller than the five-foot-four Diem. To Diem, Lodge was the sixth emissary from the president of the United States. This one, he was pretty sure, carried a knife. Agents for Diem—and for Hanoi—were sprinkled throughout the U.S. mission in Saigon. What Diem had learned of Lodge's secret schemes became clearer when the two men met in the afternoon following the presentation ceremony.

Their meeting was similar to a World Wrestling Entertainment match, with both men grappling for the advantage. Lodge struck first, keeping Diem from launching into one of his celebrated monologues. Once Lodge gained the floor, he tried to put Diem on the defensive. The opening gambit was aimed at Diem's sister-in-law Madam Ngo Dinh Nhu. "It was interesting to me," Lodge told Diem, "that people whom I had known all my life in politics thought that Madame Nhu was chief of state of Vietnam. I had met several people in Massachusetts who had seen her picture on the covers of magazines and read some of her statements about barbecuing the priests and the total destruction of the Buddhists and that this had shocked public opinion." Diem replied that he had done his best to get Madame Nhu to keep quiet, including displacing her as First Lady at the palace. "He said jokingly that he had even threatened to take a wife," Lodge said. Diem noted that Madame Nhu was also a member of the National Assembly and had the right to make public speeches. Lodge would never meet her. She would soon be in exile, a noisy foray abroad that meant her lacquered nails would sink deeper beneath the skin of the American president.

Their tête-tà-tête was in French. Lodge had studied in Paris and became fluent while a U.S. Army liaison with the French during World War II. Diem got his French from serving in the French colonial government. As he spoke, Diem pulled one cigarette after another from a tin of Phillip Morris, lit it, took one puff, and then stubbed it out. Servants quietly replaced full ashtrays with empty ones. Each man had a teapot next to his armchair. The servants would re-fill Lodge's cup. "That tea in front of me contained a diuretic which created an irresistible urge to do that thing which nobody else can do for you," Lodge said. Any doctor would explain that tea contains a natural diuretic. As Lodge squirmed, Diem held forth.

Diem had been through these sessions with Lodge's predeces-sors, who all pressed him to install some version of American democ-racy. To him, these diplomats failed to comprehend the Saigon government's struggle with the outside enemy—Hanoi and the Viet Cong—and its internal opponents. They ignored the popular approval outside of Saigon for Diem's honesty, dedication, and celibacy, and the economic vitality that Diem had fostered for nine years. "They think this is New York City," he complained to John Osborne of *Life* magazine. For Marguerite Higgins of the *New York Herald Tribune*, he imitated the emissaries wagging a finger in his face. Inevitably, the dialogue of American demands was turned aside with Diem's re-curring proclamation of independence.

"*Je ne suis pas une marionnette,*" Diem said. "*Je pas serveur.*" I am not a puppet. I will not serve. Diem would reserve these words for one of his last meetings with Lodge. In this first meeting, he indi-cated his disapproval with facial expressions. The increasingly uncom-fortable Lodge finally inserted Kennedy's chief request: Was it possible for brother Nhu to leave Saigon, at least until the end of the year? Diem's face clouded over. He looked at the ceiling. He rambled on about a different subject. Diem had been hearing this demand about Nhu from U.S. ambassadors for years. "He wouldn't talk about it," Lodge said. "It gave me a little jolt. I thought it was deplorable that he wouldn't answer questions I was bringing from the president of the United States."

With his bladder near bursting after two hours, Lodge apolo-gized and announced he must leave, but not before Diem delivered a parting shot. According to Lodge, Diem "hoped there would be discipline, particularly as regards the U.S. activities in Saigon, and there would be an end to reports of diverse activities interfering in Vietnamese affairs by various U.S. agencies." In diplomatic terms, Diem was delivering a punch in the nose. He had Lodge's number. Diem knew Lodge was already plotting a coup with army insurgents through CIA agents. Still, Lodge remained composed as he withdrew from the hot and stuffy palace.

Lodge might have wondered if the leaks to the palace came from John Richardson's CIA station in Saigon. He was unhappy with Richardson's refusal to submit to the ambassador's role as proconsul in Saigon. In his unpublished memoir, he grumbled that the CIA station "has more money, bigger houses . . . bigger salaries, more weapons, more modern equipment." Lodge's first confrontation with Richardson came when agent Conein carried to Richardson a top secret document from the Pentagon to General Harkins. Lodge walked in on the meeting and demanded Richardson hand over the document. In a menacing tone, Lodge said he would not tolerate private communications between the embassy and Washington. When *Washington Daily News* columnist Richard Starnes visited Lodge while on a Saigon trip, he picked up an important scoop. "Spooks Make Life Miserable for Ambassador Lodge," read the headline on Starnes's report concerning CIA arrogance, obstinate disregard of orders, and "an unrestrained thirst for power." Soon Richardson was on his way home. Lodge eventually seized Richardson's house and car, which was newer and larger than the one provided to the ambassador. The flap required the president to clarify the issue at a press conference where he praised Richardson's service.

Shortly after his arrival in Saigon, Lodge lectured John Mecklin, his chief of public affairs. He, not Mecklin, would control the flow of news to the top journalists. Leaking to newsmen was the ambassador's prerogative, Lodge said. Lodge's treatment of Richardson left an indelible impression in the minds of the remaining CIA operatives. "When Ambassador Lodge came to Saigon, he let everybody know who was in charge," Conein said. "He was the boss and you better execute his orders without hesitation or murmuring or you were out."

At the White House, Kennedy began to wonder if Lodge's leash was too long. "A very economic investment," McGeorge Bundy told Kennedy. In addition to being ambassador, Lodge took charge of intelligence functions and press relations.

Dunn, Lodge's deputy, sensed unhappiness at the embassy that got worse under Lodge. Lodge rarely called the U.S. missions together for "country team" meetings, a standard procedure at most American embassies. "There was an aura of distrust that absolutely dominated the entire effort from top to bottom," Dunn said. He was growing suspect of agent Conein's reports on the progress of the generals' coup. An August 27 report by Conein quoted the generals as executing the coup within seven days. "Conein had given so many false starts," Dunn said. Conein would say, "They are ready to move." "Move where, with what?" Dunn demanded. "Give me something hard. What specifically was said?"

Lodge found himself "pushing a plate of spaghetti." To Lodge it was all a disappointment. "Too much inertia and timidity among the generals," he wrote in his Vietnam memoir. "Days pass and nothing happens," he cabled Washington.

15

Laurel and Hardy

PRESIDENT KENNEDY'S INITIAL PLAN TO overthrow the most important U.S. ally in Southeast Asia was going nowhere. He had been talked into backing a handful of Saigon army generals who were ready to oust President Ngo Dinh Diem, who had been transformed from a frontline fighter of communism into a political embarrassment. Polls showed Kennedy in steady decline with American voters. Now he seemed saddled with a harebrained scheme that hinged on reluctant Saigon generals outmaneuvered by Diem. "Who the hell are all these generals?" Kennedy demanded. His politically risky scheme to oust the president of South Vietnam was fizzling a week after it was launched on Saturday. White House tape recordings on Monday, Tuesday, Wednesday, and Thursday had the president sounding like Oliver Hardy to Averell Harriman's Stan Laurel: "Well, here's another nice mess you've gotten me into!" "This shit has got to stop," Kennedy told Forrestal, who had acted as a go-between with Harriman.

The Harriman-Lodge axis had enlisted a band of senior Saigon generals who had been checkmated by the wily Diem and his ever-cunning brother Nhu. They had restricted control of troops to only his most loyal commanders, stripping the plotters of the military might needed to stage a coup d'etat. "It was a very smart move," an admiring Marine General Victor Krulak told the president. It was the only thing described as smart throughout the White House top secret meetings. As the scheme unraveled, a diplomat Kennedy respected told him bluntly that the Saigon generals lacked the guts and the skill to take on Diem. Former ambassador Nolting warned Kennedy of the immorality and treachery of ignoring solemn American pledges to support Diem over a nine-year period just because of the media uproar over the Buddhist crackdown. "A bad principle and a bad practice," Nolting told the president.

Nolting was just one of the verbal blows landed on Kennedy as he realized the slapdash quality of the plot he had approved on August 24. "If it doesn't work, if the generals don't do anything, then we have to deal with Diem as he is and Nhu as he is. Then the question is, what do we do to protect our own prestige? Anybody thought about that?" he said sharply.

Secretary of State Dean Rusk, who had deferred to Harriman's machinations, joined Kennedy in his misgivings. "What are the facts?" Rusk demanded. "Are we on the road to disaster?" In response to Kennedy's relentless questioning, Undersecretary of State Harriman kept silent. A feeble reply to Kennedy was offered by his deputy, Roger Hilsman, author of the infamous Cable 243, which had propelled the United States into this fiasco. Failure followed by an outraged Diem was an increasing reality. "That would be too horrible to contemplate, sir," Hilsman said.

By "prestige," Kennedy also meant his political fortunes, which were being eroded away by the *New York Times*. Their Washington bureau political reporter, Warren Weaver Jr., spelled it out in a front-page story a few weeks earlier. "If the polls and the politicians are to be believed, Mr. Kennedy is riding the longest steepest downgrade of his Administration with no evidence that his reputation as a national leader is doing anything but dropping steadily," Weaver wrote.

Weaver noted that Kennedy's support for civil rights legislation was hurting him with Northern voters as well. "There is growing evidence that [it] is turning voters against Mr. Kennedy in the northern suburbs where recently arrived middle-class homeowners fear the economic effects of integration."

Although Kennedy's approval rating remained high at 61 percent of those surveyed, it had dropped 15 points in eight months. The downward direction of polls terrified politicians. In addition to Weaver, the reporting that David Halberstam had been doing from Saigon was giving Kennedy an almost daily fit. Halberstam often mentioned the Roman Catholicism of Kennedy and Diem and the religious persecution of Vietnamese Buddhists. "He's wrong, he's wrong, he's wrong," Kennedy complained. The president digressed from planning the coup against Diem to portray Halberstam as an imitation of the *Times* reporter who portrayed Fidel Castro as an inspired revolutionary leader against a corrupt dictator in Havana. While this report was accurate at the time, reporter Herbert Matthews failed to anticipate Castro's emergence as the Soviet Union's ally. "Halberstam's stuff out of there reminds me very much of the stuff Matthews was writing about Castro," Kennedy complained. "He's running a most political campaign. Every sentence there calls on us to do something." Still, Kennedy recognized the power the *Times* had on his political fortunes and crucial decisions.

"When we move to eliminate a government, we want to be sure we are not doing it just because the *New York Times* is excited about it." As the crises in Saigon became more intense, Kennedy pressured publisher Arthur "Punch" Sulzberger to yank Halberstam from Saigon, an error on Kennedy's part. The *Times* editors were preparing to recall Halberstam because his reporting was too frequently over the factual line. But Kennedy's demand forced a change. After the session with Kennedy, Sulzberger vetoed the recall. "We're going to have to keep Halberstam in Saigon," Sulzberger told Washington bureau chief James "Scotty" Reston.

To Kennedy, his erosion in voter surveys was directly related to Halberstam's drumbeat of criticism. It came to dominate his crumbling relationship with Diem. In his last appeal to Diem to moderate his actions, Kennedy repeatedly stressed the disastrous impact of Saigon news.

"I have been as much irritated, as I am sure you must have been, by inaccurate press reports which tend to disparage unfairly the effectiveness of our joint effort against the Viet Cong," Kennedy wrote in a September 16 letter to Diem.

"But I cannot overemphasize to you the damage which is done to your own cause and to our common purpose," Kennedy wrote. Diem's drastic curbs on the American press in Saigon were particularly damaging. He appealed to Diem to lift the restrictions imposed after the crackdown on Buddhist protestors.

"Unless I can show the American people that the United States is wholly disassociated from acts which have raised grave questions here, I clearly cannot sustain public support for the central effort," Kennedy warned Diem.

Hilsman sought to assure the president that in pursuing the coup, the administration was not bending to media pressure. "We're not, sir," Hilsman said softly. He stressed that the key to the coup was the uniting of the Saigon generals. "Just the point you were making, sir: Could the generals coalesce?" Hilsman was a West Point graduate and Kennedy did not hide his skepticism for the brass. "Based on your experience at the Pentagon, can any generals coalesce?" Kennedy said. The Cabinet Room filled with laughter.

Then Hilsman and others called the roll on the Saigon generals Kennedy was betting on to eliminate the Diem government. There was General Le Van Kim, who promised the army would move against Diem once Kennedy gave his approval; Major General Tran Thien Khiem, who was close to the most illustrious army man, General Duong Van Minh—Big Minh, whose battlefield success put Diem in the presidency; and General Nguyen Khanh.

There was also General Tran Van Don, the chief of staff, who had warned CIA agent Conein that the potential plotters controlled no troops in the Saigon area. Perhaps the president's memory on that from Saigon cables caused him to ask the next question.

"What power do they have in Saigon?" Kennedy asked.

The answer—no one gave it directly—was none. The only general with troops to command was Khanh, and his forces were in the far north and would be unable to provide timely muscle during a coup in Saigon. The rest had been shunted to staff jobs by Diem. Big Minh wound up as adviser to the president after failing to come to Diem's rescue during the aborted 1962 coup attempt. Kennedy was getting impatient with the bobbing and weaving from Hilsman and Harriman.

Defense Secretary Robert S. McNamara piled on. He was the first to raise the most obvious question that went unspoken during Harriman's haste last Saturday. "We got our troops in there," McNamara said. "We should have some say [about] who is going to replace Diem. Get a weak man in there and we're going to be in real trouble." Names popped up and were shot down like so many hot air balloons. Kennedy then suggested Vu Van Mau, the capable foreign minister, to replace Diem. Kennedy was unaware that Mau had resigned in protest and shaved his head in sympathy with Buddhist protestors. Hilsman told the president of Mau's actions.

"We think the generals think Big Minh is the man," Hilsman said. At that point, Kennedy appeared fed up with the secondhand information from Saigon and the general lack of knowledge in the Cabinet Room. He wanted to hear from ex-ambassador Nolting, who had carried out the president's orders to charm Diem into line. "I want Nolting here tomorrow when we meet," Kennedy said. "I want to hear what he says." That was the last man Harriman wanted in the Cabinet Room discussions. In defending Diem, Nolting had clashed repeatedly with Harriman. Hilsman sought to discourage Kennedy's request. Nolting was still reeling from Diem's promising to compromise, then arresting Buddhist protestors, Hilsman said. "He's a man who has been deeply shocked," Hilsman said.

When Kennedy convened the meeting the next day, Nolting was not there. Harriman had blocked him. "He [Kennedy] just stopped the proceedings and sent for Nolting and waited until Nolting appeared before he would go ahead with the meeting," said Roswell Gilpatric, the deputy defense secretary. "President Kennedy had a very high regard [for Nolting]." When Nolting arrived, he answered the president's questions with facts certain to enrage Harriman and Hilsman.

"You know these generals, Mr. Ambassador," Kennedy said. "Are they influential?" He meant the Saigon officers recruited by Lodge.

"None of them strike me, Mr. President, as people with the guts, the sangfroid, or the drive of either Diem or Nhu," Nolting said. "I don't think they can stand up to them." For the quick and decisive coup Kennedy was planning, the generals needed a preponderance of forces and leadership. "I don't think they have either," Nolting said.

More important, he warned Kennedy that it was an immoral act of treachery that violated solemn official promises to Diem. "I have grave reservations," Nolting told Kennedy at a Cabinet Room meeting. He reminded Kennedy of a personal presidential letter to Diem in 1961 that included a vow never to interfere with Saigon domestic affairs. "Putting ourselves in a position of engineering a coup d'etat for the purpose of establishing a government with which we can deal more effectively . . . Somehow in my mind this is a bad principle and a bad practice." Nolting's comments resulted in a fiery rejoinder the next day by Harriman that left many, including Kennedy, aghast.

"Shut up," he told Nolting. "We've heard you before. No one cares what you think. You've been wrong from the beginning." Harriman then turned on Army General Maxwell Taylor, the chairman of the Joint Chiefs of Staff. He had been a leading critic of Harriman's end run on Saturday. "You've been wrong on every issue since World War II," Harriman told the celebrated wartime leader.

To Gilpatric, Harriman's outburst was unfairly critical. "I never was present at a session with the president at which someone took the dressing down that Nolting took from Harriman," Gilpatric said. "A lot of us were very surprised and rather shocked." Forrestal said Kennedy was appalled by the divisions among his advisers and the emotional outbursts. "The basic lack of information about Vietnam" also irritated the president, Forrestal said. Kennedy intervened on Nolting's behalf, telling Harriman the president wanted to hear the ex-ambassador's advice. At the end of the meeting, Harriman approached Kennedy. "I hope you're not going wobbly," Harriman said.

This series of White House meetings the last week in August established a passionate split among his top advisers that would irritate Kennedy for the next two months. Was Diem losing the war to the Viet Cong? Rusk, Harriman, Hilsman, Forrestal, and Lodge predicted a loss to Hanoi if Diem remained in power. That was countered by McNamara, Taylor, McCone, and his brother Bobby. With American advisers and weapons, the Saigon government was killing off the Viet Cong. Diem was the only competent national leader, and he would soon recover from the Buddhist turmoil.

Nolting may have had soured Kennedy on the coup. Lacking the troops to stage a coup meant it would be folly to try. "Go back to Lodge and Harkins, express our concerns about forces," Kennedy told Rusk. "I don't see how we can succeed. Those forces are almost two to one against coup." The president's second thoughts reached Saigon, where Lodge exploded. "Situation here has reached the point of no return," Lodge cabled Kennedy. "It is our considered estimate that General officers cannot retreat now. Unless the generals are neutralized before being able to launch their operation, we believe they will act and that they have goods to win." Lodge's defiance was greeted coolly by Kennedy. The president reminded Lodge that events in Saigon had not reached Kennedy's point of no return. His personal cable to Lodge reflected the lessons of the Bay of Pigs fiasco in 1961. "Until the very moment of the go signal for the operation by the generals, I must reserve a contingent right to change course and reverse previous instructions," Kennedy cabled. "While fully aware of your assessment of the consequence of such a reversal, I know from experience that failure is more destructive than the appearance of indecision."

At the end of Thursday's White House meeting, Kennedy asked who was against the coup. McNamara said Lodge should disassociate the United States from the coup and instead press Diem for the exile of Nhu. "McNamara said he sees no valid alternative to the Diem regime," recorded Bromley Smith, the National Security Council secretary.

Kennedy's August 30 order shifted authority to support a coup from Lodge to Harkins, a known opponent of the overthrow. For the record, the president had called off the coup and Rusk had instructed Lodge to seek Diem's approval for a removal of Nhu from Saigon. Then both Washington and Saigon braced for a Saigon street battle and the evacuation of Americans from South Vietnam. Just as U.S. Seventh Fleet ships moved offshore to evacuate Americans from the cross fire, General Khiem showed up at the American military headquarters in Saigon. Big Minh had canceled the coup, Khiem told General Paul Harkins. It was exactly one week after Kennedy approved American support of Diem's overthrow.

Diem and Nhu had won round one. Kennedy got the news while aboard the yacht *Honey Fitz,* enjoying a Labor Day weekend off Hyannis Port. He smoked an Upmann blunt and read the *New York Times.* Son John-John and daughter Caroline took turns at the wheel of the yacht. Kennedy watched them and smiled. These were the pleasant sunlit hours before he had to return to Washington and his stormy and badly divided government.

16

Financial Inducements

H E LIKED SCOTCH WHISKEY, SOME said too much. The CIA rated him "eccentric." Behind the Hollywood sunglasses, the tailored paratrooper fatigues, and a rakish red beret, Brigadier General Ton That Dinh had a streak of megalomania as big as all outdoors. Dinh confided that he was a "national hero" to one American reporter. To his U.S. Army adviser, Dinh portrayed himself as the finest soldier in the army of South Vietnam. Although only thirty-six, he once demanded to be appointed minister of the interior, the number two job in Diem's government. His runaway ego often pushed him over the edge. Still, Dinh became the boozy star attraction in President Kennedy's second putsch against a democratically elected ally, President Diem of South Vietnam. The first coup had collapsed a week after Kennedy's hasty approval. The aborted plan hinged on Saigon generals without the troops needed to overcome the Gia Long Palace guard. It was a mistake Kennedy would not repeat. As military governor of Saigon, Dinh controlled both troops within the city and divisions of infantry and armor within striking distance of the capital. Dinh's other chief attribute was that he was for sale. When Dinh's name first surfaced at the White House, Army General Maxwell Taylor, chairman of the Joint Chiefs, presented him as the key to overthrowing the Diem government.

"It appears," Taylor told the president, "General Dinh, the III Corps commander, is the key to this personnel situation—if he is in anyway corruptible." Roger Hilsman, a leader of the State Department faction against Diem, had a ready answer. "We have some plans about how we might corrupt Dinh," Hilsman told Kennedy. That was affirmed by Defense Secretary McNamara. "There are such additional actions specifically to buy over or persuade over or otherwise induce Dinh," McNamara assured the president.

Kennedy's order to bribe Dinh left Washington the same day—at 9:32 P.M. on August 28. It was presented in the form of questions to General Harkins and Lodge. But that was a diplomatic dodge to sugarcoat the seamy nature of the presidential decision to buy off Diem's most important military defender.

> Specifically, do you think we should:
>   —encourage Harkins and other military officers [to] discreetly hint to Gen. Dinh and other military leaders who are potential fence-sitters about continued US opposition to the Saigon government?
>   —add financial inducements as appropriate in affecting all individual decisions of uncertain key figures?

Dinh was well known to the two top U.S. agents, Rufus Phillips and Lucein Conein. Frequently, Dinh would arrive at Conein's Saigon home with a fanfare of siren-screeching escorts. In Conein's home, Dinh had installed a red phone as a direct connection to the U.S. embassy. He would say little, drink a glass of scotch, and then roar off to some nightclub party. Twelve days after Kennedy was told that Dinh was for sale, Phillips began nosing around Saigon. Phillips asked Diem's secretary of state, Nguyen Dinh Thuan, about Dinh's loyalty to the president who had given him everything. "Thuan went on to say that in his opinion, General Dinh could definitely be 'had' for an appropriate price in liquor, women, and cash," Phillips said in a top secret cable to Washington. In another CIA report to Washington on September 17, General Tran Thien Khiem mentioned a meeting with Dinh. "Khiem said that General Dinh claims that an American official offered him the amount of 20 million piasters [about $600,000 U.S.] if he, Dinh, would overthrow the government."

Dinh's power far outstripped that of any other Saigon general because of the warm, paternal feelings Diem had toward him. Dinh came out of the provinces on the recommendation of the president's brother Ngo Dinh Can, the governor of Hue. He soon qualified for paratrooper training in France, then caught the eye of the president. Dinh converted from Buddhism to become what was known as a rice-bowl Catholic, a switch to impress Diem. Dinh also became leader of the military wing of the Can Lo Party, brother Nhu's political front. Diem picked Dinh to oversee the August 20 crackdown on Buddhist demonsrators. The president later slipped Dinh a cash bonus. Senior generals had urged Diem to impose martial law to curb the protests undercutting the fight against the Viet Cong. At that palace meeting, Diem and Nhu announced that Dinh was in charge of military forces in addition to becoming military governor of Saigon. The only other Diem assignment was for General Le Quang Tung, commander of the CIA-financed Special Forces, which were in effect Diem's personal guard. A third person named by Diem, General Tran Van Don, was less important. Don, like other generals involved in the first coup, was a staff man without troops.

That Kennedy was recruiting Dinh would have made the Saigon press corps chuckle. After the mass arrests of monks and student protestors on August 21, Dinh appeared at a press conference to claim the public adulation he thought he deserved. Some of the rambunctious American journalists suspected Dinh had had a snootful that day. He was swaggering more than usual. His Cambodian bodyguards—who spoke neither French nor Vietnamese—glowered at the reporters and photographers. Dinh proclaimed that he had overcome the communist forces behind the Buddhist protest as well as the "foreign adventurers" involved. That was a tired code word for the American embassy.

Well, demanded Ray Herndon of UPI, just who are these adventurers?

Dinh ducked the question, but Herndon pressed on, using Dinh's boast to another reporter as an additional prod. After all, as a national hero you should be able to identify a national enemy, Herndon said. Perhaps, Herndon said, Dinh should call Madame Nhu to find out the names of the enemies. That produced howls of laughter. With his Cambodian gorilla shoving people out of the way, the chagrined Dinh stormed out of the press conference.

While the record shows Kennedy did bribe Dinh to join the coup against Diem, the size of the payoff remains uncertain. A 1968 reconstruction of the Saigon coup in the Paris news magazine *L'Express* reported a $1 million bribe. It quoted Australian journalist Wilfred Burchett saying Lodge negotiated the bribe with Dinh in September. Burchett, a left-wing war-horse, had important connections in Hanoi, Beijing, and Moscow.

But the payoff could have been as little as $70,000. That amount surfaced during top secret testimony by Conein to Senate investigators in 1975. Conein said he brought $70,000 worth of Vietnam piasters to coup headquarters as the generals demanded. According to Conein, the money was for families of men killed during coup battles. He had had the piasters in his safe since October 24.

A different version came from William Colby, then director of Central Intelligence. At the time of the coup, Colby was the Washington boss of CIA Saigon operations. "The generals used it [the $70,000] to attract additional support," Colby told the senators. "I can't name which ones."

Was that for a bribe? one senator asked Colby.

"I wouldn't be surprised," Colby responded.

The strongest evidence that Dinh was paid a substantial amount came from McGeorge Bundy, Kennedy's national security adviser.

After the coup was over, Bundy conducted a meeting with Rusk, Mc-Namara, Hilsman, and others. Bundy, "said we do not know what price has been paid to gain support of certain generals who backed the coup. Probably the price was rather high," reported Bromley Smith, the executive secretary of the National Security Council. Smith's finished report became part of the historical record of the meeting. However, that edited version did not reflect the original details recorded in Smith's handwritten notes of the meeting. It read: "Bundy—Dinh probably bought off at high price," which indicates a bribe closer to the $600,000 that Dinh said had been offered by an American agent. Whatever the amount, it did not last long. A decade later, Phillips had gone into the private sector and was eating at a Washington cafeteria. Spooning out food on the other side of the steam table was the former general Ton That Dinh. Years later, when Dunn, Lodge's personal assistant, was asked about the Dinh bribe, he, like Colby, refused to give amounts. "We spent a lot of money," Dunn said.

Because of his position as Lodge's right hand, Dunn found himself on the receiving end of palace invitations from Diem, who sought out Dunn as a channel to Lodge. In their meetings, Dunn grew to admire Diem's intelligence, integrity, and political achievements. "He's the one that unified the country," Dunn said. "He [Diem] spent a lot of time talking to me. He was a very shrewd article." Diem took Dunn on several trips to the countryside to view the Strategic Hamlet Program. Knowing Dunn was a military officer, Diem often discussed military strategy. Diem would unfold a map of the region and show Dunn key locations. According to Diem, with unlimited supplies from Moscow and Beijing, Hanoi was amassing division after division. "There'll be a time when they'll come at us with tanks in division strength; when they are ready," Diem said of Hanoi. Few in Saigon at the time recognized the determination of Ho Chi Minh to conquer the Saigon government; Ho's army was evolving from underfed guerrillas to an unstoppable force. "The potency of these people" was little understood, Diem told Dunn. Diem branded as nonsense that it would be an endless struggle with the Viet Cong. "We can handle the guerrillas," Diem said. It was the Hanoi juggernaut of some future year that Diem was depending on the U.S. military power to halt. He tapped invasion points on the map.

What Diem wanted from Dunn, from Lodge, from the American president was protection from that future Hanoi juggernaut. Otherwise, he told Dunn, "We have to fight and die alone." Eleven years later when Hanoi moved south with divisions and armor, Dunn got out a map. "They finally did come across the very places that he pointed out to me," Dunn said.

Dunn's religion also brought the American soldier and the Confucian mandarin closer together. "No one in the [American] mission could identify with his peculiar brand of Catholicism. I didn't have any trouble with that. I came from a background where church and state were not nearly as separable as most Americans see them." Diem, like most Catholics, saw what he wanted to see from the religion, Dunn said. "He liked some aspects better than others, as I do, as everybody does." On some Sundays, Dunn and Diem would attend the same Mass in Notre Dame, a Romanesque cathedral of rosy brick and stained-glass windows imported from Marseille and Chartres. Dunn would be in the pews after confession, absolution of his sins, and Holy Communion. Diem would sit inside the altar rail, where Archbishop Binh would frequently nod to the president.

Knowing what was in store for the Saigon government, Dunn included the small man with the intense eyes in his prayers.

17

Debacle

IN THE FALL OF 1963, turmoil in Saigon was starting to match civil rights as issues causing a daily erosion of President Kennedy's chances to win reelection to a second term in 1964. Kennedy's failed attempt to overthrow Ngo Dinh Diem made the front page of the September 2 *Times of Vietnam*, an English newspaper financed by the president of South Vietnam. "CIA Financing Coup Planned for Aug. 28 Falls Flat, Stillborn," said the headline. The next day the paper featured General Ton That Dinh underscoring the disgraceful American diplomacy. "What do you want, gentlemen of the foreign press, while our country is in real danger of an invasion?" Dinh said. "Do you want to do harm to this country while it falls into communist hands?"

That view was echoed in the U.S. Senate, where Republicans Kenneth Keating of New York and Barry Goldwater of Arizona wondered if Kennedy was about to desert Diem. Rusk, the secretary of state, told Kennedy that Lodge should be recalled from Saigon to tamp down Republican criticism. "If he were back here, he could say to those fellows, pipe down," Rusk said. More important were the misgivings of former President Eisenhower, whose support was vital to public opinion.

At a September 17 White House meeting, Kennedy asked who

could visit the old general at his farm in Gettysburg to elicit some sign of support for pressuring Diem. Director John McCone of Central Intelligence was one of the senior Republicans in the Kennedy administration who kept in touch with Ike. "You want to be careful about that," McCone said about appealing to Ike. "He remains a great admirer of him [Diem]."

"They think this is a left-wing plot by the liberals?" Kennedy said. "Yeah," McCone said. Ike had called to complain about Lodge's plunging into the chaos in Saigon. McCone then quoted Ike's viewpoint: "This is what's wrong," Ike said. "Now Diem was the toughest guy, he's a hard guy to handle, but he fights communism, he's a tough fellow. Now that crowd down there that you're associated with are going to dump him, dump Diem, and get Cabot out there and get him all screwed up and Cabot's going to be in it. And it's going to be the Republicans' fault." As McCone finished, the Cabinet Room exploded with laughter.

Another politician opposed to ousting Diem was Vice President Lyndon Johnson, who kept his advice to the president private—one on one. But in one meeting with the president's national security advisers when Kennedy was not present, Johnson exploded with criticism. "If you want to play cops and robbers, why don't you get on television, but goddamn it, let's don't go doing it with our allies," Johnson told Rusk, McNamara, Ball, Harriman, and Forrestal shortly after the first coup attempt collapsed. Johnson, as Kennedy's personal emissary, traveled to Saigon in 1961 to pledge unwavering American support. Along with other veterans of the Senate, he had little confidence in Lodge, who as a senator had a reputation for laziness and an inability to follow through.

Kennedy was unhappy with some important decisions by Lodge in Saigon who was setting his own agenda. Without first getting Washington approval, Lodge severed U.S. relations with the Saigon government agencies and ended personal contact with Diem after his initial August 26 meeting. According to Lodge, he was imposing an official cold shoulder that would force Diem to come to him. Kennedy said nothing despite grumbling by Rusk, McNamara, and McCone. "I had the impression that Kennedy was quite content to give Lodge his head in deciding how far to go against Diem," said William Colby, the CIA's expert on Vietnam who sat in most White House coup planning sessions. "Lodge's involvement and Republican credentials would protect him from recriminations, whatever developed."

The White House press corps mostly gave Kennedy a pass on pointed questions about the increasing turmoil in Saigon. Not so Walter Cronkite of CBS when he interviewed Kennedy on Labor Day at Hyannis Port. He noted Kennedy's slide among Southern voters before shifting to Vietnam. "Debacle" was the word used by Cronkite when he asked Kennedy about his policies in Vietnam. In the September 2 interview, Cronkite noted a headline that said the administration was going to use diplomacy in Vietnam. "I thought we were trying diplomacy all along," Cronkite said. "What can we do in this situation, which seems to parallel other famous debacles of dealing with unpopular governments?"

The president was quick to deplore Diem's repression of the Buddhists and he said that by becoming out of touch with the people, the Saigon government would lose the war against the communists. "There is still time," Kennedy told a nationwide audience. With changes in policy and personnel, Diem could recover the popular support necessary to win the war. It was a message from the president directly to the generals plotting the coup against Diem. With the words "change in personnel," Kennedy probably meant the downfall of Nhu. But he could also have meant Diem. Kennedy's appearance on CBS and NBC was part of what McNamara called a public education program. Included was a claim by McNamara and Taylor, after a September 28 meeting with Diem, that the war in Vietnam would end in victory in 1965. It was a dubious conclusion based on bogus facts provided by that avowed optimist General Harkins.

So suspect were Harkins's battlefield estimates that McNamara himself gave up reading them. "He placed his principal reliance on information that came to him through the CIA," said Roswell Gilpatric, the deputy defense secretary. For public consumption, however, Kennedy was switching on the light at the end of the tunnel.

So successful was the progress against the Viet Cong, McNamara and Taylor told Kennedy—and later Congress—that a thousand American advisers could be withdrawn from Vietnam. That, too, was a bit of fakery. McNamara told the president is was merely a bit of paperwork in dealing with the coming and goings of U.S. advisers to the Saigon army. "We can say to Congress and the people: We do have a plan to reduce exposure of U.S. combat personnel," McNamara said of the withdrawal of a thousand advisers. Forty-seven Americans had been killed in combat by 1963. "This will be of great value to meeting the strong view of [Senator J. William] Fulbright and those who think we are becoming bogged down in Vietnam," McNamara told Kennedy. Fulbright, chairman of the Senate Foreign Relations Committee, and Mike Mansfield, the Senate Democratic leader, were urging Kennedy to withdraw from Vietnam.

Again and again at secret White House meetings, Kennedy returned to the issue of retaining or removing President Diem. Another coup effort seemed dubious. "We did follow a policy doing our best to encourage a coup," Kennedy said. "Now, we weren't successful. Whether we should or shouldn't, I don't know. We weren't successful. I don't think Cabot [Lodge] has come up with any proposal to make it more successful." To Kennedy, Lodge was spinning his wheels in Vietnam. "There is not as yet clear support for a coup. That being true, we are going to have to work along with Diem until there is a coup or a situation that is altered so drastically that we have to take drastic action—cut off aid," Kennedy said.

Once the coup failed, Kennedy wanted Lodge to resume diplomatic talks to Diem in hopes of stabilizing Saigon Buddhists and conducting an effective war against the Viet Cong. Lodge replied that sitting down with Diem was a waste of time. To brother Bobby, a big part of the problem was Lodge. The new ambassador was convinced pressuring Diem was a waste of time. "You got a man out there who doesn't want a dialogue," Bobby said of Lodge. Bundy, Kennedy's national security adviser, said coup planning was Lodge's "other big ploy."

"Want to go ahead with coup planning?" Kennedy asked his advisers. The CIA chief, McCone, said he did not know about Lodge's coup plans. What followed in the next forty-four seconds is still censored despite the death of all the participants and the expiration of security designations after fifty years. For the record, Rusk told Lodge to suspend coup planning and resume diplomacy with Diem. In reality, Kennedy and Lodge continued to explore fomenting an overthrow by Saigon's reluctant generals.

Besides American press reports from Saigon, the Dragon Lady, Madame Nhu, was also undercutting Kennedy's public relations program. As requested, Diem exiled Beautiful Spring from Saigon. However, she was not silenced. On the road, she instilled fear and loathing in the American president. In Belgrade, she likened U.S. advisers in South Vietnam to mere "soldiers of fortune." Kennedy, at a September 23 White House meeting, raised the issue with his advisers. "I never saw a more featherheaded dame in my life than this bitch," Kennedy said. "It's all right when she was attacking me. But when she attacks junior officers in the Pentagon, we've got to crack down." When the laughter subsided, Kennedy and his advisers were still rattled over Madame Nhu's looming arrival in New York. "She strikes out and confuses the whole situation," said George Ball, undersecretary of state. "The television stations are going to have a field day when she is here." McGeorge Bundy sounded ominous when he chimed in at a later meeting. "The worse that woman becomes, the more substantial would be her elimination as an initial step."

Kennedy's inability to silence Madame Nhu, control Lodge in Saigon, or get the straight story on the course of the war against the

Viet Cong left him in turmoil about the impact of Vietnam—and civil rights—on his 1964 reelection battle. "It was on his mind all of the time," said Charles Bartlett, a personal friend and newspaper columnist. Outwardly he was confident—he predicted it at a news conference—that Senator Barry Goldwater would be the Republican presidential nominee. But privately to Bartlett, Kennedy feared a much tougher challenge from George Romney, the progressive Republican governor of Michigan who had embraced the civil rights movement ahead of Kennedy. Bartlett spent weekends with Kennedy at Camp David, Maryland, and Atoka, Virginia. "I always had the impression that he viewed George Romney as his stiffest [competition]," Bartlett said. "I don't think he ever thought he'd be lucky enough to get Barry. He had a sort of sinister feeling that George Romney would be there. He'd be sort of a surprise figure and they could be damned tough. I think what you felt in him as his life came to a close . . . sort of a gathering tension towards the election."

Politics was the topic as Kennedy and Bartlett took long walks together. One day they walked through Arlington National Cemetery, inspecting the tombstones of presidents and army privates. At the high point of the grounds near Arlington House, the Robert E. Lee Memorial, Kennedy took in the view of the nation's capital below. "Wouldn't this be a fine place to have the White House?" Kennedy told Bartlett.

Surrounded by so many graves, Bartlett wondered where Kennedy would eventually be buried. "Guess I'll have to go back to Boston," he said. Bartlett argued for Arlington. "But we left it sort of up in the air," Bartlett said.

18

Luigi

UNDERCOVER CIA AGENT LUCIEN CONEIN, known to many as Luigi, clipped his protection into place. No, it was not a Walther PPK or Kevlar body armor. For this crucial secret meeting, Conein placed around his throat the white paper that kept the bits of tooth from the dentist's drill spraying his shirt. "I would sit down in the dental chair and I'd have the little napkin around my neck, and I had my mouth wide open," said Conein. Waiting for him in the office was not the dentist but General Tran Van Don. The Paris-born Don was the most sophisticated member of the band of generals plotting the overthrow of the president of South Vietnam. Don and Conein shared a dentist, so his office seemed an ideal covert setting. Sitting in the chair with his mouth open, Conein was ready if the secret police crashed in while Don slipped out the back. It seemed everyone was being tailed as the tension in Saigon rose during the fall of 1963. President Diem and his brother, Nhu, suspected Americans and Vietnamese. "So in case anything happened, I was being treated," Conein said. "That's the way many meetings were held."

Waiting for the meeting details in Washington close to nine thousand miles away was President Kennedy. Since October 2, the coup that fizzled on August 31 was up and running again, with the same cast of characters. Instead of pushing the generals to act, as earlier, in October the American government took a passive approach to the plot: The United States would merely agree not to "thwart" the new coup; it would not actively encourage the generals. In reality, Ambassador Lodge approved all of Conein's trips to the dentist. The resumption of dealing with those plotting the coup marked the revival of a dual strategy. Lodge continued to press Diem for a diplomatic accommodation. He wanted to talk Diem into compromises with the Buddhists or some other action that might minimize the American president's political pain. At least Diem should get Madame Nhu to shut up. Meanwhile Conein, Lodge, and Kennedy encouraged the generals.

Lodge agreed to a second fruitless session with President Diem but then refused any further contacts despite being urged to deal with Diem by Kennedy. "Do not see advantage of frequent conversations with Diem if I have nothing new to bring up," Lodge cabled Kennedy on September 13. "Believe mere repetition of points already made would look weak. Visiting Diem is an extremely time-consuming procedure and it seems to me there are many better ways in which I can use my waking hours." To end recurring palace embarrassments heaped on Kennedy administration policies in South Vietnam, Lodge openly urged the removal from office of Diem and his brother Nhu. "The ship of State here is slowly sinking," Lodge messaged Secretary of State Rusk. "The time has arrived for the U.S. to use what effective sanctions it has to bring about the fall of the existing government and the installation of another."

After the first coup collapsed on August 31, Kennedy temporarily suspended the plotting by Lodge. "A certain anxiety has been expressed outside the Department on whether it is clear that [coup planning] is definitely in suspense," Rusk said in an eyes only cable to Lodge. "I am sure you share our understanding that whatever course we may decide on in the next few days, no effort should be made to stimulate coup plotting." That pleased former ambassador Nolting. He warned the president of the treachery and immorality of plotting just because Diem was unpopular in the American media. Nolting, Defense Secretary McNamara, and Director McCone of Central Intelligence opposed the coup. They feared displacing Diem would produce endless political chaos that would weaken the fight against communist North Vietnam's Viet Cong. Kennedy's suspension of the plotting caused resentment in the Averell Harriman camp, where they urged Lodge to keep pushing a coup. "I have the feeling that more and more of the town is coming around to our view that if you in Saigon and we in the [State] department stick to our guns, the rest will also come around," said Hilsman, Harriman's deputy, in a letter delivered by hand to Lodge. Rusk, the secretary of state, sent a pointed reminder to Lodge to cease and desist.

Kennedy's caution vanished when Conein "accidentally" bumped into General Tran Van Don at Tan Son Nhat airport. Don arranged for Conein to meet with Big Minh, the leader of the coup forces. Chances for a coup's success had improved because it appeared General Ton That Dinh—Diem's most trusted commander of forces around Saigon—"may join us," Don told Conein. Dinh's willingness came after Kennedy ordered Lodge to bribe the young general. The coup plotters also sought to divide Dinh from Diem. They manipulated Dinh's ego to the point that he demanded Diem make him minister of the interior. Diem reacted angrily, telling Dinh to stay out of politics. Diem then ordered Dinh to Da Lat for a cooling-off period. The exchange occurred in front of the other generals during a palace meeting in which they pressed the weakened president to include them in an expanded government. Diem refused. Angered with his brief exile, Dinh talked about deserting Diem. Troops under Dinh's command could decide the outcome of a coup. Dinh realized he had been "played for a fool," Don told Conein. Even so, Dinh's allegiance was still very iffy. There was no mention of an American bribe in Conein's reports to Washington.

More coup details came from General Big Minh. He was the hero of the 1954 Battle of Saigon, in which all of Diem's enemies were vanquished. When Minh refused to respond—too busy tending his orchids, everyone said—during the 1962 coup attempt, Diem permanently sidelined him. Minh was humiliated, and his anger fueled a desire for revenge. According to Conein, Minh needed quick approval. "General Minh stated that he must know American government's position with respect to a change in the government of Vietnam within the very near future," Conein reported October 5. "He did not expect any specific American support for an effort on the part of himself and his colleagues to change the government, but he stated he does need American assurances that the USG will not attempt to thwart his plan."

Big Minh, a warrior not known for his intellect, had put forth a clever ploy probably designed by far more clever General Don, the army chief of staff, or even by Ambassador Lodge, who was trying to find a way around Kennedy's unease over the violent overthrow of an American ally. To a wavering Washington, the general offered the perfect rhetorical compromise. Rather than encouraging or discouraging a coup—the issue that divided Kennedy's advisers—Kennedy would agree not to "thwart" one. It was an ideal option B, a masterstroke worthy of Lodge's bureaucratic genius. There is no hard evidence that Lodge was behind the ploy. But during a 1979 interview, when questioned about dealings with the coup plotters, Lodge said, "General Tran Van Don and General Minh, these generals, I use to see them all the time and they couldn't possibly have been under any kind of doubt as to what I was doing because I told them what I was doing." Lodge's statement implied that the ambassador himself—not just his CIA cutout—was personally involved in the overthrow of Diem.

Minh said the plotters had no political ambitions, adding with a laugh, except maybe General Dinh. Conein funneled more and more facts, mainly from General Don, through Lodge to White House meetings. The same day as Conein's meeting with Big Minh—October 5—Kennedy fired back approval of the revised approach.

McGeorge Bundy, the adviser on national security affairs, cabled Kennedy's approval of Lodge's recommendation. "There should, however, be urgent covert effort with closest security under broad guidance of Ambassador to identify and build contacts with possible alternative leadership as and when it appears. Essential this effort is totally secure and fully deniable."

Four days later, Kennedy elaborated. "While we do not wish to stimulate a coup, we also do not wish to leave impression that U.S. would thwart a change in government or deny economic and military assistance to a new regime." That was a green light for Lodge and Conein. Those visits to the dentist produced the names of the plotters and detailed plans for before and after Diem's overthrow. As the reality of a coup d'etat loomed, Diem's supporters became agitated with the upbeat reports from Lodge and Conein. Only two days before the November 1 coup, Defense Secretary McNamara and General Taylor were warning Kennedy that removal of Diem would produce political chaos and a series of coups by competing generals.

"We ought to take our association [with the coup] out of the very amateurish hands that have been controlling it so far," McNamara told Kennedy. "And those hands, particularly the ambassador and Conein. I don't think Conein's reports have been sound reports. He's reported a lot of gossip without proper evaluation." Kennedy sought to defend Conein, noting his close relationships with the generals involved in the coup. "They won't talk to other people," Kennedy said. McNamara refused to back down. "We are like a bunch of amateurs. I hate to be associated with this, dealing with Conein," McNamara said. He took aim at Lodge, who had been the subject of a series of favorable news stories from Saigon by reporters seduced by the ambassador. "We're dealing through a press-minded ambassador and an unstable Frenchman—five times divorced. [Conein was married five times but divorced only four.] This is the damnedest arrangement I have ever seen. This is what we have to stop." This passionate outburst was the high point of McNamara's opposition in this period before the coup. Kennedy seemed to sense a loss of control of Saigon.

"We've got a lot of variety of opinion at this table," Kennedy said. "Everybody more or less has some unanimity about reservations about Lodge's conduct. But he's there and we can't fire him, so we're going to have to give him direction. We've got to get him to end up where we want him to go and not end up where he wants us to go."

When news of McNamara's attack on Conein filtered back to Saigon, Lodge dismissed it as Ivy League criticism of a daring CIA agent who caroused in the sporting palaces of Saigon with some of the generals. Lodge and Mike Dunn, his personal assistant, were both combat veterans who admired the coarse Conein. "If you were a graduate of Exeter or Andover and then Harvard, Luigi wouldn't be necessarily your chosen role model for your eldest son," Dunn said.

19

Second Thoughts

POLITICAL ASSASSINATION IS AN INAPPROPRIATE option for the president of the United States. Richard Helms, deputy director of the CIA under President Kennedy, knew a thing or two about erasing America's enemies. In secret testimony before Senate investigators, he said the CIA sought to keep the dirty details from the Oval Office. "I think that any of us would have found it very difficult to discuss assassinations with the president," Helms said. "I just think we all had the feeling that we were hired to keep those things out of the Oval Office."

For President Kennedy, details of the CIA efforts to kill Cuban president Fidel Castro were hard to ignore. His brother Bobby, the attorney general, was directing the Castro assassination program from an office in the White House. And the likelihood of the assassination of the president of South Vietnam became apparent as Kennedy pursued the overthrow of Ngo Dinh Diem's government. Diem and Castro were painful reminders of Kennedy's inability to control events in Havana and Saigon. If they survived, both could become poster boys for the Republican presidential campaign of 1964. Castro was a nasty sliver beneath Kennedy's fingernail. Diem was a very different matter. The president had a long relationship with Diem and admired his record and integrity. Now Diem's assassination was very likely, according to CIA reports crossing the president's desk.

A September 16 CIA report from Saigon discussed ideas underlying the plot. "They generally pivot around the thought of a quick, violent attack on the palace, assassination, and then hope for substantive action," the report said. The distinct possibility that Diem and Nhu would be put to death was sprinkled through other Saigon cables. Agent Conein summed up General Big Minh's options after an October meeting with the coup leader about plans after the overthrow. "One of the options was that they would be able to allow Diem to go into exile," Conein said. "The other was that they would opt to kill Diem [and] Nhu. I reported this immediately." McCone, the CIA director, quickly told Conein that assassination would not be tolerated. Conein was ordered to go back to General Don saying there would be no U.S. support for killing Diem, Nhu, and their brother in Hue, Ngo Dinh Can. General Don brushed off the CIA's concerns. "If you don't like it, we won't talk about it anymore," Don told Conein. "We'll do it our own way."

Killing the little man with the fiery dark eyes was a worry for Kennedy. Assassination—the killing of politicians and potentates—is a fundamental part of a coup d'etat. Once he approved the military overthrow of President Ngo Dinh Diem on August 24, Kennedy was concerned about keeping Diem and his brother Nhu alive. "What about Diem and Nhu?" Kennedy asked at a meeting on August 27. "I think it is important that nothing happen to them." Initially, Roger Hilsman, the assistant secretary for the Far East, told Kennedy that the generals wanted to decide the fate of the Ngo brothers. As events progressed, Kennedy knew that this was a death warrant.

Former ambassador Nolting and other experts on the Saigon scene foresaw certain death for Diem and his brother at the hands of the generals. While Nhu was widely hated, Diem was still a national hero with the majority of South Vietnamese who lived outside of Saigon. Diem's reputation for hard work, celibacy, and integrity could quickly propel him back in office once the generals produced the inevitable political chaos. Even from abroad, Diem could stage a countercoup that would send Big Minh and his coconspirators to the guillotine or tiger cages at Con Son Prison. Killing Diem was the only way for the plotters to ensure their own safety. These men were former French colonial army sergeants made colonels and generals by Diem. Leading the coup were a band of staff officers who shared a reputation for hard drinking and sex parties. Lansdale of the CIA dismissed them as "playboys." Big Minh was the front man for army officers who deeply distrusted one another. Conein often sat at a table with two of them. When one left, the remaining general would unleash a stream of slander on his brother officer, Conein said. As a rule, Vietnamese looked down their nose at soldiers. As a regular practice, when soldiers appeared in villages, they would quickly steal all available chickens.

There is evidence that Kennedy personally reached out to Diem to avoid his assassination. Instead of acting through official channels, the president asked a personal friend to act without notifying Lodge. He recruited Congressman Torbert Macdonald, a lifelong friend from Massachusetts and a former Harvard roommate, for a top secret mission to Saigon. "Kennedy told him that there were plans to kill Diem," said Torbert Macdonald Jr. "He wanted my father to tell Diem of the assassination plans. [My father] delivered the message. He warned Diem that he would be killed. He told Diem to go—at least temporarily—to the U.S. embassy for safety." Kennedy's key aide on Vietnam, Forrestal, briefed Macdonald before the trip, his son said. All evidence of the secret mission was later erased. "He cut out the Vietnam visa from his passport," Macdonald said.

At the same time, refusing U.S. help for Diem once the coup started became one of Kennedy's last orders to Lodge. "If we give Diem help at that point, the jig is up," Rusk said. He drafted and Kennedy approved an order to Lodge that both sides be refused American support, including U.S. aircraft. That order would lead the CIA to reject a request by Saigon generals for a U.S. plane to fly Diem to exile on the second day of the coup. Lodge anticipated the ban on aircraft might cause problems in sending Diem out of the country. "The [new] government might request aircraft . . . for the evacuation of key personalities," Lodge cabled Kennedy. "I believe that there would be immediate political problems in attempting to take these personalities to another neighboring country." If Diem requested asylum in the U.S. embassy, "we would probably have to grant it." There was a precedent. Lodge had granted asylum in the U.S. embassy to leaders of the Buddhist protest.

Rusk was just one of his top advisers giving Kennedy conflicting advice seventy-two hours before the coup was launched in Saigon. Some hoped for a last-minute breakthrough agreement between Lodge and Diem. This hope stemmed from Kennedy's order to suspend U.S. commodity imports for Saigon, a decision that would quickly bring Diem's economy to its knees. The suspension resulted in Diem's invitation to Lodge, his wife Emily, and Dunn to spend the weekend in Da Lat on October 27. The mountaintop retreat, built around an artificial lake, was famous for its cool air and fresh salads. They dined in a oval-shaped house originally built by the French for Emperor Bao Dai. Emily would later remark on the silk furnishings.

In his official cable to Washington, Lodge said the session "perhaps marks a beginning. But taken by itself, it does not offer much hope." This attitude did not offer much support for any compromise as the coup loomed. But Mike Dunn saw Diem fishing for an understanding that would halt the suspension of imports. When Dunn chimed in on the discussion, Diem smiled at Lodge. Pointing to Dunn, Diem said, "Him, me—we understand each other."

In an unpublished memoir, Lodge had a more upbeat recollection of the Da Lat session. "For the first time in all of my many contacts with him, [Diem] said he was willing to discuss the matter that we wanted to discuss," Lodge wrote. "The most important of which was to have his brother, Mr. Nhu, take a vacation." That perception never reached Kennedy.

With no deal in sight, Kennedy and his senior advisers took a close look at what they were getting into at a series of meetings in the Cabinet Room. The White House tape recording system picked up a background of shrieks and laughter from John-John, Caroline, and their friends playing in the Rose Garden seeping through the French doors. The October 29 meeting left the president in turmoil. He groaned, sighed, and joined the others in sardonic laughter. William Colby, the CIA expert on Vietnam, led off with the order of battle for opposing forces in Saigon. The generals leading the coup had assembled 9,800 troops, but the charts showed Diem also had 9,800. "There is enough, in other words, to have a good fight," Colby told Kennedy.

"Thank you for your decisive . . ." said a chortling Kennedy. The laughter grew louder. The words triggered the vocal exasperation at the secret meeting. "If that is true," Kennedy said of the troop alignments, "then of course it doesn't make any sense to have a coup." Up until Colby's briefing, Kennedy and his senior advisers had expected a swift ouster of Diem with little bloodshed. Colby's prediction of a stalemate rekindled the split among Kennedy's advisers. That stuck the president with all the tough decisions. Kennedy's brother Bobby poured ice water on the plot that had been hatched without his approval on August 24.

"I just don't think this makes any sense on the face of it," Bobby said. Pointing to the CIA order of battle, he foresaw Diem as determined to put up a fight. "We are so intimately involved in this. If it's a failure, I would think he's going to tell us to get the hell out of the country." Bobby evoked the image of global humiliation that so wounded the president after the Bay of Pigs invasion. The attorney general predicted Diem's capture of the plotters, who would then finger the White House. "They're going to say the United States did it," Bobby said. "I think we are going down the road to disaster."

His outburst opened the door for the director of the CIA, John McCone. He told Kennedy that the coup was a lose-lose proposition. "We think an unsuccessful coup would be disastrous, Mr. President," McCone said. "A successful coup will create a period of political confusion that will seriously affect the war for a period of time which is not possible to estimate. It might be disastrous." He feared the rebel generals were too inept to run the embattled country. McCone was tutored by Colby, who had served as CIA station chief in Saigon. Colby had convinced McCone that Diem's removal would produce a political collapse that would only weaken Saigon's war effort and bolster Communist North Vietnam's gains. Colby had persuaded McCone to urge retaining Diem but without his troublesome brother and sister-in-law. "If I was manager of a baseball team," McCone told Kennedy at another meeting, "and I had one pitcher, I'd keep him in the box whether he was a good pitcher or not." The Saigon generals made for a hopeless bullpen. Without stable leaders in Saigon and faced with Hanoi's successes, the United States would be forced to increase its military commitment—even to the extent of sending American troops into combat—or withdraw from the ideological battlefield.

Colby's projection of a bloody Battle of Saigon created nightmare images for the president. He saw television footage and accounts of chaos by reporters Malcolm Browne, Neil Sheehan, and David Halberstam. The president sought to counter Colby's prediction of a stalemate by noting past coups where insurgent momentum wins over neutral forces. "It depends on what others will do," Kennedy said. Colby agreed, but he then gave an answer Kennedy did not want to hear. Diem had outwitted a military coup three years earlier. Reactions by others, Colby noted, foiled a military coup attempt against Diem in 1960. Rebel paratroopers seized and held Saigon for a whole day. "But they did not get the [presidential] palace," Colby noted. "Then troops from outside moved in and supported the palace." Diem called for help inside the palace and outmaneuvered his opponents, as he had continued to do since assuming the presidency in 1954.

"What does the 1960 experience tell us about this?" Kennedy asked Colby.

"It has taught Diem a lot," Colby said. The South Vietnamese president had increased his immediate defenses in Saigon and had provided troops outside the city with better radio equipment. "He has the same forces he has always maintained for his own protection," Colby said.

Bobby Kennedy hit a nerve with everyone when he argued there was progress against the Viet Cong insurgency. The president had bolstered Saigon forces with 16,000 American soldiers, including pilots of helicopters and fighter-bombers. "The war, as I understood from Bob McNamara, was going reasonably well," the attorney general said.

A central argument in favor of the coup was that Diem's army was losing the guerrilla war to the North Vietnam–backed Viet Cong. Harriman, the chief proponent of the coup, argued that retaining Diem meant a loss to the communist North Vietnam. "I feel that way very strongly," Harriman said, "I don't think Diem has the leadership to take his country through to victory."

General Taylor, chairman of the Joint Chiefs, echoed Bobby Kennedy's view that there was progress against the Viet Cong. But the old paratrooper took the issue a step further by flatly opposing the overthrow of Diem. "I agree with the attorney general," Taylor said. "I have found absolutely no suggestion that the military didn't have its heart thoroughly in the war and not in politics. If we have a successful coup, it will have an adverse effect on the war. First you will have a completely inexperienced government. These provincial chiefs so essential to combat—all will be changed," Taylor said.

Taylor's concern about the replacement of the provincial chiefs puzzled the president. "Why do we have to change all the provincial chiefs?" Kennedy asked. Taylor explained they were handpicked by Diem and crucial to the government's frontline infrastructure. Taylor foresaw gains for Hanoi.

Colby's nightmare scenario also fazed the secretary of state, who represented the hard-core supporters of the Diem overthrow—Harriman, Ball, and Roger Hilsman. Dean Rusk had seen the coup as installing a military government that would improve the conduct of the war against the South Vietnamese guerrillas and infiltrators who made up the Viet Cong. Now Rusk began thinking out loud about the ramifications of a civil war in Saigon. "If there is a change of government that can be carried out quickly with a minimum loss of life, that is one thing," Rusk said. "A protracted civil war is quite different." Diem and his chief adviser, his brother Nhu, were likely aware of the military plot in Saigon. "Coup talk is pretty rampant there," Rusk said. "If the fighting goes on for two days, both sides will almost certainly ask us for help," Rusk predicted. "What do we do there?

"If we refused to help either side, it will make a big difference to Diem. If we say we give insurgents help, we've got to make sure it will be successful." Everyone in the Cabinet Room knew an American Marine battalion could be ferried to Saigon from offshore ships by helicopter by day 2 of the coup. Ostensibly, the Marines were standing by to extract 4,300 Americans to safety. But they could end up bolstering the military coup—as Rusk implied. "If we give Diem help at that point, the jig is up and we can do nothing but support the government," Rusk said.

Rusk's projected scenario led the president to outline what was at stake. "If we miscalculate, we could overnight [lose] our position in Southeast Asia," Kennedy said. Bobby Kennedy argued that the president's knowledge of the plan was based on a flimsy connection between a single CIA agent and a single Saigon general, Tran Van Don, who refused to reveal details of the uprising. There were misgivings in the Cabinet Room about Conein.

"We are working pretty much in the dark here, and we're not going to get much more light," Rusk said. "I don't think we should put our faith in anybody on the Vietnamese side—Don or anyone else." Nevertheless, Rusk said there was a relative chance of quick success by the generals. "The leadership we have been in touch with in a relatively short time would greatly improve the situation and the war." That might have been a hint about bribing the powerful but erratic General Dinh.

The main purpose of the October 29 meeting was to draft instructions to Lodge on what to do when the coup started. Now Kennedy was vacillating. McGeorge Bundy, who always regretted urging Kennedy to go ahead with the Bay of Pigs invasion, was now reinforcing the president's second thoughts. "We don't want to have regimental combat teams making a mishmash of a three-day war," said Bundy, Kennedy's adviser on national security affairs. His job was to help Kennedy pick the right path through the conflicting advice. On the checklist he gave Kennedy before the meeting, Bundy had scrawled: "Should we cool off the whole enterprise?"

Bundy said Kennedy's goal was to avoid another fiasco. "He [the president] wanted a successful coup. He didn't want an unsuccessful coup," Bundy said. On October 25, Bundy spelled out Kennedy's fear for Lodge. "We are particularly concerned about [the] hazard that an unsuccessful [coup], however carefully we avoid direct engagement, will be laid at our door by public opinion almost everywhere. . . . We would like the option of judging and warning on any plan with poor prospects of success."

The group was trying to find just the right words to reflect Colby's prediction of street fighting for a final pre-coup cable to Lodge. "Unless he [Lodge] has information that forces could take over quite easily," Kennedy said, "we should discourage it at this time. We should close [the cable] with reiterating new evidence from the coup planners otherwise it would be a mistake to proceed."

To Rusk, however, Kennedy was trying to stop a boulder that was rolling downhill too fast. It was time Rusk told Kennedy to fulfill his role as chief executive. "I think we are on a downward slope there, Mr. President," Rusk said. "We do not have the power to delay or discourage a coup. We have to make a judgment." Rusk was echoing Eisenhower's lecture to the young president after the failure of the Bay of Pigs: There were times when there must be a success.

Still, Kennedy continued to hedge. "It would be disastrous to proceed," Kennedy said. The president sought to regain a sense of balance by citing the uncertainty surrounding past coups in South Korea and other countries. "I am sure that's the way it is with every coup," Kennedy said. "It looks foul until somebody acts."

But Taylor warned against wishful thinking. "I think it's unrealistic to line this up as if it's a football game," Taylor told Kennedy. "It all depends on a few key people. A few key people," he repeated.

Kennedy's misgivings were made clear in the final cable to Lodge, which noted the balance between the forces. There was a "substantial possibility of serious and prolonged fighting or even defeat. Either of these could be serious or even disastrous for U.S. interests." Unless Conein could get assurances of the military superiority of the opposition to Diem, "we should discourage them from proceeding since a miscalculation could result in jeopardizing U.S. position in Southeast Asia." The cable ended with a reluctant green light: "But once a coup, under responsible leadership, has begun and within these restrictions, it is in the interest of the U.S. government that it should succeed."

Lodge fired back that the coup was a Vietnamese affair. "Do not think we have the power to delay or discourage coup. It is theoretically possible for us to turn over the information, which has been given to us in confidence, to Diem and this would undoubtedly stop the coup and would make traitors of us. Heartily agreed that a miscalculation could jeopardize position in Southeast Asia. We also run tremendous risks by doing nothing." Kennedy was just as testy in reply. "We have never considered any betrayal of [the] Generals to Diem," Lodge was told. "We do not accept as a basis for U.S. policy that we have no power to delay or discourage. If you should conclude there is not clearly a high prospect of success, you should communicate this doubt to the Generals in a way calculated to persuade them to desist at least until chances are better."

Lodge agreed to do the best he could and signed off with a snarky "Thanks for your sagacious instruction." Bobby read it when he was alone in the Oval Office with his brother. "He sounds amused," Bobby said. "I told you he was going to be trouble."

"You know what's terrific about you," the president said. "You always remember when you're right."

Lodge had the bit in his teeth, but Kennedy had provided the bridle. In the end, the exchanges underlined the reality that events in Saigon were beyond Kennedy's control and had been since he approved the coup against Diem two months earlier while drifting along Cape Cod on the *Honey Fitz*. He was manipulated by Harriman on August 24, and now Lodge bordered on contempt as he blew off the president's queasiness.

It "looks to be his ass," Kennedy said of Lodge. "He's for the coup. For what he thinks are very good reasons. He is much stronger for it than we are here.

"I admire his nerve, if not his prudence."

20

Feast of the Dead

Ten-year-old Alan and Neal Dunn were scooping geckos into tennis ball cans when they heard the clanking of what turned out to be an Army of Vietnam M24 tank. From the tennis court inside the U.S. ambassador residence, they watched the 75mm gun swivel and belch thunder and fire. The blast wave washed over the twin boys, who arrived the day before the attack on President Ngo Dinh Diem. "Oh, boy," Alan said to himself, "this is going to be such a great place to play army." Just then their mother yelled, "You two get in here right now!" Rumor later said the arrival of Mike Dunn's family—his wife Fran and twin boys—was the signal to General Big Minh to launch the coup. There was no such signal that the overthrow of Diem would begin November 1. Lodge and Kennedy had expected it to start on November 2, Friday. November 1 was also All Saints' Day. In Washington and Saigon, both Catholic presidents met their obligation to attend Mass. Only Diem would attend Mass on November 2, All Souls' Day, or as it was known in Vietnam, the Feast of the Dead.

Earlier that day, Lodge attended a conventional departure cere-mony for the visiting commander of the Seventh Fleet, Admiral Harry Felt. The Pacific commander leaned over and whispered to Lodge: "Will there be a coup?" "There isn't a Vietnamese general with hair enough on his chest to make it go," Lodge told Felt, clearly irritated. He was disappointed in August when the coup fizzled. Big Minh and General Tran Van Don had refused to give an exact date, and there had been hiccups. General Harkins, the American military commander who wanted Diem to remain in power, had been cut out of coup planning cables between Lodge and Kennedy. When Don approached Harkins, the American officer said the United States was opposed to Diem's overthrow. Alarmed that U.S. support was suddenly faltering, Don contacted Conein, who in turn set up an airport meeting between Lodge and Don. Lodge assured Don that Conein had been representing the official view and it was unchanged.

President Diem, host of the ceremony for Admiral Felt, invited Lodge to the palace to ask about rumors of a coup he was now expecting. Now he seemed more willing to reach some sort of accommodation. "Please tell President Kennedy that I am a good and frank ally and I would rather be frank and settle questions now than talk about them after we have lost everything," Diem told Lodge. "Tell President Kennedy that I take all his suggestions very seriously and wish to carry them out, but it is a question of timing." Lodge thought Diem had caved. "In effect he said: Tell us what you want and we'll do it." He cabled details of the meeting to Washington but with the lowest message priority. It arrived in Washington at five P.M.—a day after coup events were almost finished in Saigon. To Lodge, Diem's surrender came too late. The next time they talked, Diem was under siege.

The swish of an overhead artillery shell announced the coup to Lodge, just as he was sitting down with the newly arrived Dunns for lunch. Marine helmets and flak jackets were supplied to his wife Emily and Fran Dunn and the two boys. They all were placed in cast-iron bathtubs in the residence's bathrooms. Gunfire and aerial bombardment around the palace grew heavy. "We're all going to die," Emily said. Lodge and Dunn, with radio nets installed, decided to stay in the residence rather than at the embassy. Conein reported in.

As planned, he had raced to coup headquarters near Tan Son Nhat airport. General Don had ordered generals and colonels to attend a staff meeting at the officers club. Once the doors were closed, General Minh sorted supporters of the coup from its opponents. Military police with machine guns filled the room as Minh asked for a show of support by standing. Those seated were forbidden to leave. Minh told Conein if the coup failed, they planned to flee to Cambodia. "You're coming with us," Minh said. As requested by Don, Conein brought a bag full of almost 5 million piasters, worth $70,000.

As Gia Long Palace came under attack, Diem and Nhu sought to rally their military supporters outside Saigon by radio and telephone as they had in 1960. This time there was little response. One of Diem's first calls was to the young general he had groomed for just this moment. An aide told Diem that Brigadier General Ton That Dinh was unavailable. Diem called again and got Dinh on the line. Diem demanded that Dinh and the other generals show their loyalty to the government in time of war. With other officers listening, Dinh launched a series of American-inspired obscenities, cursing Diem, his brothers, and Madame Nhu.

"You are finished," Dinh told Diem. "It is all over."

Dinh, bribed by Kennedy, had joined the coup late. According to Conein, Don was prepared to "neutralize" Dinh at the first sign of hesitation. One of the last efforts to woo him and his troops meant the bribing of a soothsayer to tell Dinh that the Ngo brothers faced a terrible fate. Dinh "was the key to the generals' coup," Conein informed them from Big Minh's headquarters. "When he agreed, the coup began."

Lieutenant Commander Bobbi Hovis, a U.S. Navy nurse, wandered into the middle of the Saigon chaos. She took minute-by-minute notes that wound up in the Navy History and Heritage Command files. "The next thing I knew bullets were flying," Hovis said. "Three aircraft were dive-bombing Diem's palace. As they released their bombs, antiaircraft fire was being returned from the palace. I saw one man shot. A bullet went through the back window of his car, through his chest and out the windshield. They were firing that [105mm] howitzer right into the palace. We heard [the] clank, clank, clank of tank treads. I crawled on my stomach so as not to present a target. I could just peer over the [balcony] railing. I counted twenty-seven tanks mustering right below our quarters. Between the thick cordite and smoke and the deafening blasts and concussion, we all had headaches." In Washington, Bundy and Forrestal monitored the incoming cables. In a record of the meeting, Forrestal said the coup was coming off better than anyone expected. "Bundy then commented that Diem was still holding in the palace, adding that no one wanted to go in for the kill," the report said.

At the residence, Lodge made contact with Diem about 4:30 P.M. Vietnamese accounts said the coup leaders offered Diem safe conduct before the conversation with Lodge. Dunn was listening on the second phone and taking notes. Most histories contain Dunn's account of the exchange, with Diem demanding to know the U.S. position on the army rebellion. Lodge ducked a straight answer and tells Diem he is worried about his safety. "I have a report that those in charge of the current activity offer you and your brother safe conduct out of the country if you resign. Had you heard this?" Years later, Dunn said his memo covered only a small portion of the exchange. Diem starts off by demanding protection from the U.S. Marine battalion he knew was heading for Saigon. Lodge says he is unaware of any Marines. Diem then asks Lodge to halt the coup. Not within his power, Lodge replies. "It became intense when Lodge asked him to resign," Dunn said. Diem says Lodge has no standing to make such a request of a democratically elected president. "I am the president of the Republic of Vietnam!" he shouts. "I will never leave my people."

Lodge praises Diem for his courage but seeks to focus on his survival. "Now I am very worried about your physical safety," Lodge says.

Left out of Dunn's official memo was Lodge's offer to Diem of the ambassador's personal protection, an option that did not depend on the army generals bombarding the palace. According to Dunn, he and Lodge discussed taking Diem and Nhu to the embassy. It was the same protection Kennedy urged Diem to accept in the message carried secretly by Congressman Macdonald in September. With American flags flying, Dunn would take the embassy's Checker limousine to the palace, where he knew the rebel officers were laying siege. "I knew them, they knew me. I was the American ambassador's man." He was certain he could recover the Ngo brothers and bring them to the safety of the embassy. For a combat soldier with Dunn's background, it would have been a piece of cake. Instead, Diem refuses Lodge's offer of ambassadorial protection.

As the situation at the palace worsened, brother Nhu offered a plan to rally support outside Saigon and launch a countercoup. They could split up, one going north to the highlands while the other headed south to the Mekong Delta. "We will have a greater chance of success if we take different ways," Nhu said. "Moreover, they will not dare kill one of us if we are captured as long as the other remains free." Diem rejected the plan. They decided to leave together. Nhu assembled escape supplies. In a suitcase, he placed $1 million in large U.S. denominations. He also added eighty-eight pounds of gold in two-pound ingots. (Details of the heavy, bulging case—later seized by Big Minh—were reported to Washington in a 1964 note by Lodge to Rusk. "I advised [the military junta leader] not to make this public lest it shake confidence here in all the generals," Lodge said in a top secret letter delivered by hand.) As the palace was not fully surrounded, Diem and Nhu walked out a side gate and got into a small, unassuming French sedan.

They were driven to a home in the Chinese suburb of Cholon only twenty minutes away. They were greeted by community leader Ma Tuyen, who offered the brothers tea and chicken soup. The hospitality he showed them would later lead to prison and the confiscation of his home. A communication system was rigged so that Diem could contact coup headquarters. If the generals called back, they would think Diem and Nhu were still in the palace. Throughout the night, Diem and his aides made at least five telephone calls to coup headquarters. The generals called had no idea Diem had left the Gia Long and was hiding in Cholon. At about four A.M. November 2, a nephew of Diem called coup headquarters and asked for General Don. He refused to speak to Big Minh, and the coup leader became furious. The president, the nephew said, wanted to surrender with full honors, a graceful exit from power, and safe conduct to another country. Politely Don refused. Diem himself then called and asked for Don. He, too, refused to talk to Big Minh and was once again denied honors and safe conduct. Once more Diem called and asked for Big Minh and repeated the request. A cursing Minh hung up on Diem. On his third call, Diem agreed to surrender and asked only for safe conduct.

This time Big Minh was elated. After putting on his formal uniform, Minh organized a military convoy, including his army sedan and three jeeps. At headquarters, a large table was covered with green felt. Conein thought they were preparing a press conference with newsreel cameras to capture Diem's transfer of power to Big Minh. Conein decided to avoid the press. Before he left, Minh asked for an American plane to take Diem and Nhu into exile. "Not in the books," Conein said. "This shows direct support." Kennedy's order, sent by Rusk to Lodge, prohibited U.S. support—including aircraft—to either Diem or the rebels.

So Conein called his CIA boss, acting station chief David Smith, who raised another objection—this one from Lodge. "I assumed he talked to the ambassador," Conein said later. Lodge wanted a carefully scripted flight: If Diem and Nhu were exiled, Lodge wanted them taken initially to Saipan, where Americans could control their movements. But if asylum was granted by Japan or France, Diem and Nhu should be flown there directly without the normal refueling stops in Karachi or Rome. According to Conein, the fear was that the Ngo brothers would leave the plane, form a government in exile, and rally a countercoup. The station chief told Conein it would take twenty-four hours to get an Air Force KC-135 Stratotanker from Okinawa. It could fly nonstop to Paris, Saipan, or some other distant destination out of countercoup range that offered to take in the Ngo brothers.

When he told Big Minh of the twenty-four-hour delay, the general smiled. "That's fine," Minh said, according to Conein. With his glistening brass and colorful decorations, Minh was ready for his close-up. Some years earlier, he'd had gold-rimmed replacements installed to fill the holes in his mouth caused by Japanese pliers. His convoy pulled away, leaving Don in charge. The air went out of Big Minh's optimism when his convoy quickly learned that Diem and Nhu had fled the Gia Long Palace. "Big Minh is a very proud man, and those of you who have been to Southeast Asia know that face is very important," Conein said in secret Senate testimony in 1975. "At the last moment, he lost face, going up there in all his splendor with the sedan and everything."

In a rage, Big Minh returned to headquarters. With some but not all of the officers, he demanded a vote on killing Diem and Nhu. "The pig must die," he said in French. The rest of the debate was in Vietnamese. Some wanted to preserve Diem as well as his brother. Minh voted to kill the Ngo brothers—if he could find them.

At his hideout in Cholon, Diem knew his duplicity with Big Minh had reduced his chance for survival. Dunn saw the Saigon leader as resigned to his fate. "I think he fully expected to go down with the ship," Dunn said. That conclusion stemmed from his discussion with a German priest, Father Hans DeJager, who helped organize Chinese supporters of Diem. Because Dunn was Catholic, DeJager sought the friendship of Lodge's right hand. According to Dunn, DeJager recounted a conversation he had had with Diem hours before the coup began. "I think time has run out on us," Diem said to the priest. "The sands of time have run out, and it only remains for me to do my duty."

In the house in Cholon, Diem heard the bell from the nearby

Church of St. Francis Xavier. It was about 5:15 A.M., and the bell was calling the faithful to the Feast of the Dead—All Souls' Day for Kennedy. "We will go to Mass," Diem announced to his brother and a handful of aides. In minutes his aide, Captain Do Tho, drove a Land Rover in the darkness to the front of the rococo church. Inside, it was bright from the glow of candles. In the first Mass of the day, Father Jean Tabert led them to recall their sins, plead for forgiveness, and look forward to justice through God's mercy at the final judgment. In Latin, Father Jean intoned the Catholic liturgy: "*Dies irae, dies illa*. Day of wrath, O day of mourning."

Diem and Nhu sat in the front pew and took communion. Afterward they talked to Father Jean before adjourning to the parish priest's house. Inside, Diem made a last phone call to Lodge that never made its way into declassified U.S. documents. Mike Dunn would be forever haunted by the exchange between Lodge and Diem. Dunn revered Lodge but had an emotional tie with Diem.

"Where are you?" Lodge asked. When Diem told him he was at the church in Cholon, Lodge excused himself, left the room, and handed the phone to Dunn, who talked to Diem. "He was desperate," Dunn said. "He knew they [the generals] were going to kill him. He wanted our help." Lodge returned and again, as he had the previous afternoon, offered Diem the protection of the embassy. But there was no offer to come and get him. When the call ended, Dunn immediately pressed Lodge to let him take the embassy limousine and bring Diem and Nhu to the American compound. It was a twenty-minute trip to a location unknown by the coup soldiers.

"They're going to kill him," Dunn told Lodge.

"We can't," Lodge replied. "We can't get involved." Perhaps he was following Kennedy's last order not to support Diem once the coup started. Then again, Lodge had shrugged off White House orders all along. Once again he was making the decisions. When they learned Diem had been killed, Dunn tried to discuss the day's events with

Lodge. But Lodge cut him off, looked at his watch, and shifted the discussion to dinner with his wife and the Dunn family.

"What time are cocktails?" Lodge asked.

Over a period of many years, many meals, and many drinks, the author heard Dunn frequently defend Lodge's decision as a mistake. "I firmly believe and would swear on my mother's honor, that he never foresaw that they would assassinate him." After Lodge died in 1985, Dunn admitted Diem's death was no miscalculation. Lodge's refusal was a calculated decision to rid Kennedy of this defiant would-be priest. He described it as a gangland murder.

"It was a hit," Dunn said.

21

The Hit

B Y THE TIME GENERAL BIG Minh learned the president of South Vietnam had been in St. Francis Xavier, the yellow fa-cade was dazzling in the morning sunlight. Mike Dunn was con-vinced that when Lodge excused himself during his final talk with Ngo Dinh Diem, the American ambassador informed the coup lead-ers where Diem was. Instead, it was Diem's personal military aide who first called coup headquarters. After Lodge refused to rescue him, Diem decided to take his diminishing chances with the soldier who paved the way to his presidency nine years earlier. Father Jean had recommended seeking asylum in the French or Chinese em-bassy or just in the sanctuary of St. Francis Xavier. Instead, Diem ordered Captain Do Tho to call coup headquarters. Big Minh was out, probably searching Gia Long Palace for Diem. But General Don told Captain Tho a convoy would soon be en route for the Ngo brothers. A growing number of parishioners coming to a later Mass watched the spectacle of the convoy arrival.

An M113, the green-colored armored personnel carrier, pulled into the church courtyard following three jeeps commanded by Gen-eral Mai Huu Xuan. But it was Major Duong Hieu Nghia who did most of the talking. Inside the church, he approached Diem and Nhu. "My president," Nghia said, standing at attention and saluting. After the morning's communion service, Diem was spiritually ready for anything.

The brothers followed Nghia from the church. Outside, soldiers with rifles flanked the church door. Diem walked down the steps. An aide passed Nhu's suitcase of gold and cash to General Xuan. An arrest warrant was read. Initially, Diem and Nhu balked at orders to get into the armored carrier, knowing it was a death trap. When one soldier threatened him, Nhu flicked a half-smoked cigarette in his face. Another pulled a pistol. But Diem scowled until the soldier put his gun back into its holster. Unless they got in, harsh measures would be used, said another officer. Once the rear door of the carrier was opened, the inside was a mess of pots, pans, and clothing. Nhu complained. "Why have you come for the president in a vehicle like this?" he demanded.

"There is no more president," Nghia replied.

Nhu struggled, but Diem said, "That's enough. Let's go." Nghia made sure they bowed their heads as they got in to avoid the oval metal doorway. Their hands were tied behind their backs. The door closed and Captain Nuyen Van Nhung jumped on top as the vehicle pulled away. Nhung stood in the opening for the vehicle's machine gunner. In a scabbard on his belt, Nhung wore a Poignard-Baïonnette Lebel. The French-designed trench knife had notches on the handle. Some represented Viet Cong guerrillas. Others were victims of Big Minh's orders. When the convoy left coup headquarters, Nghia saw Big Minh flash two fingers of his right hand to Nhung. He learned later that was Big Minh's order to kill both Diem and Nhu. At Nhung's feet, Diem began to pray. Nhu began a noisy argument with Nhung and the second soldier. "I don't know what it was about," said Nghia, who heard their shouts. He was in one of three jeeps following the M113.

A few minutes later—Nghia put the time at seven A.M.—the convoy was halted at a railroad crossing by a barrier for the passing train. Although muffled by the train noise, Nghia heard pistol shots. One bullet went into the back of Diem's head. Nhu also got the coup de grace with a bullet in the base of his skull. In addition, Nhung pulled his poignard from its scabbard and stabbed Nhu again and again. General Xuan, the convoy commander, did not hear the shots or realize the brothers had been murdered until they returned to coup headquarters and the M113's rear door was open. Nhung raced up to Big Minh and saluted. "Mission accomplished," he said in French.

Later, Nhung showed up at the rue Pasteur office of the Associated Press. It had been wrecked by the fighting and Malcolm Browne was clearing out the debris. "[He] tried to sell me a picture of Diem's body," Browne said. "I turned him down partly because I could not be sure the photograph was real but mostly because I was revolted by the prospect of rewarding anyone for hawking such carrion."

Someone flashed word to Lodge from coup headquarters. It was not Conein. When he thought Big Minh would be bringing Diem and Nhu back from the palace for a power transfer at coup headquarters, Conein did not want to be there when the press arrived. He went home for a shower. "I smelled like a she-goat in heat," Conein said. He missed Big Minh's angry return from the empty palace and the vote on killing Diem.

So it may have been Big Minh or General Don—the liaison between the plotters and the U.S. embassy—who called Lodge. "I knew it very soon," Lodge said. "I mean, within minutes after he was killed I got the word. I was horrified. I was absolutely horrified. Terrible. Particularly as I had friendly feelings towards him."

If Lodge knew by eight A.M. on November 2—eight P.M. on November 1 in Washington—that Diem was dead, the cable traffic indicated he delayed telling Washington for more than four hours. From Washington at 8:47 P.M.—a day behind Saigon—Rusk cabled Lodge that Kennedy would review the situation at a morning meeting. Shortly, Rusk said, the administration would spin events for the press. "We expect to background the press this evening that this is not a coup . . . but that Diem has yielded to virtually unanimous determination of military and civilian leadership," Rusk said. "This last point is of particular importance in underlining the absurdity that this national decision could have been merely a foreigner's trick." In reply at noon in Saigon—midnight in Washington—Lodge gave no hint that Diem was dead. Instead, he said Kennedy should stress the popular outpouring for the coup. "Every Vietnamese has a grin on his face today," Lodge cabled.

Conein was home when his CIA boss called saying the "highest authority"—that meant Kennedy—wanted to know about the whereabouts of Diem and Nhu. There were telephone communications between Saigon and Washington. Perhaps Lodge telephoned Rusk or the White House when coup leaders told him Diem was dead. In turn, the CIA was ordered to find out and called Conein at home. He raced back to coup headquarters. Big Minh told Conein that the Ngo brothers had committed suicide. Conein, a Catholic, knew the Catholic brothers would never commit suicide, a prohibition of the church. He filed the first report on the assassination that arrived in Washington at 12:24 A.M.—the start of November 2. "Best estimate this time is that Diem and Nhu are dead," said the CIA cable based on Conein's report. At 2:55 A.M., Harriman sent Lodge a cable asking for confirmation of suicides. "Generals must preserve to extent possible good reputation for their actions have thus far created," Harriman said. "Therefore, important to establish publicly beyond question that deaths actually suicide if this true and not by violence." Kennedy was in bed when Conein's first report arrived. McGeorge Bundy decided not to wake him.

Kennedy began November 2 with an off-the-record meeting at 9:35 A.M. Waiting for the president when he arrived were Harriman, Hilsman, and Forrestal. They had laid the foundation for Kennedy's decision to oust Diem. The leading opponents of the coup—McNamara, Taylor, McCone, and Bobby—were also there. Lodge had replied to Harriman's request for confirmation. It arrived at seven A.M. "Very reliable sources give following story about the death of Diem and Nhu," the Lodge cable began. Forrestal took a copy and handed it to Kennedy. The president read it and the color left his face. Pale, without a word, he stood and rushed from the Cabinet Room. To see their leader so shaken rattled the assembled advisers. Thoughts raced through their minds. General Taylor thought Kennedy should not have been surprised.

"What did he expect," Taylor said to himself.

Epilogue

WASHINGTON

THE MURDER OF NGO DINH Diem quickly ended David Halberstam's criticism of President Kennedy's policy in Vietnam. The Saigon bureau chief of the *New York Times* personally disliked Diem, and his one-sided reporting often angered Kennedy. Two days after Diem's overthrow, Halberstam was upbeat. "For the moment, the Americans are gratified by a sense of joy in Saigon," Halberstam reported November 4. His report reflected Lodge's exultation of "joy in the streets." The same day, Lodge cabled Kennedy, "We should not overlook what this coup can mean in the way of shortening the war and enabling Americans to come home."

But Halberstam and Lodge could not lift Kennedy's spirits on that overcast November 4 in the Oval Office. The president was full of misgivings about his decisions that led to a bullet in the head for the president of South Vietnam as he squatted, hands tied behind his back, in an armored personnel carrier. The news photo of Diem's blood-caked corpse sickened him. While he worried that Diem would be killed, Kennedy did nothing during the turmoil of the coup to ensure his safe exile. There was a touch of grief in his voice—his voice thickened—as he spoke into his office dictation machine on November 4. He knew Diem, saw an inner strength in Diem's dark eyes, and remembered the ticker-tape parade in New York City for the anticommunist miracle man.

"I was shocked by the death of Diem and Nhu," Kennedy said. "I'd met Diem with [Supreme Court] Justice Douglas many years ago. He was an extraordinary character. While he became increasingly difficult in the last months, nevertheless, over a ten-year period, he'd held his country together, maintained its independence under very adverse conditions. The way he was killed made it particularly abhorrent."

Not far from where Kennedy was sitting, press secretary Pierre Salinger was telling reporters the administration did not oppose the coup, but that it was the Saigon generals—not Kennedy—who fomented the overthrow and lost control at the end when "trigger-happy" soldiers killed Diem and Nhu. The same story was handed out by Rusk to Congress.

Kennedy was dictating a different version that would remain unheard for forty-nine years. "I feel that we must bear a good deal of responsibility for it beginning with our cable in early August in which we suggested a coup," Kennedy said. "In my judgment, that wire was badly drafted. It never should have been sent on a Saturday. I should not have given my consent to it without a roundtable conference in which McNamara and Taylor could have presented their views. That first wire encouraged Lodge along a course to which he was anyway inclined." Kennedy ticked off supporters and opponents of Diem's overthrow. "It culminated three months of conversation about a coup, a conversation that divided the government here and in Saigon." Without unanimity among his advisers, it fell to Kennedy to make the final decision. He was brooding about it when three-year-old John-John and six-year-old Caroline came shrieking into his office. A welcome diversion, they playfully added their voices to the Dictaphone. "Naughty, naughty," John-John said at one point.

At his farm in Gettysburg, Pennsylvania, Eisenhower shook his head over grisly newspaper photographs of the bloodstained Diem on the floor of the armored personnel carrier. From CIA chief Mc-Cone, Ike knew the extent of Kennedy's involvement in the events that led to the death of a man he greatly admired.

"No matter how much the [Kennedy] administration had differed with him," Eisenhower said in a November 11 letter, "I cannot believe any American would have approved the cold-blooded killing of a man who had, after all, shown great courage when he undertook the task some years ago of defeating [the] communist attempt to take over his country."

Eisenhower was responding to a note from his vice president. "I think our complicity in Diem's murder was a national disgrace," Nixon had written on November 5. A decade later, as president, with a particularly Nixonian flair, he sought to remind Americans of Kennedy's complicity: A cable intimating Kennedy's involvement was forged and leaked to *Life* magazine but never published. The bogus document was one more footnote in the Watergate scandal.

Eisenhower's anger over Kennedy's role in Diem's murder could possibly have fueled a Republican investigation of the administration's role in the Saigon coup, which would have opened a line of attack for Goldwater and others during the 1964 presidential campaign.

Kennedy's cover story was dented in Los Angeles where "that bitch," Madame Nhu, portrayed the coup as an American-inspired betrayal. "The Nhu family has been treacherously killed," she told reporters. "That will only be the beginning of the story." As for the Saigon generals—"incited and backed by Americans, official or not"—she forecast an incompetent junta. "For how long will they hold power—if they ever hold power?"

Any Senate investigation of the coup would likely invite Gordon Cox to testify. He was the Canadian member of Vietnam International Control Commission, which was created to supervise both Hanoi and Saigon as part of the 1954 peace treaty. Cox was an important supporter of Diem, and after the assassination blasted the United

States. According to Cox, the coup was engineered by the Americans, who also directed the execution of Diem and Nhu. "The coup is an absolute catastrophe which will lead to the communist takeover of Vietnam," Cox said. Secretary Rusk filed a formal protest with the Canadian government over Cox's outburst.

Where history would rank the 35th president of the United States was important to Kennedy. He had retained on his staff a Pulitzer Prize–winning historian—Arthur Schlesinger Jr.—to establish a baseline. "Put that in the book," Kennedy told Schlesinger after more than one event. But Schlesinger was not privy to many meetings where Kennedy made decisions hidden from the world. *A Thousand Days*, Schlesinger's account of Kennedy's thirty-five months in office, contained little of the reality of the Cuban missile crisis, the bugging of Martin Luther King, or the instigation of the coup and the death of Diem. His closest aides had no idea Kennedy was bequeathing to posterity tape recordings he personally engineered, turning on and off microphones at moments he considered important during high and low moments of his presidency. Kennedy's confession of culpability in the assassination of Diem was a glimpse of a man being painfully honest with himself, if not with American voters. Diem's ham-handed suppression of Buddhist protestors had triggered a political backlash just as Kennedy was preparing for his 1964 reelection campaign. Diem "became increasingly difficult" by ignoring the political backlash against Kennedy. Kennedy was explicit in August that nothing should happen to the Ngo brothers. And in September he did try to warn Diem through Congressman Macdonald. But his order to Lodge prohibiting help for Diem after the coup began contained no exception to prevent Diem's assassination. When Lodge objected to the ban, Kennedy's order was amended to mean a ban of U.S. military assistance to either side once the coup got under way. Lodge also raised the question as to whether U.S. aircraft could be used to fly Diem to safety. There is no record of Kennedy's reaction to plans for Diem to enter exile, only of his attitude about asylum for the coup plotters. Instead, the cables in the last hours were more concerned about the safety of the Reverend Tri Quang, the Buddhist leader who vowed to overthrow the Diem government. He "is of course to come and go as he pleases," Rusk told Lodge the day the coup started.

Perhaps Kennedy had Diem's safety in mind when Rusk sent a cable to Lodge to remind the coup leaders to behave. "Following are points we hope the Generals will bear in mind," Rusk said. "Safe passage for family to exile." No mention of Diem and Nhu. It could have meant Nhu's children, who were later flown to Italy. The reminder was too late anyway. It was timed out in Washington at 6:53 P.M.— 6:53 A.M. in Saigon. Seven minutes later the Ngo brothers were dead. CIA agent Rufus Phillips, who regretted his role in the downfall of Diem, thought the assassination could easily have been avoided. "Just require Diem's safety as a condition of U.S. recognition of the new government," Phillips said. This was never mentioned in cables between Washington and Saigon. The absence of presidential direction may have affected Lodge's final decision. In the end, Lodge threw Diem and his brother to the wolves.

In orchestrating the coup, Kennedy overrode top military advisers who warned the loss of Diem would weaken the war against Hanoi's communist aggression. These thoughts were with him on a gray Monday in the Oval Office as he dictated. "The question now is, Can the generals stay together and build a stable government?" Kennedy said. It was a legitimate worry. Lodge had cabled that day—two days after Diem's murder—that the generals were arguing over the composition of the junta government. Major General Ton That Dinh, the man Kennedy bribed to stage the coup, wanted to be minister of the interior, over the strong objections of others. And there were bitter complaints from the formidable General Nguyen Khanh. "General Khanh's only stipulation for joining the coup was that the President not be killed," Lodge cabled. One of Diem's last requests was relayed to General Khanh by the president's military aide. Khanh had come to Diem's side in the 1960 attempted coup. "Tell Khanh to avenge me," Diem said as he fled to Cholon with Captain Do Tho.

A week later, Kennedy was in a brighter mood as he made plans for his 1964 reelection campaign. The Democratic National Convention would be in Atlantic City, a gift to New Jersey supporters, who consistently put the Garden State in the Democratic presidential column. George Stevens Jr. would produce the films for the convention. "The guy is fantastic," Kennedy said. "These should be made in color. They come over TV in black and white. But they will come over NBC in color. I don't know how expensive it is. But color at the convention is damn good if you do it right." A film biography would feature his family and clips from his inaugural, West Berlin, Dublin, and American University speeches. Khrushchev might even have a cameo in the portion on the Cuban missile crisis. Then the film would show personal moments along Cape Cod with John-John, Caroline, and Jackie.

More fundamental was Kennedy's search for just the right issues to be the focus of his campaign. "What can we do to make them decide to vote for us, the Democrats and Kennedy?" Kennedy told his political advisers. "What is it we have to sell them?" Prosperity for the average voter? "We hope we have to sell them prosperity, but he's not very prosperous. And the people who really are well off hate our guts. I am trying to think what else. Like Negroes." Then again, his campaign for civil rights was hurting him with voters in the South and the North where African-Americans were moving into all-white neighborhoods for the first time. Kennedy had misgivings about making that a campaign issue. Civil rights as a campaign issue was quickly discarded. "We're the ones who are shoving Negroes down their throat," Kennedy said. Also off the list was Vietnam. Kennedy anticipated pressure from both Democrats and Republicans on the 1964 campaign trail. With Diem dead, Senate Majority Leader Mansfield was ready to push for total withdrawal from Vietnam. It could become a liberal cause in Atlantic City. Senator Goldwater, the likely GOP presidential candidate in 1964, was leading Republican criticism of the overthrow of Diem and of losing ground in the war against the communists.

So despicable was Diem's execution that Kennedy was planning to offer up Henry Cabot Lodge Jr. as a sacrifice to stanch political outrage over American foreign policy in Vietnam, just as former president Eisenhower had predicted. Kennedy set Lodge up for the fall with a note of gushing praise for his total control of events in Saigon. Kennedy would spring the trap when Lodge arrived in the Oval Office on November 25. Brother Bobby looked forward to Lodge's demise. "Henry Cabot Lodge was being brought back—and the president discussed with me in detail how he could be fired—because he would not communicate," said Bobby in 1965. In fact, his brother was against overthrowing Diem, Bobby said. "The person who really did that was Henry Cabot Lodge." Lodge's political antennae sensed the possibility in Saigon. "They're going to try to blame this on me," Lodge told Bob Healy, a reporter for the *Boston Globe* who flew to Saigon after Diem's assassination. "Equally absurd is the statement [that] the president did not know that a coup was coming," Lodge said. "He was thoroughly informed about everything." As Diem was buried, Lodge's image was enhanced by the media as a patriotic Republican, a straight shooter rising above lies and treachery. In Saigon, he was above the partisan fray at home, where fellow progressives were organizing a stop Barry Goldwater drive. The Arizona conservative was working to lock up the 1964 GOP presidential nomination. In Saigon, Lodge was in a prominent but politically neutral situation, similar to that of General Eisenhower when Lodge had induced him to run for the presidency. Eisenhower, reluctant to leave his post in Paris as the Supreme Commander Allied Expeditionary Force, became a candidate only after winning the Minnesota primary in 1952 as a write-in candidate. Senator Lodge orchestrated the upset victory before steamrollering conservative opponents of

Eisenhower. Lodge planned on meeting with Ike after seeing Kennedy on Monday morning, November 25. Perhaps a write-in candidacy in some primary might work for him as it did Ike.

On the afternoon of November 22—the clock atop the Texas School Book Depository said 12:30 P.M.—many in Dealey Plaza thought they heard firecrackers. Not Merriman Smith of United Press International. He was riding eighty yards behind Kennedy's limousine, part of the official convoy in the designated wire service car equipped with a radiotelephone. Smith was a hunter and a marksman. To him, the overhead *pop*, pause, *pop, pop* that interrupted the applause and cheers for Kennedy were unmistakable. "Those are shots," Smith said to the driver and three other newsmen in the rear seat. They all were jerked back in their seats as the motorcade hurtled out of Dealey.

Smith picked up the radiotelephone and gave the operator the number of the Dallas UPI bureau. Around the world, teletype machines rang five bells as Smith's bulletin told anchormen and editors:

THREE SHOTS WERE FIRED AT PRESIDENT KENNEDY'S MOTORCADE IN DOWNTOWN DALLAS.

The teletype operator timed it off at 12:34 P.M.—four minutes after Lee Harvey Oswald fired from the sixth floor of the depository. In the backseat of the wire car, Jack Bell of the Associated Press heard his competitor dictating an earthshaker of a news report. The wire car was now doing ninety to keep up with the Kennedy limo. Bell reached over Smith's shoulder and said, "Give me that goddamned phone." Smith refused, saying the Dallas bureau had trouble hearing him. He leaned over the phone. Bell began hitting him on the back. Smith threw the phone at Bell as the wire car pulled into the emergency entrance at Parkland Hospital. Smith got out and walked over to Kennedy's open car. Jacqueline Kennedy had the president in her lap in a puddle of blood and brains. Secret Service agent Clint Hill was covering Kennedy with his coat as Smith walked up. "How badly was he hit, Clint?" Smith said. "He's dead, Smitty," Hill answered. Smith walked into the emergency room and got on the phone. Now fifteen bells rang on global teletype machines to herald a flash.

FLASH FLASH KENNEDY SERIOUSLY WOUNDED, PERHAPS FATALLY BY ASSASSINS BULLETS.

That was timed off at 12:39 P.M. By 12:41, Smith had dictated a full story that newspapers could use. A generation would remember exactly what they were doing when they heard Smith's news. So far nothing had appeared on the AP wire because of Bell's bumbling. Smith did not stick around after the formal 1:40 P.M. announcement of Kennedy's death. He had raced to Air Force One at Love Field to witness Lyndon Johnson being sworn in as the 36th president of the United States. Bell and the AP missed that, too.

In France, it was 7:30 P.M. when Kennedy was killed. In a Paris hotel, CIA agent Néstor Sánchez handed over Dr. Edward Gunn's fabulous Paper Mate. With a click, the ballpoint pen would extend a syringe so fine that Fidel Castro would barely feel the injection of poison. The CIA's Dr. Do Harm recommended Black Leaf 40, a commonly available insecticide with a lethal dose of nicotine. The man willing to assassinate Castro, Major Rolando Cubela Secades, was not impressed with the Paper Mate or Black Leaf 40. "Cubela didn't think much of the pen," Sánchez reported. As a medical doctor, he could come up with a better poison and delivery system, Cubela said. What he really wanted were twenty hand grenades, two high-powered rifles with telescopic sights, and twenty pounds of C4 plastic explosive. Yet he put the Paper Mate in his pocket. The syringe was empty. As they left the hotel meeting, they learned of Kennedy's assassination. "Cubela was visibly moved," Sanchez said. The man who had been recruited to kill Castro looked at Sanchez and said, "Why do such things happen to good people?" Three years later, Cubela was arrested and the Cuban police seized his CIA-supplied rifle mounted with a 4×40 scope. He was sentenced to death by firing squad. Castro called for leniency. Cubela's sentenced was reduced to twenty-five years in jail. But he was released after ten years and then emigrated to Spain.

Two days after Kennedy's death, President Johnson told the architects of U.S. policy in Vietnam they had produced a disaster. "This was a mistake," Johnson said of the Diem overthrow. "This was a decision we did not have to make." Johnson was opposed to the overthrow of Diem, didn't care for Harriman and Hilsman's campaign for the coup, personally disliked Lodge, and thought it stupid to push demands for democratic reforms on Vietnam. Johnson laid out his feelings to Rusk, McNamara, McCone, Lodge, and McGeorge Bundy who took notes at the 3:00 P.M. meeting in the Executive Office Building. The meeting started off with an upbeat assessment by Lodge, who showed photographs of Saigon celebrations after Diem's death. He gave "the impression that we are on the road to victory," Bundy said. Setting what Bundy called a new "tone," Johnson unloaded. The new president noted misgivings about the coup and "strong voices" in Congress for withdrawal from Vietnam. This had caused Johnson considerable concern, and "he was not at all sure we took the right course in upsetting the Diem regime." Bundy noted the inference: Johnson would not have supported the action, which led to the coup. Yet he was resigned to the situation. "It was a fait accompli" to Johnson. In his account of the meeting, the ex-Harvard dean probably chose to put this French phrase in the mouth of the West Texan. From his service with Lodge in the Senate, Johnson knew the Saigon ambassador to be easily bored with the grind of duty, often outright lazy, with a very short attention span. "He ain't worth a damn," Johnson would say later. "He can't work with anybody." Even so, Johnson would reappoint Lodge to the Saigon post two years later in hopes of winning Republican support in Congress—just as Kennedy had done.

At the November 24 meeting, Johnson focused on the chaos at the embassy in Saigon. "The president then stated he has never been happy with our operations in Vietnam," Bundy noted. "He said there had been serious dissension and divisions within the American community and he told the ambassador that he was in total charge and wanted the situation cleaned up." Johnson knew Lodge cut General Harkins out of all the cables leading up to Diem's overthrow. He wanted an end to bickering and urged the ouster of anyone who failed to conform to policy. "The president was holding the ambassador personally responsible," Bundy said. Soon after the meeting, Johnson ordered Harriman excluded from policy decisions about Vietnam. And he triggered a competition between Rusk and Undersecretary George Ball as to who would fire Hilsman, the assistant secretary of state for the Far East.

Almost instantly, the news from the battlefield in Vietnam went from bad to worse. With the death of Diem, the Viet Cong guerrillas, surging throughout South Vietnam during 1963, increased their offensive operations. Hanoi, astounded at the execution of its archenemy, made dramatic military inroads as an important obstacle to the Viet Cong—the Strategic Hamlet Program—was abandoned. In the first ninety days after Diem's death, the Viet Cong destroyed seventy-five strategic hamlets in Binh Dinh province alone. "They were gifts from heaven for us," said Nguyen Huu Tho, chairman of the National Liberation Front, the Viet Cong political group. "Our enemy has been seriously weakened from all points of view—military, political, and administrative." To the U.S. military commander in Saigon, the Viet Cong upsurge went unchallenged as the new junta scrambled for control. "While it cannot be directly linked, unusual pattern of VC attacks reported in Vinh Long," General Harkins reported the day Diem was killed. The Viet Cong, staged a truly massive attack—two hundred guerrillas wearing blue uniforms—to overrun Strategic Hamlets in the province.

Two months after Diem's assassination, Khanh moved to avenge Diem's death. He arrested Big Minh, Tran Van Don, and Ton That Dinh—leaders of the Diem overthrow—in a January 30 bloodless coup. Khanh also arrested Nhung, the military aide to Big Minh who had killed Diem and Nhu. Nhung, it was announced, committed suicide in his cell. In reality, Khanh personally executed Nhung. "He just took him out and shot him," said Colby of the CIA. "There's no doubt about it."

Lodge shifted easily from Big Minh, who was once the solution to Diem, to Khanh, who seemed to be more determined to take on the Viet Cong. Two days after the second coup, Lodge told the new president that the thirty-six-year-old Khanh was able. With American military aid and increasing Saigon army forces, the new junta leader had only to press the fight. "This requires a tough, ruthless commander," Lodge cabled on February 1. "Perhaps Khanh is it." A month later, Johnson was told Khanh and the Saigon army were on the verge of defeat. The grim outlook came from McNamara, who had told Kennedy six months earlier that victory was likely in 1965. "The situation has unquestionably been growing worse at least since September," McNamara told Johnson in a March 16 report. Half of South Vietnam was under Viet Cong control, and in some provinces, 75 to 90 percent were dominated by Hanoi's guerrilla force. The Saigon army was beset by desertions and draft dodgers, while South Vietnamese were joining the Viet Cong at record rates. Popular support for Hanoi was growing while "large groups of the population are now showing apathy and indifference." Diem, who once brandished his telephone as his weapon to keep the province chiefs in line, had taken a working infrastructure with him to the grave. "The political control structure extending from Saigon down into the hamlets disappeared following the November coup [against Diem]," McNamara told Johnson.

The president's options, McNamara outlined, were a deeper commitment to a prolonged ground war or the neutralization of South

Vietnam, which, he said, was the same as turning Saigon over to communist Hanoi. With Johnson's approval, Army General Earle Wheeler, chairman of the Joint Chiefs of Staff, began planning an American air war against North Vietnam. Those plans blossomed into Operation Pierce Arrow. U.S. warplanes bombed North Vietnam in retaliation for what Johnson called "a new and grave turn" with Hanoi's August 2, 1964, attack on the destroyer USS *Maddox* in the Gulf of Tonkin. One carrier pilot, Lieutenant JG Everett Alvarez Jr., was shot down and captured August 5. He was held prisoner for eight years. Years later, it was established that U.S. warships provoked Hanoi. Instead of innocent patrols, the USS *Maddox* was on spy missions and supporting secret Saigon attacks on North Vietnam island and coastal military installations. At the time, American voters and Congress were told it was a provocation by Hanoi. And both the House and Senate approved a joint resolution "to promote the maintenance of international peace."

Johnson used it as a license for an unlimited war on Hanoi without resort to nuclear weapons. Senator Mansfield, who had succeeded Johnson as the majority leader, tried to get the president to think twice. Two weeks after Johnson took office, Mansfield warned that with Diem gone, the United States risked committing ground troops to a jungle war. "What national interests in Asia would steel the American people for that massive costs of ever-deepening involvement of that kind?" Mansfield wrote. He reminded Johnson that Eisenhower won political support by negotiating an end to the Korean War in 1953, not by expanding it. He urged Johnson to enlist Russia, France, and Britain in a new Vietnam peace conference. Johnson's answer was to order his staff to come up with a point-by-point refutation of Mansfield's letter.

While Vietnam threatened to be a campaign problem for Kennedy in 1964, it vanished as an issue for Johnson in the presidential race with Republican Arizona senator Goldwater. One reason was that Goldwater refused to make it an issue. After the party conventions,

Goldwater met secretly with Johnson. "I do believe it is in the best interest of the United States not to make the Vietnam War a political issue," he told Johnson. "I've come to promise I will not do so." In exchange, Goldwater asked Johnson not to challenge the Republican's stance on civil rights. "We shook hands. I kept my promises and Lyndon Johnson kept his." Goldwater carried Arizona and the Bible Belt—Louisiana, Mississippi, Alabama, Georgia, and South Carolina. Johnson carried the rest in what remains the third largest landslide in U.S. history. At the time of the secret deal, Goldwater knew he had no chance. Goldwater blamed his loss on attacks on him by the moderate wing of the Republican Party led by Henry Cabot Lodge. In a surprise upset, Lodge won the New Hampshire presidential primary with a noncampaign in Saigon. He would fly to Manila and other cities to make phone calls to political supporters. Lodge's presidential ambitions were doused by a defeat in the Oregon primary by New York governor Nelson Rockefeller.

In the White House, the war in Vietnam preoccupied the newly elected president. As the Saigon government and its army disintegrated, Johnson more and more saw the killing of Diem as the cause of all his problems. Saigon's collapse was forcing the United States to take over the fight. Johnson's frustrations grew after hearing Saigon's 200,000-man army was being defeated by 34,000 Viet Cong. "How can 34,000 lick 200,000?" Johnson asked. If Saigon's army refused to take on the communists, perhaps he could threaten U.S. withdrawal. "Why not say, 'This is it!' " Johnson said. "Not send Johnson City [Texas] boys out to die if they [are] acting as they are." General Taylor, who had replaced Lodge as ambassador to South Vietnam, was in Washington to hand-deliver the bad news at a December 1, 1964, meeting. "[It] won't collapse immediately, but [it is] a losing game," Taylor said of the Saigon government.

"How did Diem do it?" Johnson asked. "[He] ran a tight ship," Taylor replied. "We could have kept Diem," Johnson said, adding later that Taylor should "create another Diem." The president was resigned to spending more on Saigon army equipment and training. "[We do] not want to send the widow woman to slap Jack Dempsey," Johnson said. "[The] day of reckoning is coming." Instead of following advice from Mansfield and Undersecretary of State George Ball to negotiate the United States out of Vietnam, Johnson deferred to General Eisenhower. Without some clear success on the battlefield, Ike told Johnson that it would be a mistake to seek talks with Hanoi with a weak hand. It would be up to the Saigon army to halt Viet Cong infiltration. "We can, however, play a major role in destroying the will of the enemy to continue the war," Ike said. It was advice that led to Johnson's day of reckoning as he ordered more bombing—Operation Rolling Thunder—of North Vietnam. What Johnson got was more political turmoil in Saigon. General Nguyen Cao Ky, the flashy chief of the Saigon air force with a playboy reputation, became the third junta leader. "Hot damn, I'm getting sick and tired of this goddamn coup shit in Vietnam," Johnson told an aide. "It's got to stop."

By 1965, the Saigon army had collapsed to the point where it could not provide perimeter defense for the American-supported air base in Da Nang. U.S. Marines waded ashore on Red Beach March 8. The 3,500 infantrymen were greeted by women with leis and signs: "Welcome, Gallant Marines." To Maxwell Taylor, who had replaced Lodge as ambassador, the Marines were the "nose of the camel under the tent." They were the first of 8 million Americans who came and went in the Vietnam Theater of Operations over the next decade.

Under the Johnson and Nixon administrations, 58,209 Americans were killed—almost an even division. Another 211,454 were wounded by punji sticks, old women and boys planting booby traps, and raggedy-ass little bastards with a ferocious perseverance that only Diem understood. When some of the wounded came home to the United States without arms or legs or faces or genitals, they were despised by many as war criminals. Some were. U.S. Army Lieutenant William "Rusty" Calley's platoon massacred at least 600 old men, women, children and infants in My Lai. His men were in a rage at the death of a popular sergeant killed by a booby trap set near the village.

This happened in 1968, a year later marked by Army psychiatrists as the end of the "good" war. Before 1968, soldiers saluted, followed orders and sought to defend villagers against the communist threat. After that the "bad war" began, when soldiers—many drugged on heroin and marijuana—would kill an unpopular commander. A hand grenade rolled into an officer's tent became known as a fragging. American grassroots opposition to the war dramatically affected troops in the field. It shredded the morale of many of the 539,000 men and women in the country in 1969. Many officers, such as Army Lieutenant Colonel Alexander Haig, would spend one year in the country, get his ticket punched and leave. Haig wound up working for Henry Kissinger at the White House, where he would tell President Richard Nixon—and me, for that matter—that there would be victory in Vietnam.

The real warriors, such as Major H. Norman Schwarzkopf Jr., would spend tour after tour getting wounded four times in one firefight, earning two Silver Stars for bravery. "I hated Vietnam," Schwarzkopf said. "I hated what it did to the army." In 1992, he led the massive Desert Storm army to victory in Kuwait and ticker-tape parades down Broadway.

By 1966, Johnson was sounding as if he was locked in a back room at the Hanoi Hilton with other American prisoners of the Vietnam War. There were 385,000 American troops in Vietnam, and Johnson was being pressured to send more. Killed so far were 8,494 Americans, and thousands more were wounded. As more Democrats in Congress joined Senator Mansfield in calling for a withdrawal of American troops, Johnson described his plight to Senator Eugene McCarthy. The Minnesota Democratic-Farmer-Labor liberal was one of Johnson's few personal friends from his Senate days. The president spoke as if his will was being broken by Hanoi and the *New York Times.*

"Well, I know we oughtn't to be there, but I can't get out," Johnson told McCarthy on February l, 1966. "I just can't be the architect of surrender. I'm willing to do damn near anything. I am willing to do near anything a human can do if I can do it with any honor at all. But they don't have the pressure on them to bring them to the table as of yet. We don't know if they ever will.

"They started with me on Diem, you remember? He was corrupt and he ought to be killed. So we killed him. We all got together and got a goddamned bunch of thugs and we went in and assassinated him. Now we really have no political stability since then." He was aiming for a settlement through the United Nations once Hanoi buckled to his policy of "attrition." More North Vietnamese would be killed than American losses, which were soaring. Trouble was, Johnson explained, Hanoi was convinced they would win. "They got it, and they know it," Johnson told McCarthy.

"The most helpful thing they have is the belief that I have more problems on my hands than Ho [Chi Minh, the premier of North Vietnam] has on his. And I have the *New York Times*. It's awful hard to have a foreign policy they don't approve of." He described how his critics were elevated by the newspaper with stories that "have four dirty cracks against me. And they've [Hanoi] got it made. It has a hell of an effect." In a background meeting with reporters, Johnson famously explained how Hanoi was ignoring American feelers for negotiations to end the conflict. Through a variety of diplomatic avenues, he sought Hanoi's approval for an exit that would somehow leave South Vietnam an independent country. He was listening for a reply, he told a group of reporters who asked him about signals from Hanoi.

"Signals?" Johnson shot back. "I'll tell you about signals. I got my antenna out in Washington. I got my antenna out in London. I got my antenna out in Paris. I got my antenna out in Tokyo. I even got my antenna out in Rangoon. You know what signals all my antennae are picking up from Hanoi?" The newsmen became silent as

Johnson scanned their faces. "I'll tell you what the signals from Hanoi are saying: 'Fuck you, Lyndon Johnson.'"

Johnson took one body blow after another as the nation divided over a war they saw nightly on television. Parents with sons old enough to be forced into military service—the draft—were early opponents to the Vietnam War. Not far behind were their children and college students. Some fled to Canada to dodge the draft. As the war continued, the draft's inequities became the heart of antiwar demonstrations in which draft cards were burned. Those with resources, such as Richard B. Cheney engineered deferments to avoid combat in Vietnam. As a White House adviser, congressman, secretary of defense, and vice president, Cheney consistently favored sending Americans into war. Cheney was frequently criticized as a "chicken hawk." Another American vice president, Dan Quayle, used family connections to win a spot in what was then a safe haven, the National Guard. George W. Bush, who would become the 43rd president of the United States, enlisted in the Texas National Guard in 1968. He sat out Vietnam in Houston and Montgomery, Alabama. The rich went to one graduate school after another. African-Americans and poor whites answered the call.

Johnson at one point went to see off a unit of the 82nd Airborne at Fort Bragg. "About 50 percent of them were Negroes," Johnson said. "I understand they volunteered because of the high morale in the Airborne and the extra pay. Those boys expressed no sentiment, but it was obvious to me that none of them was happy to be going." Perhaps because he struggled with poverty as a boy, Johnson had a deeper feeling for the plight of African-Americans than most of his Democratic predecessors. Within eight months of assuming the presidency, Johnson manipulated the House of Representatives and enlisted Senate Republicans to pass the landmark civil rights legislation that was beyond Kennedy's legislative skills.

"Let us close the springs of racial poison," Johnson said at the ceremony marking the signing of the bill. He shook hands and gave a memorial pen to King. The exchange was watched by Hoover and his boss, Robert Kennedy, the attorney general. They also attended the ceremony. With Johnson's approval, the FBI would continue its surveillance of King until April 4, 1968, the day he was assassinated in Memphis, Tennessee. Before he was killed, King made the civil rights movement one of the leading opponents of Johnson's war in Vietnam. "If America's soul become totally poisoned, part of the autopsy must read 'Vietnam,'" King said in 1967.

King reflected the black community's anger over the disproportionate use of their sons and husbands.

Blacks were suffering high casualty rates in Vietnam, and in 1965 alone they comprised almost one out of every four combat deaths. With the draft increasing calls for more soldiers, the Pentagon significantly lowered its admission standards. In October 1966, McNamara launched Project 100,000, which further lowered military standards for 100,000 additional draftees per year. McNamara claimed this program would provide valuable training, skills, and opportunity to America's poor—a promise that was never carried out. Many black men who had previously been ineligible could now be drafted, along with many poor and racially intolerant white men from Southern states. The number of U.S. military personnel in Vietnam jumped from 23,300 in 1965 to 465,600 by the end of 1967. Between October 1966 and June 1969, 246,000 soldiers were recruited through Project 100,000, of which 41 percent were black, while blacks made up only about 11 percent of the population.

Passage of the civil rights law was achievement enough for any president. But Johnson's domestic record rivaled that of Franklin Delano Roosevelt. By 1965, Johnson had signed into law Medicare for the elderly and Medicaid for the poor. Other progressive legislation would clear the air and the water in U.S. cities and set safety standards for automobiles, leading to the lifesaving cars of today. All this was blotted out by Johnson's handling of the Vietnam War. In the end, Vietnam ended his hopes for a second full four-year term in the 1968 presidential election.

Johnson saw himself a victim of media attacks. "They call me a murderer," he told one Senate colleague. "But Ho [Chi Minh] has a great image. I wish Mike [Mansfield] would make a speech about Ho Chi Minh."

Despite their friendship, McCarthy would lead the nation's opposition to the war and Johnson's presidency. Hanoi's massive attack on South Vietnam's cities launched on January 30, 1968, the Tet Offensive, forever ended Washington's talk of victory. McCarthy made a strong second-place showing against Johnson in the March 12, 1968, New Hampshire primary. The media turned McCarthy's defeat into a "moral victory." New York senator Robert F. Kennedy soon announced he, too, would challenge Johnson for the presidential nomination. Nineteen days later, Johnson echoed Lincoln in describing the nation as a house divided—"a house that cannot stand." He shocked the American political establishment by announcing he would not run for reelection to a second term.

Only a few knew of Johnson's plans to withdraw. One was Senator Mansfield, who sat through an evening at the White House as Johnson went over his speech. Mansfield had only a low-key response to Johnson's dramatic gesture. "I couldn't get out of there soon enough," Mansfield said. His inability to sway Johnson or Kennedy out of military solutions to Vietnam would forever haunt him. Mansfield became the center of the debate about whether Kennedy would have sent combat troops to Vietnam.

"He told me he would get out of Vietnam, a complete withdrawal," Mansfield said. "But he said, 'Mike, I can't do it until after I am reelected [in 1964].' I believed him." And I believed Mansfield. But events swept away Kennedy's promises. In eliminating the Diem government, Kennedy created the first of a series of military juntas that followed Washington orders until Hanoi's army rolled into Saigon and changed its name to Ho Chi Minh City. The predicted instability of military governors came on schedule. There were four changes of government in Saigon as the generals and colonels staged coup after coup.

Would the reelected Kennedy have withdrawn as the Saigon army folded? His closest adviser, his brother Bobby, repeatedly said no. Rather than abandon the field to the communists, Bobby, McNamara, Rusk, and other Kennedy appointees said Jack would never have left Saigon undefended. However, Roswell Gilpatric, number two at the Pentagon, saw Kennedy as steadily opposed to sending combat troops and against a deeper and more costly commitment. But confronted with the collapse of the infrastructure that followed Diem's overthrow and a more aggressive Hanoi, Gilpatric said he was uncertain if Kennedy would have made the same decisions as his successor. "No one can say what he would have done, but my view is that consistent with everything he did and said before his death, he would have been reluctant to involve ourselves to the extent the country did after President Johnson took over," Gilpatric said.

As Kennedy's spirit was lifted to elsewhere—he was a believer in the soul's immortality—he wound up in a pantheon where few presidents reside. Myth overtook reality. One debate that would intensify as millions died in Vietnam and American society divided in bitterness was Kennedy was ready to withdraw when he was struck down. Oliver Stone's ludicrous film *JFK* had Vice President Johnson killing Kennedy to thwart such a withdrawal. As did "eyeball-to-eyeball," another myth was inserted in the American psyche.

Kennedy's order to get rid of Diem was the real beginning of the American war in Vietnam. My viewpoint is shared by the three men most bloodstained from that war who consistently opposed Kennedy's decision to replace the mandarinate with a series of hapless military juntas. One was Robert Strange McNamara. He warned Kennedy the coup would lead to chaos. Yet McNamara led the American military to a stupendous defeat while unleashing strategic bombers that dropped three times more tonnage on North Vietnam than all the bombs in Europe and the Pacific during World War II. He estimated that between 2 million and 3 million Vietnamese died, North and South. He became a haunted relic of Vietnam, refusing to leave Washington, coauthoring books and appearing in films. At one point, he admitted knowing in 1965 that the war was hopeless. Still, he kept up the pressure for more troops and more bombing until the Tet Offensive three years later.

Confessing his own skewed judgment, McNamara wallowed in a pool of regret for the rest of his life. Thirty years would pass before McNamara spelled out the disastrous dimensions of the 1963 coup. "Had Diem lived, I'm inclined to think he would neither have requested or accepted the introduction of large numbers of U.S. combat forces," said McNamara. "I think the war would have taken a totally different course."

Of all Kennedy's advisers, only General Taylor foresaw the destruction of South Vietnam's governmental infrastructure if Diem was overthrown. He wound up replacing Lodge as ambassador in 1964 and personally witnessed the collapse of the Saigon government and its military. "Our responsibility for the overthrow and the murder of Diem certainly contributed to our [military] contribution to South Vietnam," Taylor said. "Diem's overthrow set in motion a sequence of crises, political and military, over the next two years which eventually forced President Johnson in 1965 to choose between accepting defeat or introducing American combat forces. . . . What we could not know was that the American-supported coup would remove Diem and with him the lid from the political Pandora's box in which Diem confined the genies of political turbulence."

Diem's assassination and the series of events it set into motion was just the sort of thing Kennedy was once determined to avoid. After blundering into the Bay of Pigs shortly after his inauguration, the new president resolved to never again make such an unwitting commitment. He took to heart the lesson of Gavrilo Princip's shooting of

Archduke Franz Ferdinand. That assassination unleashed a string of seeming unrelated events that produced World War I. Historian Barbara Tuchman's 1962 best seller, *The Guns of August*, detailed the bumbling and miscalculation by world statesmen. The book had two Germans puzzling over the events of 1914. "How did it all happen?" said one. "Ah," the other replied, "if one only knew." After reading the book, Kennedy summoned Army Secretary Elvis Stahr to the White House and handed him Tuchman's book. "I want you to read this," Kennedy told Stahr. "And I want every officer in the army to read it."

Still, Kennedy ignored repeated warnings—from Hilsman, McNamara, Taylor, McCone, and Colby—that Diem's assassination could lead to chaos and the collapse of the Saigon government. But with every warning, every meeting, every briefing, Kennedy brushed them aside. Diem posed an unacceptable threat to his 1964 reelection campaign. His choice was clear and fateful for his vice president and the Americans who spent ten years in the jungles of Indochina.

Johnson saved his most bitter recriminations for reporters who visited him at his ranch near Johnson City, Texas. He wore his white hair down to the collar and started smoking cigarettes again. The Diem overthrow "was a terrible mistake upon the part of our officials, and I don't think we ever really recovered from it," Johnson told Walter Cronkite. "And it has cost us many American lives, in my judgment." To other reporters, Johnson saw Kennedy forced into ousting Diem because of political attacks by the press. "He couldn't take the heat from the press," Johnson said.

Two more presidents—Richard M. Nixon and Gerald R. Ford—would get the same response picked up by Johnson's antennae from Hanoi's negotiators in Paris. As Diem predicted, the Americans did not fathom Hanoi's determination to seize South Vietnam and create a nationalist state with communist ties. Division after division began spilling over the North Vietnamese border at the exact points that Diem had predicted to Mike Dunn.

America's defeat was complete in 1975 when its diplomats, some employees, and their Marine guards flew to safety in helicopters that landed on the U.S. embassy roof. General Big Minh, who helped place Diem in the presidential palace and later ordered his murder, was chosen to handle South Vietnam's last official act. Big Minh chose a business suit over his uniform on April 30, 1975. Civilians, not soldiers, surrendered. President Nguyen Van Thieu, one of Minh's coconspirators in the overthrow of Diem, had fled the presidential palace. Minh would hand over the Saigon government to North Vietnam. North Vietnamese tanks knocked down the iron gates around the palace. The tank commander, Colonel Bui Tin, stalked in.

"I have been waiting since early morning to transfer power to you," Minh said.

"There is no question of your transferring power," Tin said. "Your power has crumbled. You cannot give up what you do not have."

With the arrival of Hanoi's troops, Americans were ordered out. Malcolm Browne, now a science reporter for the *New York Times,* showed up in Saigon on special assignment. Along with other reporters and photographers, Browne was warned there would be a departure signal. American Forces Network would start playing Irving Berlin's "White Christmas." Dirck Halstead, for years the UPI photo editor in Saigon, had returned to photograph the final moments for *Time* magazine. He thought the departure signal was more of a spooky funeral dirge.

"You could hear Bing Crosby all over town," Halstead said.

ACKNOWLEDGMENTS

When President John F. Kennedy was buried on what he thought was a grand spot overlooking Washington, the reality of his presidency was lowered into the grave with him. A small army of historians attached to the Kennedy family, the Kennedy Library, and the Kennedy mystique produced something close to an Irish wake, where everyone says of the body, "He looks wonderful." It took thirty years for the first sober judgment. Richard Reeves's *President Kennedy: Profile of Power* in 1993 gave us a clear-eyed look at Kennedy the president. Reeves offers insight into every president's struggle as they scramble for facts surrounding a crisis, which of course changes daily. Kennedy the man comes into view in *An Unfinished Life* by Robert Dallek. Dallek and Reeves were points on the compass for me. For 1963 in Saigon, two books provide a bedrock of insight: Ellen J. Hammer's *A Death in November* and William Prochnau's *Once Upon a Distant War*. For Kennedy thoughts, laughter, and keen awareness of the world he dealt with, I am indebted to thirty-two CDs produced by the staff of the John F. Kennedy Library. Often I had to replay many again and again to get just the right word. Clicking, tapping, kids shrieking, coughing—all made for difficult research. One day Kennedy seemed to be missing from a crucial meeting when, finally, I realized he had been there, his voice disguised by a bad cold. Sheldon

M. Stern's *Averting "The Final Failure"* was a big help in getting through the Cuban missile crisis. The staff of the LBJ Library in Austin, Texas, was very helpful, as were the men and women at the Eisenhower Library in Abilene, Kansas, and the Ford Library in Ann Arbor, Michigan. I want to thank Roger Harrison for reading the early drafts of this book and making valuable suggestions. Two men who served America in peace and war provided fascinating insights into events in the Saigon embassy in 1963. I am indebted to and still miss the late John Michael Dunn, who served as top assistant to Ambassador Lodge on two tours in South Vietnam. The other was Rufus Phillips, who served in the Central Intelligence Agency. As do I, Dunn and Phillips look back on Kennedy's overthrow of President Diem as a blunder that opened the door to a decade of jungle warfare for American troops. Colleagues Carl Pisano and John Hall generously read the manuscript. My daughter, Nora, also uncovered some key State Department testimony.

NOTES

The abbreviation FRUS stands for *Foreign Relations of the United States*.

PROLOGUE: JFK

2 *Well, if we have to have:* Arthur M. Schlesinger Jr., *Robert Kennedy and His Times* (Boston: Houghton Mifflin, 1978), 131.

3 *Why, even:* Robert Dallek, *An Unfinished Life: John F. Kennedy, 1917–1963* (Boston: Little, Brown, 2003), 196.

1 GENERAL LEMAY'S THREAT

11 *Kennedy's head start:* dictated to a recorder (Dictabelt #40) microphone while preparing for his 1960 presidential race.

12 *Lemay:* White House tape recording 111.

14 *The order came down:* Travis interview, 2013.

15 *Surrounding Russia:* Aleksandr Fursenko and Timothy Naftali, *One Hell of a Gamble: Khrushchev, Castro, and Kennedy, 1958–1964: The Secret History of the Cuban Missile Crisis* (New York: W. W. Norton, 1997).

15 *However:* Philip Nash, *The Other Missiles of October: Eisenhower, Kennedy, and the Jupiters, 1957–1963* (Chapel Hill: University of North Carolina Press, 1997).

15 *The Jupiters:* 1991 BBC interview with Alexi Adzhubei, Khruschev's son-in-law.

16   *We were not:* Nikita Khrushchev, *Khrushchev Remembers: The Glasnost Tapes,* translated and edited by Jerrold L. Schecter with V. V. Luhkov (Boston: Little, Brown, 1970).

16   *In the end:* Fursenko and Naftali, *One Hell of a Gamble.*

17   *This trade:* White House tape recording A41, October 17.

17   *Kennedy's concession:* Oral History, Kennedy Library.

18   *Bobby said:* White House tape recording, October 16.

18   *The vice president:* White House tape recording, October 27.

20   *Lemnitzer recalled:* Letter to a CIA official, Dino A. Brugioni. Also Dino A. Brugioni, *Eyeball to Eyeball: The Inside Story of the Cuban Missile Crisis* (New York: Random House, 1991).

21   *Lemnitzer would say:* Brugioni interview, June 2013.

21   *But Johnson stressed:* Lyndon Baines Johnson, *Vantage Point: Perspectives on the Presidency 1963–1968* (New York: Holt, 1971).

21   *Bobby's contention:* Robert Kennedy, *Robert Kennedy in His Own Words,* edited by Edwin O. Guthman and Jeffrey Shulman (New York: Bantam, 1988).

21   *The missile swap:* Richard Ned Lebow and Janice Stein, *We All Lost the Cold War* (Princeton, NJ: Princeton University Press, 1994); Russian Foreign Ministry archives, obtained and translated by NHK, Japanese Broadcasting.

22   *The American version:* A record of the interview is contained in the Richard B. Russell Library for Political Research, part of the University of Georgia Library holdings in Athens, Georgia. The book is *As I Saw It: Dean Rusk as Told to Richard Rusk,* edited by Daniel S. Papp (New York: W. W. Norton, 1990).

25   *If there is:* Brugioni, *Eyeball to Eyeball,* 377.

26   *I think that:* White House tape recording 31.2, October 19.

27   *He was just:* Gilpatric Oral History, JFK Library, 1970.

30   *His diary was:* Bruce J. Allyn, James G. Blight, and David A. Welch, eds. *Back to the Brink: Proceedings of the Moscow Conference on the Cuban Missile Crisis,* January 27–28, 1989 (Lanham, MD: University Press of America, 1992), 92–93.

30   *In a 1988 book, Bundy:* McGeorge Bundy, *Danger and Survival: Choices about the Bomb in the First Fifty Years* (New York: Random House, 1988), 432–441.

31   *But in a later:* Fursenko and Naftali, *One Hell of a Gamble.*

31 *We then issued:* White House telephone recording, October 28.

32 *I think the:* Bartlett Oral History, JFK Library.

33 *According to Bundy:* Bundy Oral History, 1964, JFK Library.

34 *The president never: Robert Kennedy in His Own Words.*

34 *I cut his:* Michael R. Beschloss, *The Crisis Years: Kennedy and Khrushchev, 1960–1963.* (New York: Edward Burlingame Books, 1991).

35 *LeMay rudely rejected:* Richard Reeves, *President Kennedy: Profile of Power* (New York: Simon & Schuster, 1993), 425.

2 ZR/RIFLE

37 *See the poll:* White House tape recording, 90.3, 1963.

38 *The worse you:* Arthur Schlesinger Jr., *A Thousand Days: John F. Kennedy in the White House* (Boston: Houghton Mifflin, 1965), 292.

38 *The general took:* Eisenhower's record of the meeting of April 22, 1961, Eisenhower Library, Abilene, Kansas.

39 *A more direct:* Inspector General John Earman of the Central Intelligence Agency, *Report on Plots to Assassinate Fidel Castro,* 1967.

41 *The only thing:* Richard N. Goodwin, *Remembering America: A Voice from the Sixties,* (Boston: Little, Brown, 1988), 189.

44 *It was an:* William Attwood interview, 1982.

44 *Any word that:* White House tape recording 119, November 5, 1963.

45 *He said the:* Attwood interview.

3 THE CROCODILE

50 *He's going to make:* Rudy Abramson, *Spanning the Century: The Life of Averell Harriman* (New York: William Morrow, 1992).

50 *An act of:* Arthur M. Schlesinger Jr., *Robert Kennedy and His Times* (Boston: Houghton Mifflin, 1978).

51 *[Harriman] put me:* William Colby, *Honorable Men* (New York: Simon & Schuster, 1978).

52 *I don't want:* Interview, Hugh Sidey of *Time,* 1961.

52 *He was a:* Evan Thomas, *Ike's Bluff: President Eisenhower's Secret Battle to Save the World* (Boston: Little, Brown, 2012).

53 *I would have:* Richard Reeves, *President Kennedy: Profile of Power* (New York: Simon & Schuster, 1993); also Thomas J. Schoenbaum,

Waging Peace and War: Dean Rusk in the Truman, Kennedy, and John-son Years (New York: Simon & Schuster, 1988).

54   *Our job is:* Abramson, *Spanning the Century,* 583.

55   *The effectiveness of:* Frederick Nolting, *From Trust to Tragedy: The Po-litical Memoirs of Frederick Nolting, Kennedy's Ambassador to Diem's Vietnam* (New York: Praeger Publishers, 1988).

57   *It was very:* Ellen J. Hammer, *A Death in November* (New York: E. P. Dutton, 1987).

4 MIRACLES

61   *Kennedy's father, Joseph:* Don Oberdorfer, *Senator Mansfield: The Ex-traordinary Life of a Great American Statesman and Diplomat* (Wash-ington, D.C.: Smithsonian Books, 2003), 140.

61   *According to Malachi:* John Cooney, *The American Pope* (New York: Times Books, 1984).

61   *There are only:* Rufus Phillips, *Why Vietnam Matters* (Annapolis, MD.: Naval Institute Press, 2008), 17.

62   *His calmness and:* Mike Moyar, *Triumph Forsaken: The Vietnam War, 1954–1965* (New York: Cambridge University Press, 2006), 66–67.

62   *We rejoice that: New York Times* editorial, February 24, 1957.

63   *Although the French:* Stanley Karnow, *Vietnam: A History* (New York: Penguin Books, 1983).

64   *We must keep:* FRUS, August 24, 1954. October 22, 1954.

64   *In the event:* Senate Report on South Vietnam, 1954.

65   *A losing game:* November 15, 1954.

66   *The president decided:* Seth Jacobs, *America's Miracle Man in Vietnam* (Durham, NC: Duke University Press, 2004).

67   *Just what happened:* David L. Anderson, *Trapped by Success: The Eisen-hower Administration and Vietnam, 1953–1961* (New York: Columbia University Press, 1991).

67   *It was a:* John Osborne, *Life,* May 13, 1957.

68   *Lansdale made sure of the:* Stanley Karnow, *Vietnam: A History,* 222.

69   *The U.S. cannot undertake:* FRUS, May 8, 1955.

5 HEAD BUTTS

73   *They meant to:* John Osborne, "The Tough Miracle Man of Vietnam," *Life,* May 13, 1957.

75   *I got two shots:* Elbridge Durbrow, Oral History, 1981, LBJ Library. Austin, Texas.

76   *Express your opinion:* A. J. Langguth, *Our Vietnam: The War 1954–1975* (New York: Simon & Schuster, 2000).

76   *He didn't like:* William J. Rust, *Kennedy in Vietnam* (New York: Scribner's, 1985).

78   *I was absolutely:* Rust, *Kennedy in Vietnam.*

78   *The U.S. ought:* Langguth, *Our Vietnam.*

79   *I strongly disagreed:* William Colby, with James McCargar, *Lost Victory: A Firsthand Account of America in Vietnam* (Chicago: Contemporary Books, 1989).

81   *Another report had:* Denis Warner, *The Last Confucian* (New York: Macmillan, 1963), 221.

82   *Frail and broken:* Durbrow Oral History.

83   *One conversation dealt:* Roger Hilsman, *To Move a Nation* (Garden City, NY: Doubleday, 1967).

87   *The U.S. should:* Edward Lansdale, *Saturday Evening Post,* May 20, 1961.

87   *This is going:* Walt Whitman Rostow, *The Diffusion of Power: An Essay in Recent History* (Macmillan, New York, 1972).

88   *If we went:* Ball interview, WGBH Open Vault, 1981.

88   *The loss of:* Memo, Presidential Office files, Nov. 11, 1961.

88   *There are limits:* Harris Wofford, *Of Kennedys and Kings: Making Sense of the Sixties* (Pittsburgh: University of Pittsburgh Press, 1992), 379.

88   *The American embassy:* J. Graham Parsons, Oral History, JFK Library, p. 30.

88   *The outcome of:* Frederick Nolting, *From Trust to Tragedy: The Political Memoirs of Frederick Nolting, Kennedy's Ambassador to Diem's Vietnam* (New York: Praeger Publishers, 1988).

89   *Mr. President, I:* Richard Reeves, *President Kennedy: Profile of Power* (New York: Simon & Schuster, 1993), 118.

89   *You're going tonight:* Howard Burris interview, 2001.

90   *Diem said the:* FRUS, Vol. I, Vietnam, 1961, document 54.

90   *Johnson countered with:* John M. Newman, *JFK and Vietnam: Deception, Intrigue, and the Struggle for Power* (New York: Warner Books, 1992), 72.

91   *I found him:* Nolting, *From Trust to Tragedy,* 41.

6 DUE COURSE

94 *Splinter the CIA:* New York Times, April 25, 1966, page 1.

94 *He always thought:* Jean Kennedy Smith, interview, March 17, 1995.

95 *We put on:* Harris Wofford, *Of Kennedy and Kings: Making Sense of the Sixties* (New York: Farrar, Straus and Giroux 1980), 125.

96 *When I feel:* Senator Hubert H. Humphrey, Oral History, JFK Library.

97 *What the hell:* Taylor Branch, *Parting the Waters: America in the King Years 1954–63* (New York: Simon & Schuster, 1988).

98 *Can't you tell:* Wofford, *Of Kennedy and Kings,* 127.

99 *If you mean:* McGeorge Bundy, Oral History, JFK Library, March 1964.

100 *There are three:* Wofford, *Of Kennedys and Kings,* 122.

7 WHOPPERS

101 *Malcolm Wilde Browne:* Malcolm W. Browne, *Muddy Boots & Red Socks* (New York: Times Books, 1993); Browne, *The New Face of War* (Indianapolis: Bobbs-Merrill, 1965).

103 *The muscular:* John M. Newman, *JFK and Vietnam: Deception, Intrigue, and the Struggle for Power* (New York: Warner Books, 1992), 127.

103 *Browne exposed Kennedy's:* FRUS, Vol. III, 7, 1/2/63, Hilsman Memo of Conversation.

103 *He personally approved:* Jean Mager Stellman, "The Extent and Patterns of Usage of Agent Orange and Other Herbicides in Vietnam," *Nature,* Vol. 442, 2003.

104 *Not known at the time:* FRUS, 1–8, 1963, document 77. U.S. Institute of Medicine report on Agent Orange, 1996, National Academy Press, Washington, DC.

104 *As the results of:* Library of Congress History of the Vietnam War, 1984.

104 *Thomas Hughes, head:* The Man Nobody Knew, film documentary about William Colby of the CIA, Carl Colby, 2011.

105 *When the first:* Stanley Karnow, *Vietnam: A History* (New York: Penguin Books, 1983).

105 *Supersedes all:* Newman, 152.

105 *Roger Hilsman at:* Hilsman Papers, JFK Library.

106 *Project Tiger:* John Prados, *William Colby and the CIA: The Secret Wars of a Controversial Spymaster* (Lawrence: University Press of Kansas, 2009).

112 *Harkins, class of:* Karnow, *Vietnam*; David Halberstam, *The Best and the Brightest* (New York: Random House, New York, 1972).

113 *In Washington, success:* William Colby, *Honorable Men* (New York: Simon & Schuster, 1978); Mike Moyar, *Triumph Forsaken: The Vietnam War, 1954–1965* (New York: Cambridge University Press, 2006).

114 *Waves of American:* Neil Sheehan, *A Bright Shining Lie: John Paul Vann and America in Vietnam* (New York: Random House, 1988); William Prochnau, *Once Upon a Distant War* (New York: Vintage Books, 1996).

8 A NAIL IN THE COFFIN

120 *Say something about:* White House tape recording 69, January 8, 1963.

123 *Mansfield was just:* Interviews with Mansfield, 1964–1995.

125 *A Secret Service:* Don Oberdorfer, *Senator Mansfield: The Extraordinary Life of a Great American Statesman and Diplomat* (Washington, D.C.: Smithsonian Books, 2003), 194.

126 *The Saigon government:* Kenneth P. O'Donnell and David F. Powers, *Johnny, We Hardly Knew Ye: Memories of John Fitzgerald Kennedy* (Boston: Little, Brown, 1972).

127 *The exile's reception:* Douglas Oral History, JFK Library, 1964.

131 *This guy, I think:* Hanes Oral Interview, John Foster Dulles collection, Seeley Mudd Library, Princeton University.

131 *Andrew J. Goodpaster:* CNN, Cold War Series, 1999.
    Once installed in: FRUS, Vol. 1, Vietnam, Document 109, April 9, 1955.

131 *And that's how:* Amory Oral History, JFK Library, February 9, 1966.

132 *I think:* Frederick Nolting, *From Trust to Tragedy: The Political Memoirs of Frederick Nolting, Kennedy's Ambassador to Diem's Vietnam* (New York: Praeger Publishers, 1988).

9 RATHOLES

133 *That practice contributed:* William Prochnau, *Once Upon a Distant War* (New York: Vintage Books, 1996).

134 *It started with:* Rufus Phillips, *Why Vietnam Matters* (Annapolis, MD: Naval Institute Press, 2008).

135 *Diem was sensitive:* Seth Jacobs, *Cold War Mandarin* (Lanham, MD: Rowman & Littlefield, 2006).

136 *Tri Quang was:* Anne Blair, *Lodge in Vietnam* (New Haven: Yale University Press, 1995), 27.

136 *At his post:* Elbridge Durbrow, Oral History, LBJ Library.

137 *Can wanted a:* Ellen J. Hammer, *A Death in November* (New York: E. P. Dutton, 1987).

137 *The sky is:* Prochnau, *Once Upon a Distant War.*

138 *They never gave:* Frederick Nolting, *From Trust to Tragedy: The Political Memoirs of Frederick Nolting, Kennedy's Ambassador to Diem's Vietnam* (New York: Praeger Publishers, 1988).

139 *He sent the: Reporting America at War: An Oral History,* compiled by Michelle Ferrari (New York: Hyperion, 2003).

140 *It took him:* YouTube.Com has several videos of Quang Duc's death, including one taken with a movie camera (http://www.youtube.com /watch?v=tVS4iZXkkaU).

141 *The whole trick:* Patrick Witty, *Time,* August 28, 2012.

142 *If Diem does:* FRUS, Vol. III, January to August, 167.

143 *I'd never drink:* Prochnau, *Once Upon a Distant War.*

144 *Once the picture:* Interview, 1976.

10 HARD CONDITION

146 *The New Frontier:* Harris Wofford, *Of Kennedy and Kings: Making Sense of the Sixties* (New York: Farrar, Straus and Giroux, 1980), 140.

146 *I think it's:* White House tape recording 85. May 4, 1963.

147 *You could make:* White House tape recording 90.3, June 1, 1963.

148 *I think Birmingham:* King Oral History, JFK Library.

149 *Jesus Christ!:* Arthur Schlesinger Jr., *Robert Kennedy and His Times* (New York: Houghton Mifflin, 1978).

149 *He felt like:* Lincoln Diary, October 23–28, JFK Library; Robert Dallek, *An Unfinished Life: John F. Kennedy, 1917–1963* (Boston: Little, Brown, 2003).

149 *I was actually:* McGeorge Bundy, Oral History 1, JFK Library.

150 *Civil rights," Albert:* White House recording, Dictabelt 22A.2m, June 12, 1963.

151 *I know the risks:* Tape recording of Vice President Johnson's telephone call to Theodore Sorensen, LBJ Audio Library, June 3, 1963.

152 *I can kiss:* David Lawrence, Oral History, JFK Library.

152 *There's no reason:* William Doyle, *Inside the Oval Office: The White House Tapes from FDR to Clinton* (New York: Kodansha USA, 1999).

152 *During his presidency:* Merle Miller, *Los Angeles Times,* July 18, 2003.

154 *King is so hot:* White House tape recording 86.2, May 20, 1963.

154 *Despite years of:* David J. Garrow, *The FBI and Martin Luther King Jr.* (New York: W. W. Norton, 1981).

155 *I assume you:* Taylor Branch, *Parting the Waters* (New York: Simon & Schuster, 1988).

155 *The president was:* Antony Lewis, Oral History, JFK Library.

156 *I may lose:* Branch, *Parting the Waters.*

156 *King admitted that:* King Oral History, JFK Library; Reeves, *President Kennedy,* 531; Dallek, *An Unfinished Life,* 635.

158 *They will destroy:* Garrow, *The FBI and Martin Luther King Jr.,* 106.

159 *One package of:* Select Committee to Study Governmental Operations with Respect to Intelligence, *The FBI, Cointelpro and Martin Luther King Jr., Final Report,* 1975.

159 *How he was calling:* Jacqueline Kennedy, tape-recorded interview with Arthur Schlesinger Jr., 1964.

11 THE PROCONSUL

161 *It is so good:* Lodge interview, Beverly, Massachusetts, 1981.

163 *I marvel how:* Lodge files, June 18, 1963, Massachusetts Historical Society.

163 *They all will:* White House tape recording 104, August 15, 1963.

163 *I think we:* White House tape recording 96, July 4, 1963.

167 *I am not bound:* William J. Miller, *Henry Cabot Lodge: A Biography* (New York: James H. Heineman, 1967), 336.

168 *While a portion:* Lodge files, Massachusetts Historical Society.

12 THE GUY NEXT TO THE GUY

169 *I want you to:* John Michael Dunn, interviews.

170 *I needed someone:* Lodge interview.

170 *It was a fun:* Dunn, Oral History, LBJ Library.

171 *Death threats:* William Prochnau, *Once Upon a Distant War* (New York: Vintage Books, New York, 1996).

172 *I liked him:* Malcolm W. Browne, *Muddy Boots & Red Socks* (New York: Times Books, 1993), 163.

172 *This was the first glimpse:* John Mecklin, *Mission in Torment: An Intimate Account of the U.S. Role in Vietnam* (Garden City, NY: Doubleday, 1965), 190.

173 *A dangerous man:* Rufus Phillips, *Why Vietnam Matters: An Eyewitness Account of Lessons Not Learned* (Annapolis, MD: Naval Institute Press, 2008).

174 *Honey was a:* Henry Cabot Lodge Jr., *The Storm Has Many Eyes: A Personal Narrative* (New York: W. W. Norton, 1973), 207.

176 *According to Conein:* FRUS, Vol. III, January to August 1963, 275.

176 *The key question:* FRUS, Vol. III, January to August 1963, 274.

177 *Suggestion has been made:* FRUS, Vol. III, 276, August 24, 11 P.M. (Saigon Time).

13 END RUN

179 *They are pushing:* White House tape recording 96, July 4, 1963.

180 *The more important:* Rudy Abramson, *Spanning the Century: The Life of W. Averell Harriman 1891–1986* (New York: William Morrow, 1992), 589.

180 *In agreement at:* David L. Di Leo, *George Ball* (Chapel Hill: University of North Carolina Press, 1991), 59.

180 *Harriman actually thought:* Frederick Nolting, *From Trust to Tragedy: The Political Memoirs of Frederick Nolting, Kennedy's Ambassador to Diem's Vietnam* (New York: Praeger Publishers, 1988), 126.

181 *Forrestal became: The Death of Diem*, NBC News White Paper, 1971; also William J. Rust, *Kennedy in Vietnam* (New York: Scribner's, 1985).

184 *He viewed it:* Roswell Gilpatric, Oral History, JFK Library.

184 *He knew what:* George Ball, Oral History, LBJ Library.

184 *The president on:* Rust, *Kennedy in Vietnam,* 115.

185 *The president polled:* Roger Hilsman, *To Move a Nation: The Politics of Foreign Policy in the Administration of John F. Kennedy* (Garden City, NY: Doubleday, 1967), 493.

186 *I should not:* White House Dictaphone recording, November 4, 1963.

186 *The fact of:* George Ball, Memorandum of Conversation with the President, JFK Library.

14 PERFIDY

187 *They were asking:* International Herald Tribune, July 26, 1975.

187 *In case they:* John Michael Dunn, interview.

188 *Their meeting was:* FRUS, Vol. IV, August–December 1963, 11.

191 *When Ambassador Lodge:* Lucein Conein, WGBH Vault, Boston, Massachusetts.

15 LAUREL AND HARDY

193 *White House tape:* White House tape recording 107, August 26–28, 1963.

193 *This shit:* Gordon M. Goldstein, *Lessons in Disaster: McGeorge Bundy and the Path to War in Vietnam,* Gordon M. Goldstein (New York: Times Books/Holt, 2008).

199 *The basic lack:* William J. Rust and the editors of U.S. News Books, *Kennedy in Vietnam* (New York: Scribner's, 1985).

199 *Situation here has:* FRUS, Vol. IV, Vietnam, August–December, Lodge Telegram, August 29, 1963, 12.

200 *At the end:* FRUS, Vol. IV, Memorandum of Conference with the President, 15, August 29.

200 *Kennedy's August 30:* FRUS, Vol. IV, Vietnam, August–December, 18.

200 *He smoked a:* Photographs of White House photographer Cecil Stoughton, August 31, 1963.

16 FINANCIAL INDUCEMENTS

202 *It appears," Taylor:* White House tape recording 107, August 28, 1963.

202 *Kennedy's order to:* FRUS, Vol. IV, August–December 1963, 8.

202 *Dinh was well:* Rufus Phillips, *Why Vietnam Matters: An Eyewitness Account of Lessons Not Learned* (Annapolis, MD: Naval Institute Press, 2008).

204 *The strongest evidence:* FRUS, Vol. IV, August–December 1963, November 4, 288.

205 *However, that edited:* Bromley Smith, original notes, November 4, 1963, LBJ Library.

17 DEBACLE

207 *At a September:* White House tape recording, 111, and reel 1.

208 *If you want:* President Lyndon B. Johnson, recorded White House telephone conversation.

209 *I had the impression:* William Colby, *Honorable Men* (New York: Simon & Schuster, 1978).

210 *He placed his:* Roswell Gilpatric, Oral History, LBJ Library.

210 *We can say:* White House tape recording 114, A9, reel 3.

211 *I never saw:* White House tape recording 112.

212 *It was on his:* Charles Bartlett, Oral History, JFK Library.

18 LUIGI

213 *I would sit:* Lucien Conein, WGBH Open Vault, Boston, Massachusetts, May 7, 1981.

214 *Do not see:* FRUS, Vol. IV, Vietnam, August–December, September 17, 1963.

215 *Don arranged for:* FRUS, Vol. IV, August–December 1963, October 5, 177.

216 *But during a:* Lodge interview, WGBH Open Vault, Boston, Massachusetts, 1979.

216 *Kennedy fired back:* FRUS, Vol. IV, August–December 1963, October 5, 1963, 182.

218 *We've got a:* White House tape recording 118/A54, October 29, 1963.

19 SECOND THOUGHTS

220 *I think that:* U.S. Senate Select Committee to Study Governmental Operations with Respect to Intelligence Activities, 1975. Chaired by Democratic Senator Frank Church, Idaho.

220 *One of the:* WGBH Media Files and Archives, 1979.

220 *If you don't:* Church committee, 1975.

220 *What about Diem:* White House tape recording 108, reel 3, August 29, 1963.

221 *Kennedy told him:* Macdonald interview, 2012.

221 *If we give:* White House tape recording 117 A53, October 24, 1963.

222 *The [new] government:* FRUS, Vol. IV, Vietnam, August–December, 242, October 30, 1963.

222 *For the first:* Henry Cabot Lodge unpublished Vietnam memoir, Lodge Papers, Massachusetts Historical Society, Boston, Massachusetts.

227 *He [the president] wanted a:* McGeorge Bundy Oral History, JFK Library.

227 *We are particularly:* FRUS, Vol. IV, August–December, 217, October 25, 1963.

228 *Noted the balance:* FRUS, Vol. IV, Vietnam, August–December, 236, October 29.

228 *Do not think:* FRUS, Vol. IV, Vietnam, August–December, 242, October 30.

229 *Thanks for your:* Richard Reeves, *President Kennedy: Profile of Power* (New York: Simon & Schuster, 1993), 642.

229 *You know what's:* Robert Kennedy, *Robert Kennedy in His Own Words*, edited by Edwin O. Guthman and Jeffrey Shulman (New York: Bantam, 1988), 398.

20 FEAST OF THE DEAD

231 *There isn't a:* U.S. News & World Report, October 10, 1983.

233 *You are finished:* Stanley Karnow, *Vietnam: A History* (New York: Penguin Books, 1983).

233 *When he agreed:* Rufus Phillips, *Why Vietnam Matters: An Eyewitness Account of Lessons Not Learned* (Annapolis, MD: Naval Institute Press, 2008). Controlled American Source 2135, CIA documents.

234 *Bundy then commented:* FRUS, Vol. IV, Vietnam, August–December, 263, November 1, 1963.

235 *We will have: Captain Do Tho Diary* (Saigon: Hoa Binh Publishing House, 1970), 260.

237 *When he told:* Conein testimony before the Church Committee, June 20, 1975.

237 *In a rage:* An NBC News White Paper, *Vietnam Hindsight*, December 22, 1971.

21 THE HIT

241 *My president," Nghia:* Interview, 2012.

242 *Why have you:* Cong Luan newspaper, No. 882, November 26, 1970; Luong Khai Minh, Cao Vi Hoang (Cao The Dung), *How to Kill a President: A Historical Record,* unpublished; Nguyen Ngoc Huy, "Ngo Dinh Diem's Execution," *World View*, November 1976.

242 *Nhu flicked a: Captain Do Tho Diary* (Saigon: Hoa Binh Publishing House, 1970), 260–265.

243 *Later, Nhung showed:* Malcolm W. Browne, *Muddy Boots & Red* Socks (New York: Times Books, 1993), 167.

244 *Every Vietnamese has:* FRUS, Vol. IV, Vietnam, August–December 1963, November 2, 269, 270.

244 *Generals must preserve:* FRUS 2271, November 2.

245 *What did he:* Oral History, LBJ Library.

EPILOGUE: WASHINGTON

248 *I was shocked:* White House Dictabelt, 52.1, November 4, 1963.

251 *Just require Diem's:* Interview, 2012.

251 *It was a legitimate:* FRUS, Vol. IV, Vietnam, August–December, 289, November 4.

252 *Tell Khanh to: Captain Do Tho Diary* (Saigon: Hoa Binh Publishing House, 1970).

253 *Henry Cabot Lodge:* Robert Kennedy, *Robert Kennedy in His Own Words,* edited by Edwin O. Guthman and Jeffrey Shulman (New York: Bantam, 1988). 17.

253 *They're going to:* Healy interview, 1981.

254 *On the afternoon:* Patrick J. Sloyan, "Total Domination," *American Journalism Review,* May 1998.

255 *In France, it:* Inspector General John Earman of the Central Intelligence Agency, *Report on Plots to Assassinate Fidel Castro,* 1967. Declassified in 1999.

256 *President Johnson told:* FRUS, Vol. IV, Vietnam, August–December, 330, November 24.

256 *He ain't worth:* Mike Moyar, *Triumph Forsaken: The Vietnam War, 1954–1965* (New York: Cambridge University Press, 2006), 293.

257 *They were gifts:* Ellen J. Hammer, *A Death in November: America in Vietnam 1963* (New York: E. P. Dutton, 1987), 309.

258 *This requires a:* FRUS, Vol. I, Vietnam, 1964, 30, February 1.

259 *While Vietnam threatened:* Barry M. Goldwater, *With No Apologies: The Personal and Political Memoirs of United States Senator Barry M. Goldwater* (New York: William Morrow, 1979), 193.

260 *As the Saigon:* FRUS, Vol. I, Vietnam, 1964, 432.

261 *Hot damn, I'm:* Interview, Jack Valenti, 1981.

263 *Through a variety:* William Tuohy, *Dangerous Company: Inside the*

World's Hottest Trouble Spots with a Pulitzer Prize–Winning War Correspondent (New York: William Morrow, 1987).

264 *African-Americans and:* FRUS, Vol. VI, Vietnam, 1968, 80, February 20.

265 *Blacks were suffering* James Maycock, "War Within War," *The Guardian*, September 14, 2001.

266 *He told me:* Mansfield interview, 1986.

267 *However, Roswell Gilpatric:* Oral History, LBJ Library.

268 *Had Diem lived:* CNN, *Cold War*, Episode 11, 1998.

268 *Diem's overthrow set:* Maxwell D. Taylor, *Swords and Plowshares* (New York: W. W. Norton, 1972), 302.

269 *I want you to read this:* Richard Reeves, *President Kennedy: Profile of Power* (New York: Simon & Schuster, 1993), 305.

269 *The Diem overthrow:* CBS News, 1969.

BIBLIOGRAPHY

Abramson, Rudy. *Spanning the Century: The Life of Averell Harriman, 1891–1986.* New York: William Morrow, 1992.

Adams, Sam. *War of Numbers: An Intelligence Memoir.* South Royalton, VT: Steerforth Press, 1994.

Allyn, Bruck J., James G. Blight, and David A. Welch, eds. *Back to the Brink: Proceedings of the Moscow Conference on the Cuban Missile Crisis, January 27–28, 1989.* Lanham, MD: University Press of America, 1992.

Anderson, David L. *Trapped by Success: The Eisenhower Administration and Vietnam, 1953–1961.* New York: Columbia University Press, 1991.

Beschloss, Michael R. *The Crisis Years: Kennedy and Khrushchev, 1960–1963.* New York: Edward Burlingame Books, 1991.

Bill, James A. *George Ball.* New Haven, CT: Yale University Press, 1997.

Blair, Anne E. *Lodge in Vietnam: A Patriot Abroad.* New Haven, CT: Yale University Press, 1995.

Blight, James G., and Janet M. Lang. *The Fog of War: Lessons from the Life of Robert S. McNamara.* Lanham, MD: Rowman & Littlefield Publishers, 2005.

Branch, Taylor. *Parting the Waters: America in the King Years, 1954–63.* New York: Simon & Schuster, 1988.

———. *Pillar of Fire: America in the King Years, 1963–65.* New York: Simon & Schuster, 1998.

Browne, Malcolm W. *Muddy Boots & Red Socks.* New York: Times Books, 1993.

———. *The New Face of War.* Indianapolis: Bobbs-Merrill, 1965.

Brugioni, Dino A. *Eyeball to Eyeball: The Inside Story of the Cuban Missile Crisis.* New York: Random House, 1991.

Bundy, McGeorge. *Danger and Survival: Choices about the Bomb in the First Fifty Years.* New York: Random House, 1988.

Colby, William. *Honorable Men.* New York: Simon & Schuster, 1978.

Colby, William E. *Lost Victory: A Firsthand Account of America's Sixteen-Year Involvement in Vietnam.* Chicago: Contemporary Books, 1989.

Cooney, John. *The American Pope: The Life and Times of Francis Cardinal Spellman.* New York: Times Books, 1984.

Dallek, Robert. *An Unfinished Life: John F. Kennedy, 1917–1963.* Boston: Little, Brown, 2003.

Dobbs, Michael. *One Minute to Midnight: Kennedy, Khrushchev, and Castro on the Brink of Nuclear War.* New York: Knopf, 2008.

Fursenko, Aleksandr, and Timothy Naftali. *One Hell of a Gamble: Khrushchev, Castro, and Kennedy, 1958–1964.* New York: W. W. Norton, 1997.

Galbraith, John Kenneth. *Letters to Kennedy.* Edited by James Goodman. Cambridge: Harvard University Press, 1998.

Garrow, David J. *The FBI and Martin Luther King, Jr.* New York: Penguin Books, 1983.

Goldwater, Barry M. *With No Apologies: The Personal and Political Memoirs of United States Senator Barry M. Goldwater.* New York: William Morrow, 1976.

Grant, Zalin. *Facing the Phoenix.* New York: W. W. Norton, 1991.

Halberstam, David. *The Best and the Brightest.* New York: Random House, 1972.

Hammer, Ellen J. *A Death in November.* New York: E. P. Dutton, 1987.

Higgins, Marguerite. *Our Vietnam Nightmare.* New York: Harper & Row, 1965.

Hilsman, Roger. *To Move a Nation: The Politics of Foreign Policy in the Administration of John F. Kennedy.* Garden City, NY: Doubleday, 1967.

Jacobs, Seth. *America's Miracle Man in Vietnam.* Durham, NC: Duke University Press, 2004.

Johnson, Lyndon Baines. *Vantage Point: Perspectives of the Presidency, 1963–1968,* New York: Holt, 1971.

Jones, Howard. *Death of a Generation.* New York: Oxford University Press, 2003.

Karnow, Stanley. *Vietnam: A History.* New York: Penguin Books, 1983.

Kattenburg, Paul M. *The Vietnam Trauma in American Foreign Policy, 1945–75*. New Brunswick, NJ: Transaction Books, 1980.

Kennedy, Robert. *Robert Kennedy in His Own Words*. Edited by Edwin O. Guthman and Jeffrey Shulman. New York: Bantam, 1988.

Khrushchev, Nikita. *Khrushchev Remembers: The Glasnost Tapes*. Translated and edited by Jerrold L. Schecter with V. V. Luhkov. Boston: Little, Brown, 1970.

Langguth, A. J. *Our Vietnam: The War, 1954–1975*. New York: Simon & Schuster, 2000.

Lodge, Henry Cabot. *The Storm Has Many Eyes: A Personal Narrative*. New York: W. W. Norton, 1973.

McNamara, Robert S. et al. *Argument Without End: In Search of Answers to the Vietnam Tragedy*. New York: Public Affairs, 1999.

——— et al. *In Retrospect: The Tragedy and Lessons of Vietnam*. New York: Vintage Books, 1995.

Mecklin, John. *Mission in Torment: An Intimate Account of the U.S. Role in Vietnam*. Garden City, NY: Doubleday, 1965.

Miller, William J. *Henry Cabot Lodge: A Biography*. New York: James H. Heineman, Inc., 1967.

Morgan, Joseph G. *The Vietnam Lobby: The American Friends of Vietnam, 1955–1975*. Chapel Hill: University of North Carolina Press, 1997.

Moyar, Mark. *Triumph Forsaken: The Vietnam War, 1954–1965*. New York: Cambridge University Press, 2006.

Nash, Philip. *The Other Missiles of October: Eisenhower, Kennedy, and Jupiters, 1957–1963*. Chapel Hill: University of North Carolina Press, 1997.

Newman, John M. *JFK and Vietnam: Deception, Intrigue, and the Struggle for Power*. New York: Warner Books, 1992.

Nolting, Frederick. *From Trust to Tragedy: The Political Memoirs of Frederick Nolting, Kennedy's Ambassador to Diem's Vietnam*. New York: Praeger, New York, 1988.

Oberdorfer, Don. *Senator Mansfield: The Extraordinary Life of a Great Statesman and Diplomat*. Washington, D.C.: Smithsonian Books, 2003.

O'Donnell, Kenneth P., and David F. Powers. *Johnny, We Hardly Knew Ye: Memories of John Fitzgerald Kennedy*. Boston: Little, Brown, 1972.

Parmet, Herbert S. *JFK: The Presidency of John F. Kennedy*. New York: Penguin Books, 1983.

Phillips, Rufus. *Why Vietnam Matters: An Eyewitness Account of Lessons Not Learned*. Annapolis, MD: Naval Institute Press, 2008.

Prados, John. *William Colby and the CIA: The Secret Wars of a Controversial Spymaster*. Lawrence: University Press of Kansas, 2009.

Prochnau, William. *Once Upon a Distant War*. New York: Vintage Books, 1996.

Reeves, Richard. *President Kennedy: Profile of Power*. New York: Simon & Schuster, 1993.

Reeves, Thomas C. *A Question of Character*. New York: Prime Publishing, 1991.

Reporting Vietnam. New York: Library of America, 1998.

Rostow, W. W. *The Diffusion of Power: An Essay in Recent History*. New York: Macmillan, 1972.

Rusk, Dean. *As I Saw It: Dean Rusk as Told to Richard Rusk*. New York: W. W. Norton, 1990.

Rust, William J. *Kennedy in Vietnam*. New York: Scribner's, 1985.

Schlesinger, Arthur M., Jr. *Jacqueline Kennedy: Historic Conversations*. New York: Hyperion, 2011.

———. *Robert Kennedy and His Times*. Boston: Houghton Mifflin, 1978.

———. *A Thousand Days*. New York: Houghton Mifflin, 1965.

Schoenbaum, Thomas J. *Waging Peace and War: Dean Rusk in the Truman, Kennedy, and Johnson Years*. New York: Simon & Schuster, 1988.

Sheehan, Neil. *A Bright Shining Lie*. New York: Random House, 1988.

Sorensen, Theodore C. *Kennedy*. New York: Harper & Row, 1965.

Stern, Sheldon M. *Averting 'The Final Failure': John F. Kennedy and the Secret Cuban Missile Crisis Meetings*. Stanford: Stanford University Press, 2003.

Taylor, Maxwell D. *Swords and Plowshares*. New York: W. W. Norton, 1972.

Tran, Van Don. *Our Endless War: Inside Vietnam*. San Rafael, CA: Presidio Press, 1978.

Warner, Denis. *The Last Confucian*. New York: Macmillan, 1963.

Weber, Ralph E. *Spymasters: Ten CIA Officers in Their Own Words*. Wilmington, DE: SR Books, 1999.

Winters, Francis X. *The Year of the Hare: America in Vietnam, January 25, 1963–February 15, 1964*. Athens: University of Georgia Press, 1997.

INDEX

Haig, Alexander, 262
Halberstam, David, 133–34, 136,
    143–44, 172, 224
  Kennedy's relationship with,
    4, 195–96, 247
Hall of Mirrors brothel, Saigon, 63
Halstead, Dirck, 270
Hamer, Fannie Lou, 147
Ha Minh Tri, 61–62, 70
Hamlett, Barksdale, Jr., 169
Hanes, John, 131
Hanoi, 101, 103–5, 107–17, 189,
    205–6. *See also* Ho Chi Minh;
    Vietnam conflict
  countries backing, 54, 102
  Diem overthrow's impact on, 60,
    163–64, 199, 209–10, 212, 215,
    224–25, 251, 257–70
  Laos Treaty's impact on, 52–58
  spy operations of, 106
Harkins, Paul Donal, 110, 112–17, 121,
    190, 209–10
  Diem's overthrow and, 143, 172–73,
    187, 200, 232, 257
Harriman, Averell, 45, 47–51, 142, 257
  Diem's overthrow engineered by, 50,
    143, 163, 175, 177, 179–86,
    193–94, 197–99, 208, 215,
    225–26, 229, 244–45, 256
  Laos treaty negotiations by, 54–58,
    143
Harriman, Marie, 50
Harvard Law School, 148
Healy, Bob, 167, 253
Hearst, William Randolph, Jr., 62
Heath, Donald, 64
Helms, Richard, 39, 184, 219
Henry V, 149–50
Herndon, Ray, 204
Hesburgh, Theodore, 148

Higgins, Marguerite, 189
Hill, Clint, 255
Hilsman, Roger, 83, 105, 202
  Diem's overthrow and, 142, 163,
    181–83, 194, 196–99, 202, 205,
    215, 220, 226, 244–45, 256–57,
    269
Hitler, Adolf, 14, 27, 33, 48–49
Hoa Hao religious sect, South
    Vietnam, 66–68, 70
Ho Chi Minh, 128–29, 138, 263, 266.
    See also North Vietnam
  determination of, 205–6, 269
  Diem assassination plots by, 59,
    61–62, 70
  French defeat by, 124, 130
  Laos treaty's impact on, 52–58
Ho Chi Minh City, Vietnam (formerly
    Saigon), 267
Honey Fitz (presidential yacht), 125,
    200, 229
Honey, Patrick J., 174
Hoover, Herbert, 2
Hoover, J. Edgar, 265
  wiretapping by, 154–55, 157–59
Hovis, Bobbi, 233–34
Hudson, Bill, 145, 149
Hue, Vietnam, Buddhist uprising in,
    134–37, 141
Huey helicopters, 114–15, 121
Hughes, Thomas, 104–5
Humphrey, Hubert H., 96, 152
hydrogen bombs, U.S., 25

"I Have a Dream" speech (King), 156
Inter American Press Association, 45
"In Time of Crisis" (Bartlett), 13

Jefferson, Thomas, 1
JFK (movie), 267